APR 2 6 2005

P9-DCC-011

Haverhill Public Library
Founded 1874
Haverhill, Massachusetts

COOKING AT HOME
with The Culinary Institute of America

COOKING AT HOME
with *The Culinary Institute of America*

JOHN WILEY & SONS, INC.

641.5
Cooking

THE CULINARY INSTITUTE OF AMERICA
Vice President, Continuing Education: Mark Erickson
Director of Marketing and Product Development: Sue Cussen
Editorial Project Manager: Mary D. Donovan

JOHN WILEY & SONS, INC.
Vice President and Executive Group Publisher: Robert Garber
Vice President and Publisher: Natalie Chapman
Senior Editor: Pamela Chirls
Assistant Editor: Pamela Adler
Production Director: Diana Cisek
Art Director: Edwin Kuo
Associate Marketing Director: Valerie Peterson
Marketing Manager: Adrianne Maher

WELDON OWEN INC.
Chief Executive Officer: John Owen
President: Terry Newell
Creative Director: Gaye Allen
Associate Creative Director: Leslie Harrington
Project Editor: Sarah Putman Clegg
Designer and Photo Director: Kyrie Forbes
Assistant Editor: Mitch Goldman
Production Director: Chris Hemesath
Color Manager: Teri Bell
Shipping and Production Coordinator: Libby Temple

A WELDON OWEN PRODUCTION
Weldon Owen Inc.
814 Montgomery Street
San Francisco, CA 94133

Text copyright © 2003 by The Culinary Institute of America.
Photographs copyright © 2003 by Weldon Owen Inc.

Published by John Wiley & Sons, Inc., Hoboken, New Jersey.

All rights reserved, including the right of reproduction in
whole or in part in any form.

Library of Congress Cataloging-in-Publication Data is available.

Photographs by Michael Falconer.
Front cover bell pepper photograph and endpaper
photograph by Quentin Bacon.

Set in Adobe Garamond and Berthold Akzidenz Grotesk.

Color separations by Embassy Graphics.

Printed in China by Midas Printing, Ltd.

First printed in 2003.

10   9   8   7   6   5   4   3   2

THE CULINARY INSTITUTE OF AMERICA wishes to thank the faculty, students, administration, and staff for their support and assistance throughout the development of this book, especially our recipe testers, Lisa Lahey, Margaret Otterstrom, Jessica Bard, Belinda Treu, and Lynn Tonelli. We also gratefully acknowledge the assistance of Chefs Frederick C. Brash, Mark Ainsworth, and Ryan Baxter.

JOHN WILEY & SONS and WELDON OWEN wish to thank the following people for their generous assistance and support in the production of this book: Editor and Writer Mary Donovan; Consulting Editors Thy Tran and Sharon Silva; Copy Editor Ann Martin Rolke; Writer Stephanie Rosenbaum; Photographer Michael Falconer; Photographer's Assistants Michelle de Greeve and Faiza Ali; Food and Prop Stylists Kim Konecny and Erin Quon; Assistant Food Stylist Annie Salisbury; Photographer Quentin Bacon, Photographer's Assistants Amy Sims and Jeremiah Dart, Food Stylist Alison Attenborough, and Assistant Food Stylist Jamie Kimm (front cover bell pepper and endpaper photographs); Proofreaders Carrie Bradley, Sharron Wood, and Desne Ahlers; Production Designers Linda Bouchard and Joan Olson; and Indexer Ken DellaPenta.

CONTENTS

Introduction

Since its founding in 1946, The Culinary Institute of America has provided its students the world's best professional culinary education through a practical, logical approach to food and cooking that emphasizes excellence in all aspects of the culinary arts. Our graduates master far more than the fundamentals of culinary technique, however. They also learn to think critically about cooking. Once the day's assignments are prepared and the students have gathered around the table, they talk about what they are eating, what it tasted like the last time they tried it, or how they might change it next time. Their professors send them into the library to research the history, culture, and business of food. Even when they leave the classroom or the library, they talk—and argue— about all things culinary.

Students come away from this rich experience knowing that it isn't enough to simply follow the steps in a recipe. They must also learn how to look at, touch, smell, and taste a dish to judge whether it is coming together. They learn to watch closely for changes in appearance, texture, color, and shape at every stage of cooking.

Although you may not spend every day as deeply immersed in cooking as they do, you can learn about cooking and dining the same way that our students learn the culinary arts. The way to learn about cooking is by cooking.

One of the first topics our students tackle is the identification of ingredients and equipment. This introduction gives students a common language. They learn to assess the flavors, aromas, and textures of ingredients ranging from saffron to beef. We maintain that using the best possible ingredients is essential for good cooking. And just as chefs seek out high-quality ingredients from a wide range of sources, so too should home cooks. Whether you choose ingredients from your own garden, a farmers' market, or the shelves of a mega-market, the moment of selection is when cooking begins.

Then, when students of the culinary arts have truly grasped fundamental techniques, their culinary world expands. Instead of depending on the rote following of a recipe, cooking becomes a highly creative act. Inspired cooks are the ones who thrive on finding solutions to culinary challenges. Faced with a favorite recipe that calls for an out-of-season ingredient, they may choose to substitute an ingredient that is in season now, or they may adjust the cooking method to introduce extra flavor. Similarly, if an ingredient is perfectly ripe and flavorful, they might tone down the rest of the flavors in the recipe, the better to appreciate it. If their favorite kitchen gadget breaks or they don't have a filleting knife, they figure out how to manage without it. Where do good cooks learn these skills? They learn them in the marketplace, in the kitchen, and at the table, through the daily acts of shopping, cooking, and eating.

Using this book

Understanding cooking techniques is critical to your success in the kitchen. In the beginning of this book, you'll find a discussion of the fundamental cooking methods: grilling and broiling, roasting and baking, sautéing and stir-frying, pan-frying, deep-frying, steaming, boiling and simmering, shallow poaching, poaching, braising, and stewing. We then reinforce those lessons in the chapters that follow by illustrating techniques that apply to specific foods and providing recipes for plenty of hands-on practice.

The recipes were developed with an eye toward using commonly available ingredients. We anticipate that when you visit your market, the seasonal selections there will inspire you to try them in one of our recipes. And although we'd love to be with you as you examine tomatoes and thump melons, we know that it is in the doing that you become more expert at finding great quality.

That said, we don't want you to feel restricted by recipes. We've included suggestions for variations on a number of "master recipes" to give you a sense of how our students and their teachers might play with colors, textures, or flavors to change things just a little or to create an entirely new dish, without drastically altering the essential technique. Once you understand how cooking works, making such changes will become second nature.

Enjoying food

Just as we at the CIA believe strongly that the best cooking begins with the selection of first-rate ingredients, we also believe that, as cooks, our work is not done until the meal is served and enjoyed. The way the food looks when it arrives at the table—its presentation—is the final step. Presentation can be as elaborate or as simple as you like. Use these simple principles as a starting point: Highlight food's natural shapes, colors, and textures as you place it on plates or platters. Serve hot foods hot and cold foods cold. Wipe plate rims clean.

Memorable meals slow us down for a moment and allow us to enjoy ourselves with our family and friends. There is no guarantee that our efforts in the kitchen will always translate into a fine dining experience, but cooking with intelligence and care and sharing food with the people who are most important to us will always be rewarding.

Preparing and measuring ingredients for a recipe.

Preheating ovens

Most modern ovens require 10–15 minutes to reach maximum temperature. Some older models, however, require 45 minutes or more to heat to very high temperatures, especially if you are using a baking stone. Although some dishes, such as casseroles or roasts, will tolerate low initial temperatures, it is best to heat your oven fully to the temperature directed in a recipe before placing the food in it. Using an oven thermometer will take the guesswork out of preheating.

Preheating ingredients and equipment

When you take the time to preheat ingredients and equipment properly, the entire cooking process goes more smoothly. As you read a recipe, notice what temperature an ingredient should be when you add it to the dish, and plan accordingly. Preheat pans for sautés, pan-fries, or stir-fries. When you add oil to a preheated pan, it heats more quickly.

MISE EN PLACE

Understanding the French culinary term *mise en place,* or "putting in place," is essential for the professional chef and home cook alike. At its most basic level, it refers to assembling all ingredients, tools, and pans required to prepare a meal. But mise en place is also a state of mind. In a busy restaurant kitchen, careful planning allows a chef to keep many tasks in mind simultaneously, arranging steps and assigning priorities as needed. In your own kitchen, the same methodical approach will make the process of cooking less hectic and more enjoyable.

The first step is to read through a recipe completely, and then gather or purchase all the necessary ingredients and equipment. When everything is at hand, you can begin washing, trimming, cutting, and measuring raw ingredients as described in the ingredients list. Mise en place also includes the first few tasks mentioned in the recipe method, such as preheating the oven or lining baking sheets. Once everything is washed, cut or sliced, and measured, then you're ready to start following a recipe method.

Every meal that coordinates several dishes is made simpler with some thoughtful planning. When choosing the recipes for a meal, read through the ingredient lists and methods. Make it easy on yourself: The more courses you want to serve and the shorter their cooking times, the more organized you will need to be. Try to balance your selections so that not every dish needs last-minute attention. Some dishes, such as soups and stews, taste best when cooked a day or two in advance, then reheated just before serving. You can prepare certain simple dishes an hour or two in advance, then reserve them for a final heating. Deep-fried, grilled, and sautéed foods, on the other hand, are best served immediately after cooking. Break your menu down into stages, determining which components can be prepared in advance and which ones might be grouped together to make preparation easier.

When you're ready to start cooking, assemble and prepare your ingredients, from washing greens to dicing onions to seasoning meat. Group together similar steps from different recipes—for example, peel and mince all the garlic at once.

Keep in mind that convenience products can shave valuable time from meal preparation. Canned broths and frozen vegetables, which can be real time-savers, certainly have their places in the home cook's pantry. Sample different brands until you find ones that best suit your taste. Remember that the goal of mise en place is to prepare good food with ease and efficiency.

EQUIPMENT

There are many clever kitchen gadgets available, but a basic collection of cookware and tools is all you will need to prepare even the most intricate recipe. Certain tools are essential; others save time and ease the preparation of specific ingredients or types of dishes. This guide will help you gather the most useful pieces for the home kitchen. There's no shortage of options, but whatever you choose, invest in good quality and maintain your tools well. Each one should feel solid and comfortable in your hand.

Cookware

You'll find pots and pans constructed from a variety of metals, each conducting heat with varying speed and evenness. A kitchen is better equipped with pans of different metals that suit the pan's purpose rather than a single collection of matching cookware.

Saucepans are basic pans with straight sides. They are designed for making and reducing sauces, but they are versatile enough to be used for many other preparations, from steaming rice to making soup. It's helpful to have more than one size.

Stockpots and soup pots, large, deep pots with straight sides, are used for simmering stocks and soups. They are also excellent for boiling pasta, as they allow plenty of room, which prevents sticking.

Skillets and sauté pans are wide, shallow pans, each with one long handle, and are generally interchangeable. Skillets usually have sloped sides, allowing for stirring, while sauté pans often have straight sides, helping to contain ingredients as they are tossed.

Dutch ovens are also called casseroles. Typically the sides are as high as the pot is wide and it has a lid and loop handles. Dutch ovens are used both on a burner and in the oven.

Steamers are large, lidded pots with perforated inserts or stacking layers. As water boils in the pot, steam rises and circulates in the insert, cooking food gently.

Baking pans and sheets are large rectangular pans with low sides (or, in the case of some sheets, no sides) that allow for free circulation of heat in the oven.

Woks are large bowl-shaped pans that distribute heat evenly while allowing the rapid stirring and tossing used in stir-frying.

Omelet and crêpe pans are small, shallow skillets with very short, slightly sloping sides that make it easier to swirl, shape, and quickly cook omelets and crêpes.

Stockpot, saucepan, and sauté pan.

Metals that heat evenly
Copper, cast iron

Metals that heat quickly
Copper, aluminum, steel

Metals that react with acidic foods
Uncoated aluminum, copper, cast iron

Metals that don't react with acidic foods
Stainless steel, anodized aluminum, enameled cast iron, nonstick-coated metals

Keeping food warm

You may need to set aside a chicken breast while you make a pan sauce, hold food as you cook several batches, or keep dinner warm until the last of your guests arrives. To keep a small amount of food warm for just a few minutes, place it on a warm plate and cover it loosely with a sheet of foil, a pot lid, or an upside-down bowl. For larger amounts of food, use a low oven. Arrange the food in a single layer on a baking pan or sheet and place it in an oven set to 200°F. Be sure to check the food frequently while you are holding it.

Standard whisk, sauce whisk, and balloon whisk.

Measuring dry and liquid ingredients

To measure a dry ingredient, spoon it into a nested measuring cup, overfilling the cup. Use the spine of a knife to scrape off the excess and level the cup.

To measure a liquid ingredient, set a graduated measuring cup on a level surface and pour the ingredient into it, filling until the level of the ingredient rises to the appropriate indicator mark. You must be eye level with the cup to take an accurate reading.

Tools

In the process of preparing a meal, you might measure, weigh, strain, and mix ingredients numerous times. Equipping your kitchen with the following tools will allow you to prepare dishes quickly and easily with a minimum of fuss.

Tools for accurate measuring

Measuring cups come in two different styles, for dry and liquid ingredients. Stocking two sets of dry measuring cups and two or three different sizes of graduated liquid measures will help you prepare recipes more quickly.

Measuring spoons are for ingredients used in small amounts. Look for long handles with easy-to-read numbers and narrow bowls that will fit into spice bottles.

Thermometers are available for specific uses. An instant-read thermometer, inserted into cooked meat, helps determine proper doneness. Candy and deep-fat thermometers are designed to remain in sugar syrup or hot oil throughout the cooking time.

Tools for mixing and stirring

Whisks come in a variety of shapes for different tasks. Sphere-shaped balloon whisks incorporate plenty of air into beaten egg whites or whipped cream. Sauce whisks, with a flat, narrow shape and fewer wires, are ideal for deglazing pans and stirring sauces.

Spoons are essential for stirring, mixing, basting, and serving. Slotted or perforated spoons strain food from cooking liquid, while deep ladles are useful for transferring sauces or soups to a blender or serving bowl.

Rubber spatulas are soft and flexible utensils for folding together foams and batters, scraping bowls clean, and keeping delicate ingredients from sticking to the bottom of pans. Look for heatproof spatulas made of silicone for the most versatility.

Mixing bowls come in a wide range of sizes. A nonreactive material, such as stainless steel, is best. Aluminum, for example, reacts with eggs, turning them gray, and with lemon, causing a metallic flavor. Unlined copper bowls, however, react with egg whites in a positive way, to help stabilize the whites as they foam.

Tools for holding and turning

Tongs allow quick turning and mixing of large pieces of food during cooking. Long-handled tongs are ideal for grills, while shorter ones are useful for the stove top.

Metal spatulas are good for lifting and turning foods, especially more delicate items that could be torn by tongs. Common spatulas, also known as pancake turners, have a bend near the handle to protect hands from hot pans and are available in a variety of lengths. Long, narrow icing spatulas are used for spreading fillings and icing.

Kitchen forks are used to test the doneness of meats and vegetables, to lift large items, and to steady meat or poultry while carving.

Tools for straining and puréeing

Sieves, made from fine mesh, can be shaped like cones, drums, or bowls. Strainers are perforated metal bowls. Use sieves for sifting flour or puréeing raspberries. Strainers are handy for washing fruit or, when lined with a double layer of dampened cheesecloth, for straining solids from soups. Colanders are strainers with plenty of large holes for quickly draining foods such as pasta or blanched vegetables.

Skimmers, made of perforated metal or mesh, are useful for removing foods from hot fat or liquids or skimming foam from a simmering stock.

Cheesecloth is light, fine-mesh gauze made from white cotton. It can be used alone or to line a colander or sieve for straining fine sauces. Small squares are used to make spice sachets for infusing stocks and sauces with flavor.

Food mills purée soft or cooked foods. Resembling strainers, they have a curved blade at the bottom that rests flat against a perforated disk. Turning a crank attached to the blade forces food through the disk's holes, puréeing it while straining out solids such as seeds and peels. A set of disks offers a range of textures, from coarse to fine.

Tools for peeling and cutting

Vegetable peelers remove the skins from fruits and vegetables in a thin layer. Most are equipped with a swivel blade to follow the irregular contours of food. Sharpened on both sides, the blade will peel in both an upward and downward motion. With practice, the same task can be performed with a paring knife.

Shears are useful for performing a wide variety of tasks in the kitchen, from cutting twine for trussing poultry to snipping herbs for garnishing a dish. Heavy-duty or poultry shears have a small indentation in one blade to allow cutting through bones.

Mandolines are convenient tools for slicing vegetables. Their blades may be adjusted to create slices, julienne, potato chips, and French fries in a range of thicknesses.

Two styles of sieve.

Food processors and blenders

Food processors and blenders can do one another's work in a pinch, but they are not always interchangeable.

The shape of the bowl and the size of the blade in a food processor encourage even chopping. A processor is also good for mixing dough for pasta, bread, or pie. A powerful motor purées foods without needing much, if any, additional liquid.

Blenders have flared pitchers instead of a straight-sided bowl to hold the ingredients; their blades are smaller, but typically have four arms and are slightly bent. They can produce finer, smoother, and lighter purées than processors since they incorporate more air. To purée foods that are relatively dry in a blender, add a bit of liquid to loosen the ingredients.

Knives

A set of knives may be used more often than any other equipment in your kitchen. Look for knives that will last. A blade made from high-carbon stainless steel will take and keep a sharp edge, and it will not discolor or rust readily. Taper-ground blades, forged from a single sheet of metal, will last longer and have better balance than hollow-ground blades, which are made by fusing together two thinner sheets of metal. A basic set should include the following types.

Chef's knife, slicer, paring knife, and boning knife.

Chef's or French knives are used for a wide variety of cutting tasks, from chopping onions to mincing herbs to slicing meat. Their blades, 6 to 14 inches long, taper from sturdy heels that can slice through small bones to thin tips that slice mushrooms smoothly.

Specialized knives

Filleting knives are similar to boning knives, but with thin, flexible blades for cutting between the delicate flesh and bones of fish.

Cleavers, with their large, rectangular blades, are used widely in Asia. Heavy cleavers can cut cleanly through bones, while lighter ones are used for vegetables and garnishes.

Paring knives, with 2- to 4-inch blades, are designed for peeling and trimming vegetables.

Boning knives, whose narrow, sharply pointed blades offer good maneuverability, are used for separating raw meat cleanly from bones.

Slicers, with long blades, often serrated, are good for cutting even slices of cooked meat or bread. Some slicers have an offset handle for a more comfortable grip, or a fluted edge to ease the blade smoothly through food.

Keep the blades of your knives sharp and well honed. A sharp knife not only cuts better, but also is safer to use. The more pressure you need to apply to the knife to cut food, the more damage you can do with a slip of the blade. Using a cutting board made of wood, plastic, or polyethylene helps preserve a knife's edge. Cutting on metal, glass, or marble surfaces, on the other hand, will dull and eventually damage the blades. Store knives in racks or holders, not loose in a drawer where their blades may be damaged.

Knife skills

Learning good knife skills makes for better finished dishes because precise, uniform cuts allow ingredients to cook at the same rate. For most cutting, grip the knife high on the handle, at the point where it meets the blade. This grip offers greater stability, control, and balance than holding the handle farther away from the blade. Grasp the handle with three fingers, resting your index finger and thumb flat against the blade on either side. When chopping bones or cutting through harder foods, grip the handle with all four fingers and rest your thumb firmly along the top of the blade, close to where it meets the handle. For smaller knives, wrap all four fingers around the handle but leave your thumb pressed against the side of the blade.

In all cases, the hand not holding the knife—your guiding hand—maneuvers the food, prevents the item from slipping, and helps control the size of the cut. Hold food with your fingertips, tucking them slightly under and holding your thumb out of the way. The flat of the blade should rest against your knuckles so you don't cut your fingertips.

Always try to cut food into pieces of the same shape and size. The basic cuts follow.

1 **Chopping** is used for rustic dishes or for ingredients that will be puréed or strained out of a finished dish. Slice or chop the food at nearly regular intervals. The pieces need not be perfectly even in shape, but all the pieces should be roughly the same size.

2 **Mincing** reduces food to a relatively fine, even cut, useful for vegetables, herbs, and other flavoring ingredients such as garlic or gingerroot. Roughly chop the food first and gather it into a pile. Then, holding the knife tip against the cutting board with your free hand and using a rocking motion, mince firmly and rapidly to the desired fineness.

3 **Julienne** are long, rectangular cuts, such as for matchstick carrots or French fries. Cut a thin slice from one side of round vegetables to make them more stable as you cut. Slice the food lengthwise, using parallel cuts of the desired thickness. Stack these rectangular slices, aligning their edges, and make a second set of lengthwise cuts through the stack. Julienne should be very narrow, ⅛ inch. A wider cut, about ¼ inch, is called batonnet. Straw *(paille)* is similar to julienne, but cut even more finely. Depending on the food itself or your preference, the length can vary from 1 to 2½ inches.

4 **Dicing** produces small, neat cubes. Brunoise, the finest size (⅛ inch), is often used for a delicate garnish. Fine, medium, and large dice, ranging in size from ¼ inch to ½ inch to ¾ inch, appear in a wide variety of preparations. To dice, cut the food lengthwise into slices as thick as the dice you want. Stack these slices and slice again lengthwise to make strips. Gather the strips into a neat stack or line, then cut crosswise into dice.

5 **Oblique or roll cut** is used with long, cylindrical vegetables such as carrots and celery, especially if they will be braised or roasted. Make a diagonal cut to remove the stem end. Holding the knife in the same position, roll the vegetable a half turn (180 degrees) and slice again to create pieces with different angles at each end. Repeat to cut up the rest of the vegetable.

6 **Shredding and chiffonade** are strips of leafy vegetables and herbs, chiffonade being a finer cut than shredded. Stack a few leaves and roll them tightly lengthwise. With a sharp knife, make thin crosswise cuts. Before using the shreds, loosen them with your fingertips.

PANTRY INGREDIENTS

A finished dish is only as good as its raw ingredients. From the oil in a sauté pan to the herbs sprinkled as garnish, every ingredient can lend delicious flavor to a dish. In addition to stocking the familiar staples, look for new flavors to add to your pantry. Unusual ingredients from around the world, whether highlighted in traditional dishes or blended into new creations, will enhance your menus. Although many pantry ingredients are dry staples, the term also includes others, like butter or fresh herbs, that are best stored in the refrigerator. How much to stock depends on your cooking habits—how often you cook, how many people you cook for, and how much space you have for storage—as well as the specific shelf life of each product. For the best flavor, buy food in amounts that you can store and use readily.

Rosemary, thyme, sage, and parsley.

Using herbs

For the best flavor, wash, dry, and chop fresh herbs just before using. To replace fresh herbs with dried, start with one-third the quantity of fresh. Taste, then add more, bit by bit, throughout the cooking process, to reach the desired flavor. Before adding fresh or dried herbs, roll and crush them between thumb and forefinger to release essential oils.

Herbs, spices, and aromatics

Herbs, spices, and such aromatic ingredients as onions, garlic, leeks, mushrooms, celery, wines, and citrus fruits are employed by cooks and chefs everywhere to give their dishes character. Each cuisine owes its characteristic flavors to unique combinations of these elements. For example, consider humble chicken soup. You can stir into the pot ginger and green onion for an Asian version, lime and chile for a Mexican creation, paprika and parsley for an eastern European taste, or thyme and bay leaves for a Mediterranean flavor. Each simple combination of ingredients creates an altogether different dish.

Herbs

Herbs are the leaves and stems of plants that contain distinctive aromatic oils. Common herbs include parsley, cilantro, oregano, thyme, and dill. Most herbs are available both fresh and dried. Dried herbs are used in different ways and at different times than fresh herbs. For example, dried herbs are commonly used in coatings and breadings and in long-simmering stews, braises, and soups. They are generally added early in the cooking process to develop the best flavor. Herbs with woody stems and strong aromatic oils, such as rosemary, sage, and bay, keep well dried, but other, more delicate herbs, such as tarragon and dill, retain their flavor and aroma for a shorter time after they are dried.

Check both fresh and dried herbs for flavor by rubbing or crushing the leaves or needles and smelling; they should smell strong and pleasant, not musty. Crushing herbs also releases their essential oils, bringing more flavor to the dish in which they are used.

For the deepest flavor, add herbs at two different stages in long-cooked sauces. Sprinkle fresh herbs both at the beginning and at the end of cooking for layers of flavor, or supplement dried herbs used at the beginning of long cooking with the bright flavor and color of fresh ones as garnish.

Most fresh herbs are best stored in the refrigerator, wrapped first in damp paper towels and then loosely in plastic, though some, such as parsley and basil, benefit from being kept in a jar of water, much like a bouquet of flowers. Dried herbs should be kept in airtight containers in a cool, dark cupboard. Avoid storing them near the heat of the stove or in direct light. For the best flavor, wash and chop fresh herbs close to the time of use. Before adding dried herbs to dishes, roll and crush their leaves between your palms to release more of their aromatic oils.

Spices

Spices generally come from the root, bark, and seeds of plants, where aromatic oils are naturally concentrated. Intense in flavor, most spices are used in small amounts. Among the most popular spices for sweet and savory dishes are cardamom, cinnamon, cloves, cumin, fennel seed, mustard, nutmeg, saffron, star anise, and turmeric. Nearly always sold in dried form, they are available whole or ground.

Cooks around the world use distinctive spice blends to flavor classic dishes. Indian garam masala, French quatre épices, American chili powder, and Chinese five-spice powder each combine several spices to add color as well as complex layers of flavor to foods. Premixed spice blends are widely available, but feel free to create your own blends as needed.

Whole spices retain their aromatic oils significantly longer than already-ground spices. For the best flavor, grind whole spices as close to the time of cooking as possible. Store spices in airtight containers in a cool, dark place; exposure to air, heat, and light will diminish their flavor.

Salt

Among the most prized of all seasonings, salt highlights the natural flavors of foods when used judiciously, and adds its own flavor when used in slightly greater amounts. Stock a variety of salts for the greatest flexibility in your cooking.

Table salt has small, dense grains; it is often fortified with iodine. Kosher salt is compressed into flakes that adhere to foods readily and dissolve quickly. Sea salts are produced

Cinnamon, cloves, saffron, and nutmeg.

Using spices

To bring out the flavor of whole spices before grinding them, gently toast in a dry skillet or sauté in a small amount of oil, just until they take on slight color and become aromatic. Take care not to scorch them, or they will taste bitter. Transfer to a plate to cool.

Salting cooking water

When boiling pasta or blanching vegetables, be sure to add salt to the cooking water—enough to give it a discernibly salty taste, like that of seawater. Seasoning the water will result in a fuller flavor in the finished dish.

Using kosher salt

Substitute 1 teaspoon kosher salt for each ½ teaspoon table salt for use in recipes.

Seasoning with salt and pepper

These two ingredients are taken so much for granted that some cooks fail to apply them early enough during cooking or in enough quantity to bring out the best flavor in cooked foods. Adding salt and pepper before cooking highlights the inherent flavors in foods. If they are added only after the cooking is complete, they can dominate the flavor of the finished dish. (An exception: salt is not added to legumes until they have begun to soften during simmering. The salt may have the effect of toughening the beans' outer layer.)

Apply salt and pepper separately. Apply salt with dry fingertips, to control the amount you use and ensure an even coat. Use freshly ground pepper for the best flavor.

Roasting garlic

Slice the top off a garlic head to expose the cloves. Rub the head with oil, then place cut side down in a small baking dish and roast at 350°F until soft, 30–45 minutes. Remove the outer papery layers, separate into cloves, squeeze out the roasted garlic, and mash to a purée with a fork. Use the roasted garlic in soups, vegetable purées, sauces, and vinaigrettes, or as a spread on sandwiches or grilled bread.

when briny sea or marsh waters evaporate, leaving minerals and other "impurities" that give sea salts their unique colors and flavors. Kosher and sea salts have tastes noticeably different from table salt. Salts are sold in varying degrees of fineness, from the ultrafine popcorn salt to extremely coarse sea salt grains.

Peppercorns

Dried from the still-green berries of the pepper vine, black peppercorns have a sharper, hotter flavor than white or green peppercorns. Less pungent white peppercorns are fully ripened berries that have had their husks removed before drying. Chefs use them for their pale color when preparing light-colored sauces. Tart, pungent green peppercorns, the soft, unripe berries of the pepper plant, are most commonly available packed in vinegar or brine.

Pink peppercorns are actually the dried berries of the Baies rose plant. Available freeze-dried or brined, they lend a hint of sweetness and a sprinkle of light red color to sauces. Szechwan peppercorns come from the prickly ash tree that grows in China. The seeds of the tree's brown berries have a distinctly warm, spicy flavor with hints of anise.

Garlic

A member of the genus Allium, which also includes onions, leeks, and shallots, garlic grows in a bulb covered with papery white or purple-streaked skin. Strong and pungent when raw, garlic sweetens and mellows as it cooks. So many recipes call for a garlic clove or two that cooks often take the aromatic bulb for granted. Garlic appears slivered on flat breads, minced in marinades, or roasted to smoky richness for sauces. Each clove is also encased in a thin skin. Crushing the clove gently loosens the peel for easier removal. Finely mincing or puréeing the garlic brings out its flavor more than simply slicing or roughly chopping it. Cut garlic as close to when you intend to use it as possible for the best flavor. For more details on preparing garlic, see page 181.

Ginger

The rhizome of a tropical plant, fresh ginger has a bright, peppery flavor. Spicy yet slightly sweet, it plays an important role in marinades, soups, and sauces. Ginger adds a distinctive flavor to food, yet it also proves extremely versatile. Recipes may call for grinding the root for curry paste, slicing it thickly to infuse a stock, or cutting it into slivers for garnish. When selecting fresh gingerroot, look for plump, firm knobs with smooth, shiny skin. Peel fresh ginger before using it. Store in the refrigerator, loosely wrapped in a damp paper towel and then placed in a plastic bag. Freezing ginger, excellent for longer storage of large amounts, makes the root easier to grate and mince. For more detail on preparing ginger, see page 181.

Aromatic combinations

Curry, chili powder, and pickling spices are examples of spice and herb combinations used to season dishes. Fresh herbs are used singly and in combinations such as *fines herbes* or *herbes de Provence*. Mirepoix, consisting of onions, carrots, and celery, is just one of many aromatic vegetable mixtures. Cajun and Creole dishes feature "the Holy Trinity" (onions, peppers, and celery), while Italian dishes feature *battuto* (onions, peppers, celery, garlic, and herbs sautéed in olive oil) and Spanish dishes employ a *sofrito* (onions, peppers, garlic, herbs, and annatto seeds sautéed in rendered pork fat). Flavors that can supplement or change one of these aromatic bases include lemongrass, chiles, tomatoes, mushrooms, ginger, and ham.

Fats

Fat carries and blends the flavors of other foods. In cooking, it transfers heat to foods and can prevent sticking. It also holds the heat in food, emulsifies or thickens sauces, and creates a crisp texture when used frying. Butter and shortening are cooking fats used both as ingredients in a mixture and as a cooking medium. Because these fats are solid, they can be creamed or rubbed into batters for tender or flaky results. Fats like duck fat, bacon drippings, or lard give dishes a special flavor. Oils are so versatile as both a cooking medium and an ingredient that good cooks often stock several types in their cupboards.

Oils

Plants that naturally contain a high amount of oil, such as olives, nuts, and corn, can be pressed to produce cooking oils. When heated to a high enough temperature, oils begin smoking, develop a bitter flavor, and break down. The exact smoke point varies depending on the type of oil, but refined vegetable and seed oils tend to have higher smoke points. They also retain less fruity or nutty flavor. The best oils for cooking, especially high-heat cooking such as frying, tend to be these refined oils with high smoke points and neutral flavors, which make them versatile for use in many different dishes. Oils for salads and other uncooked dishes, on the other hand, are intended to add flavor to a dish, so they should be less refined. For example, the first, most flavorful pressing of olive oil and nut oils is often chosen for dressings. Flavored oils, infused with ingredients such as garlic, lemon, basil, chiles, or truffles, are popular for sauces and vinaigrettes and for garnishing finished dishes. Stock several different types of oils in your pantry, depending on the

Classic mirepoix.

Best oils for sautéing

Canola oil
Grapeseed oil
Light sesame oil
Pure olive oil
Sunflower oil

Best oils for deep-frying

Canola oil
Corn oil
Peanut oil
Safflower oil
Vegetable oil

Best oils for salad dressings

Almond oil
Avocado oil
Extra-virgin olive oil
Pumpkin seed oil
Walnut oil

Oil and butter.

Making clarified butter

Melting butter and removing its milk solids and water allows you to heat it to higher temperatures for sautéing and frying. Heat butter over medium heat until foam rises to the surface and the milk solids drop to the bottom. As the liquid becomes clear, skim the surface to remove all traces of the foam. Pour or ladle off the butterfat into another container, leaving behind the water and milk solids at the bottom of the pan. After the clarified butter is poured off, it is ready to use for cooking.

Making bread crumbs

Remove the crust of fine-textured white bread, tear the bread into pieces, and pulse in a food processor. For dried bread crumbs, use stale bread or toast the bread in a 275°F oven until dried before processing into crumbs.

Toasting nuts

Spread nuts on a baking sheet and toast in a 325°F oven until deeper in color and fragrant, 7–15 minutes, depending on the type and size of nut.

types of dishes you like to make. Oil becomes rancid with age, and this process is hurried by exposure to air, heat, or light. Purchase oils in small quantities and store in an airtight container in a cool cupboard.

Butter

Good-quality butter has the fresh flavor of the sweet cream used to make it. The color of butter will vary depending on the breed of the cow and the time of the year, but it is usually a pale yellow. Most chefs prefer to use unsalted butter so they can control the amount of salt they add to their dishes during cooking. The salt in salted butter should be barely detectable. Since salt extends the shelf life of butter, it may mask old or "off" flavors. For the best flavor, buy grade AA unsalted butter. (Note that the label "sweet butter" indicates only that the butter is made from sweet cream; it may still contain salt.)

Butter foams and burns easily when used to sauté or fry foods. Clarifying butter allows you to heat it to higher temperatures. When clarified butter is served alone as a sauce for seafood, it is known as drawn butter. To make ghee, Indian cooks continue to heat clarified butter until it turns a golden brown and develops a rich, nutty flavor.

Other pantry ingredients

Bread crumbs

Bread crumbs can be used fresh or dried. Fresh bread crumbs are soft and light in texture, while the smaller grains of dried crumbs readily absorb moisture. The two function differently and should not be substituted for each other in recipes. Bread crumbs are often mixed into stuffing or sprinkled on food before filling to absorb flavorful juices and maintain the texture of surrounding ingredients. Coating food with bread crumbs creates a crisp crust during frying. Fresh bread crumbs keep best in the freezer, but dried crumbs can be stored in a cool, dark cupboard or cabinet.

Nuts

Except for peanuts, which are the underground seeds of a legume, nuts are the fruits of various trees. Walnuts, almonds, hazelnuts, pine nuts, pecans, and pistachios are among the most popular in the kitchen. Rich in flavor, whole or chopped nuts add a crunchy texture to a wide variety of sweet and savory dishes. Nuts can also be puréed to a creamy paste or pressed into flavorful nut oil. For the longest shelf life, store nuts in an airtight container in the freezer or refrigerator. Purchase whole nuts, which keep longer, and chop them as needed. Toast nuts just before you use them to improve both flavor and texture.

COOKING BASICS

The science of cooking is a field unto itself, but knowing a few basic principles will help you understand how food is transformed during cooking and how to control those changes.

Dry versus moist heat

Dry-heat cooking methods cook food either by direct, radiant heat, like the heat of a grill, or by indirect heat contained in a closed environment, such as an oven. No water or broth is added to the food during cooking. Dry-heat cooking *can* involve fats or oils as a cooking medium, or it can be carried out without them.

In the dry-heat methods of grilling, broiling, and roasting, any butter, oil, or fat added during cooking is intended for flavor only and does not act as a cooking medium. Using these techniques, you'll get a highly flavored exterior and a moist interior.

Sautéing, stir-frying, pan-frying, and deep-frying all involve cooking by dry heat with fat or oil. One difference among these methods is the amount of oil used in relation to the quantity of food being cooked. In sautéing and stir-frying, only small amounts of oil are used to develop flavor. Pan-frying and deep-frying call for larger amounts of oil to create a crisp crust that contrasts with the food's moist interior. These cooking methods are all relatively quick, depend on high heat, and are used for small pieces of tender food.

Moist-heat cooking methods cook food in a liquid bath or a vapor. You can prepare an entire meal—meats, fish, vegetables, and grains—in a single pot. The classic dishes of many cuisines, from an Italian osso buco to a French *poule au pot,* involve slow, moist cooking. In addition to producing moist, tender, and delicately flavored food, these techniques also produce a good quantity of rich broth. This broth can be served as a separate soup course, or it can form the basis for a sauce.

The primary moist-heat cooking methods are steaming, poaching, boiling and simmering, braising, and stewing. The amount of liquid varies from one technique to another, from a few drops of moisture to complete submersion. Because no browning occurs when foods are steamed and poached, the flavor remains delicate. (Sauces or broths made from poaching liquids capture the full flavor of the dish and add succulence to the finished dish.) In braising and stewing, foods are first seared and browned to give deep color and flavor to the dish. Stews generally feature bite-sized pieces cooked in enough liquid to cover them. Braises are ideal for large cuts or pieces; you use less cooking liquid than for a stew in order to produce a reduced sauce to serve with the food.

Food safety

If not prepared or stored properly, foods can become contaminated with enough pathogens to cause illness. The higher the amount of protein in a food and the less acidic the food, the greater the danger. Do not leave protein-rich foods—especially meat, poultry, and fish, but also cooked rice, beans, pasta, and potatoes—at room temperature for more than 2 hours. Store fish and shellfish at 30°–34°F, meat and poultry at 32°–36°F. The back and bottom shelves of a refrigerator tend to be the coldest areas. Wash your hands thoroughly with soap and warm water before and after handling raw ingredients. Use separate cutting boards and knives for raw and cooked foods, or wash your equipment with hot, soapy water between uses. All food should be stored in a way that prevents contact between cooked and raw ingredients.

Cooling in an ice bath

Putting hot food directly into the refrigerator for chilling or storing raises the temperature of the refrigerator and endangers the other foods stored there, but letting warm food sit out at room temperature is also a food safety risk. To cool down food quickly before placing it in the refrigerator, transfer the food to a deep container and place it in a larger container or a sink filled partly with iced water. Stir frequently for fast, even cooling.

Serving food

Warmed serving platters or plates keep your food hot and delicious between leaving the stove and arriving at the table. Place serving platters, dinner plates, or soup bowls in an oven set to the lowest temperature for about 10 minutes. Be careful that the serving dishes don't become too hot to touch.

For cold soups, salads, appetizers, or desserts, chill dishes or bowls for 10–12 minutes in the refrigerator or freezer before serving to keep these foods cool and refreshing.

Grilling and broiling, with their dry, direct heat and quick cooking times, are ideal for cooking tender pieces of meat, poultry, fish, or vegetables.

1 Preparing the grill

Scour the grill well with a stiff brush between uses to remove any charred particles. Preheat a gas grill, or use a chimney starter to start coals and let smolder until covered with white ash. You can create zones of varying temperature by gathering the coals into a pile to one side of the grill. Sear or grill foods with short cooking times over the direct heat, right above the coals. Cook larger pieces of food more slowly over indirect heat, in the areas with fewer or no coals. To gauge the heat level, count how long you can hold your hand 1 inch above the grill: 1–2 seconds is high heat, 3–5 is medium, and 6 or more is low.

2 Coating with oil

For the best appearance and flavor, as well as to prevent sticking, lightly coat food with oil before grilling or broiling. If using skewers, oil metal ones to prevent sticking, or soak wooden ones to keep them from burning.

3 Marking the first side

Place the best-looking side of the food face down on the grill. When the food comes into contact with the heated rods, distinct marks are charred onto its surface. Let it cook undisturbed on the first side until it is time to turn. This develops better flavor and allows the food to release naturally from the grill without sticking or tearing. Use a spatula or tongs to avoid piercing the food and losing juices. Grill baskets ease turning of multiple items, large items, and delicate fish. To mark foods with a crosshatch, rotate the food when it is three-fourths of the way through cooking on the first side.

4 Glazing and finishing

Because many grilling sauces and glazes contain sugar, which burns readily, cook the food partially before applying them so that they will caramelize lightly but not burn. Brush a single coat on each side, or build up a coating with several layers. Larger pieces of meat may need to be transferred to a cooler part of the grill to allow the center of the food to finish cooking before the surface scorches.

5 Cutting uniform thicknesses

If grilling more than one type of food for the same meal, cut the foods into uniform thicknesses and start cooking denser foods a few minutes earlier than tender foods. For example, crisp bell peppers may need to cook a little longer than tender mushrooms.

6 Broiling

The heat source for broiling is above, rather than below, the food. Smaller or more delicate foods, such as cut vegetables or fish fillets, are good choices for broiling. Preheat the broiler and the broiler pan completely first; surrounding the food with heat will prevent sticking and develop good texture and color. Leave the door of the broiler or oven slightly ajar to allow steam to escape, since dry heat will develop a crisper texture and deeper flavor. Raise or lower the broiler rack to control the heat level.

Roasting and baking surround food with the dry, indirect heat of an oven, for crusty exteriors and tender, juicy interiors. The term *roasting* is commonly used for large cuts of meats and whole poultry or fish, while *baking* more often refers to portion-sized foods—but the terms are frequently used interchangeably.

1 Preparing the ingredients
Pat food dry for roasting to prevent it from steaming in its own moisture. Truss whole poultry or tie large roasts with string to give them a compact shape, encouraging even cooking (see pages 69, 97). Brush the food with oil to help it brown in the oven, or sear it briefly on the stove top before roasting.

2 Choosing the equipment
Using a low-sided roasting pan and a rack helps improve the circulation of hot air for even cooking. The pan or rack should be large enough to hold the food comfortably, without crowding. If you are roasting several large items, plan to leave several inches of space between them to allow hot air to circulate freely.

3 Basting
The heat of the oven can dry out certain foods, especially those that require longer cooking times. Basting returns moisture to the food and imparts additional flavor. The fat and juices released by the food itself form the traditional basting liquid, but you can also baste with flavored oil or melted butter.

4 Adding mirepoix

If you will be preparing gravy from the pan drippings, add mirepoix—a classic mixture of diced onion, celery, and carrot—or other aromatic ingredients to the roasting pan during the last 30–45 minutes of cooking time. These ingredients will contribute their color and flavor to the pan drippings and the final gravy. Do not let these ingredients burn, or the gravy will taste bitter. For information on making gravy and other pan sauces, see page 98.

5 Resting

Allow a resting period before cutting and serving roasted meat or poultry. Resting allows the juices to redistribute evenly throughout the meat and the temperature to equalize, for better texture and flavor. Place in a warm spot, cover loosely with aluminum foil, and let sit for 5–20 minutes, depending on the size of the food.

6 Baking

The main distinction between roasting and baking has to do with the cut of meat or poultry used. Generally, roasts are made with large cuts or whole birds, while portion-sized pieces (breasts, thighs, drumsticks, or chops) are usually considered baked.

Sautéing and stir-frying cook food rapidly in a small amount of fat over high heat. Derived from the French word for *jump,* sautéing refers to the motion of food tossed in a hot pan. Stir-frying, a similar method, is used in many Asian cuisines.

1 Choosing a fat

Depending on the flavors of the dish, you can use butter, bacon or duck fat, or oils such as olive, canola, or grapeseed for sautéing. Butter may be used alone, but it has a tendency to burn; a mixture of butter and oil gives a dish a good butter flavor and also allows heating to a higher temperature before burning occurs. Clarified butter (see page 26) may be heated to a higher temperature than regular butter.

2 Heating the pan and fat

Preheat a dry sauté pan over medium-high heat, then add enough oil or other fat to cover the bottom with a thin, even film. A well-seasoned or nonstick pan may require significantly less oil. Heat butter or solid fat until it melts. Heat oil until it shimmers for red meat; for other meats, poultry, fish, and vegetables, oil should be hot, but not hot enough to shimmer.

3 Adding and turning the food

Some sautés call for cooking aromatic ingredients first for additional flavor. When you add larger cuts of food to the pan, make sure that each piece comes in direct contact with the hot fat to avoid sticking. Avoid overlapping the pieces or crowding the pan, as this will make the food steam in its own moisture and prevent browning and caramelization. To develop flavor and color, let the food cook undisturbed until it is time to turn it. Large pieces should be turned only once, but small pieces, such as shrimp or diced vegetables, may be tossed or turned more often, in order to cook them evenly on all sides.

4 Deglazing to make a pan sauce

To make a pan sauce, remove the food from the pan and keep warm. Pour off all but a thin coating of fat or oil and return the pan to high heat. Add aromatic ingredients or garnishes and cook them briefly to release their flavor. Deglaze the pan, pouring in wine, spirits, broth, or water and using a wooden spoon or spatula to scrape up the flavorful browned bits from the bottom of the pan. Let the liquid reduce to a saucelike consistency, or add a starch slurry (see page 46) if desired to help thicken the sauce. Add other flavoring ingredients as directed in a recipe or as desired.

5 Setting up for a stir-fry

For stir-frying, a method that shares many characteristics with sautéing, use a wok or a wide, heavy skillet. A large pot or Dutch oven would create steam rather than the dry, intense heat you need for stir-frying. Because stir-frying involves very short cooking times, prepare all ingredients ahead of time, including the sauce, and arrange them near your stove in order of their use.

6 Stir-frying in sequence

When stir-frying, add the ingredients in the sequence given in a recipe. You'll start with foods that require the longest cooking time, such as onions and carrots, and finish with those that cook in only a few moments. Some ingredients may be blanched, or partially cooked, in advance. This advance cooking ensures even cooking throughout and sets vegetables' bright color.

Pan-frying lean cuts of meat or small, even pieces of sturdy vegetables creates a rich crust and a moist interior. Dredging, breading, and battering may be used to create different textures in the crust. Moderately heated oil cooks the food quickly while sealing in its natural juices.

1 Dredging, breading, and battering
Dry the food well with absorbent towels and season with salt and pepper before adding the coating. Dredge the foods lightly in flour, then batter or bread them if directed in a recipe (see page 68). You can bread foods up to 4 hours in advance, but batter them just before pan-frying.

2 Heating the oil
Pour enough oil into a skillet to come one-third to one-half of the way up the side of the food. For the proper development of the crust's crisp texture and golden brown color, allow the pan and the cooking fat to reach 350°F before the food is added. To test the temperature without a thermometer, dip a corner of the food in the fat. If the fat is hot enough, it will bubble and the coating will start to brown within 45 seconds.

3 Cooking and draining
Add the food gently to the pan and pan-fry on the first side until a golden brown crust forms. To cook the second side, carefully turn the food away from you to prevent splashes. Work in batches if needed to avoid crowding the pan and steaming the food in its own moisture. Between batches, skim the oil of any debris and let the oil return to 350°F. Drain or blot the fried food on absorbent towels. Hold pan-fried foods only briefly before serving, as they tend to turn soggy.

Deep-frying submerges tender food completely in fat or oil, to develop a crisp, brown exterior while maintaining a juicy interior.

1 Setting up

Choose a pan deep enough to hold the amount of oil specified in a recipe and allow at least 3 inches above the level of oil to the top of the pan, since the oil will expand as it heats and foam up when food is added. Have ready a plate or platter lined with absorbent towels for draining the fried food. To cook rapidly, the food must be cut into a uniform size and shape. Be sure to season all the pieces before coating them, and batter or bread them as directed in a recipe.

2 Heating the oil

Heat the oil over medium to medium-high heat to the specified temperature. Generally, foods are deep-fried at 350°F, but check the recipe you are using; some foods are cooked at lower temperatures for longer periods, others at higher temperatures for shorter periods. Use a deep-fat frying thermometer to check the temperature. The temperature may decrease for a short time as food is added, but it should return to the correct temperature within a few seconds.

3 Cooking and draining

Use tongs or a skimmer to lift battered foods carefully in and out of the oil. Breaded items can be conveniently deep-fried in a wire basket. Work in small batches to prevent the food from sticking together, and let the fat return to the proper frying temperature between batches. Skim the oil of debris between batches. Let excess oil drip back into the pan, then drain or blot the food on the towels. Do not hold the food too long, or its crust will become soggy.

Steaming surrounds delicate ingredients with gentle, moist heat. Bright colors and clean flavors stay true.

1 Setting up

Use a pot with a tight-fitting lid and a steamer insert or collapsible basket. To cook more than one layer of food at a time, use a tiered steamer. Lettuce leaves are excellent for lining steaming racks to prevent food from sticking. Add enough liquid to the pot to last throughout the cooking, as adding more during cooking releases steam and slows the cooking. (If you do need to add liquid during cooking, preheat it before you add all the food.) Bring the liquid to a boil.

2 Arranging the food

Naturally tender foods cut into small or thin shapes are ideal for steaming. Arrange the ingredients in a single layer on the steamer insert. Allow enough room for the steam to circulate completely around the food for even, rapid cooking.

3 Maintaining even heat

Once the water has come to a boil, adjust the heat to maintain an even, moderate simmer. Add the steamer insert and cover the steamer tightly with a lid. Avoid removing the lid unnecessarily, as the drop in temperature will affect flavor and quality. Steamed foods should be served immediately after cooking, since they'll become rubbery and dry if held too long.

Boiling and simmering are fundamental techniques for cooking vegetables, grains, pastas, and beans. These techniques make food tender, colorful, and flavorful.

1 Setting up

Select a pot large enough to hold the vegetables comfortably and add enough water or broth to cover them by a few inches. Stir in salt, seasonings, or aromatic ingredients. Start dense or starchy root vegetables in cold water to allow the heat to penetrate evenly. Add other vegetables to fully boiling liquid, working in small batches to maintain the liquid's rapid bubbling.

2 Boiling, parboiling, or blanching

Cook the vegetables to the desired doneness. Tender-crisp vegetables still offer slight resistance and a sense of the original texture, while fully cooked vegetables will be quite tender. To boil vegetables for a purée, cook them until they almost fall apart on their own. Parboiling, or parcooking, calls for cooking vegetables for a shorter time, to partial doneness, to prepare them for later grilling, sautéing, or stewing. To blanch vegetables, for easier peeling, setting color, or reducing strong flavors, use a strainer to immerse them in boiling water for only 30–60 seconds.

3 Draining and cooling

Remove the vegetables from the liquid by draining them through a colander or by lifting them from the pot with a large skimmer. If they will not be finished or served immediately, cool the vegetables by plunging them into very cold or ice water. Drain them again and refrigerate until needed.

Shallow poaching combines the speed of a sauté with the delicate heat of poaching, and the poaching liquid may be used to create a flavorful pan sauce.

1 Choosing the ingredients
By partially submerging food in a liquid and placing it over gentle heat, you can combine steaming and simmering for quick yet delicate cooking. This is an excellent method for cooking small, tender cuts. Arrange individual servings in a buttered pan. Carefully add the cooking liquid, letting it come no higher than halfway up the food. For fish and shellfish, choose fish broth or wine. For poultry and meat, use a flavorful broth. Aromatic ingredients such as herbs, spices, citrus zest, vegetables, vegetable juice, or wine will enhance the flavors of the dish.

2 Maintaining gentle heat
Bring the liquid to a boil. Place a round of parchment paper that just fits the pan over the food to capture some of the steam, then gently simmer and steam over low heat on the stove top or in a moderate oven.

3 Making a sauce
Once the food is properly cooked, it can be removed from the pan and kept warm while you make a sauce from the remaining poaching liquid. Return the pan to high heat and let the poaching liquid boil until reduced by half. You can swirl in butter or flavored butter, minced herbs, or other flavorings. Or, add a little heavy cream to the poaching liquid and reduce it for a quick cream sauce.

Poaching food by submerging it in liquid and cooking at a constant, moderate temperature preserves the texture and flavor of naturally tender fish, shellfish, chicken, eggs, and fruit.

1 Choosing the ingredients

Large cuts of very tender meat and whole fish or poultry are ideal for deep-poaching. Wrap dressed fish in cheesecloth, truss whole poultry, or tie meats to help retain their shape as they cook. To cook poultry evenly, you may prefer to separate the bird into breast and leg portions. The breast portions cook more quickly, so you can either start cooking the breast portions a little later than the legs, or start both at the same time and remove the breasts when they finish cooking.

2 Submerging the ingredients

Some foods are started in cool liquid, whereas others are lowered into preheated liquid. It is easiest to place the food in the pot, then add the liquid, covering the food by at least 1 inch.

3 Maintaining the temperature

Make sure the poaching liquid does not boil. Adjust the heat to maintain the poaching liquid at 160°–185°F. A thermometer is useful, as even a few degrees can make a difference in texture. The surface of the liquid may show slight motion, sometimes called shivering, but no air bubbles should break the surface. Certain tougher meats may require simmering at higher temperature, 185°–200°F, to become tender. Skim as needed throughout the cooking time to remove foam and ensure a clear broth. Once the food is fully cooked, transfer it to a serving dish or carving board. Strain the broth through a sieve or cheesecloth. You can serve the broth as part of the dish, make a sauce from it, or save it to use as an ingredient in other dishes.

Braising and stewing are gentle, slow cooking techniques that transform tough cuts of meat into tender morsels in a rich, flavorful sauce. Braising is used for larger cuts, stewing for bite-sized pieces.

1 Browning the meat

The first step in many braises or stews is to brown the surface of the meat or poultry quickly in fat over high heat. This gives it a more appetizing appearance than if it were cooked only in liquid, and also contributes good flavor to the final dish. Brown the meat in batches without crowding, to avoid steaming it in its own moisture. The meat should not be cooked through at this stage, and the browning should be done in the same pot that will be used for braising. Choose a heavy-gauge ovenproof pan with a lid, such as a Dutch oven, that is just large enough to hold all the ingredients.

2 Sautéing the aromatics

After the meat is browned, remove it from the pot and sauté a mixture of aromatics in the same fat (adding more oil or butter if needed). Mirepoix—a mixture of finely chopped onion, carrot, and celery—is commonly used to add a base of flavor. Other vegetables may be added, including mushrooms and tomatoes. Be sure to sauté them until they release their flavorful liquid.

3 Adding the liquid

Once all the ingredients are sautéed, add the braising liquid, often a mixture of broth and wine. Spices and herbs may be added as well; if they are not edible, wrap them in cheesecloth to make a spice sachet, for easy retrieval later. For a braise, the liquid should come only one-third of the way up the meat. Stews usually call for enough liquid to cover the food completely.

4 Returning the meat to the pot

Put the meat into the liquid in the pot, bring the liquid to a gentle simmer, then cover and place the pot in a 350°F oven. Cooking in the oven rather than on the stove top is a more reliable way to braise, since cooking over a flame can lead to overly rapid cooking and scorching. Because stews have more liquid, they are fine to simmer on the stove top. In either case, maintain a slow and gentle cooking speed, in order to extract as much flavor as possible without drying out the food.

5 Degreasing the liquid

When the meat is tender, remove it from the pot along with larger chunks of vegetable and keep it warm. Use a spoon or skimmer to degrease the liquid, spooning off as much of the floating fat as possible, in order to give the final sauce a better consistency. Or, since most stews and braises benefit from 24 hours of rest, let cool and refrigerate them overnight. Any fat will lift off easily and completely.

6 Thickening the liquid

If the braising liquid is a little thin, bring it to a boil and let it reduce and thicken to a saucelike consistency. If it is very thin, add just a drizzle of cornstarch slurry—a blend of cornstarch and water—and simmer until thickened. Stews often include ingredients that thicken the sauce, such as potatoes.

1 Soups

From light, clear broths and creamy purées to cool fruit soups and rib-sticking chowders, there is a soup to suit every season and nearly every occasion. Delicately flavored or simply garnished, soups make good starters for an elegant menu, soothing but not dulling the appetite. Or a soup may be the centerpiece of a meal, flanked with good bread and a simple green salad. When properly prepared and served, soups are satisfying in ways that permanently etch them in your culinary memory.

Most soup recipes are extraordinarily adaptable and can be adjusted to incorporate the ingredients you have on hand or the leftovers you want to use up. For example, a broth-based soup with lots of vegetables can usually accommodate a handful of beans or lentils, some pasta, or some diced meat to become a hearty main course. And when you want to prepare satisfying meals for busy days ahead, soups are convenient because most recipes can be doubled or tripled, and the soup refrigerated or frozen until needed.

Soups are the best teachers of some important culinary lessons, especially flavor development and seasoning. Eating soup gives you a simultaneous experience of aroma, texture, taste, and temperature. You can evaluate soups at virtually any stage of preparation, making seasoning adjustments as you go.

Types of soup

The four basic styles of soup addressed in this cookbook are broths, purée soups, cream soups, and hearty soups. A broth, made by simmering poultry, meat, fish, or vegetables in water, can be either a sustaining cup of soup on its own or the basis of countless other dishes. Broth-based soups include such classics as chicken noodle soup, onion soup, and bouillon. If your broth-based soup includes vegetables, grains, or pasta, add these ingredients in the sequence indicated in a recipe to ensure that everything finishes cooking at the same time. Finish a full-bodied broth with simple, carefully chosen garnishes: grilled or baked croutons, poached eggs, wontons or tortellini, a few sprigs of a fresh herb, or tender new peas.

Purée soups and cream soups share several characteristics, although they also differ in a few essential ways. Purée soups are made from dried legumes or starchy vegetables such as lentils, potatoes, pumpkins and other squashes, or carrots. Their hearty texture and substantial body come from these main ingredients. The base of a cream soup may be nothing more than a purée soup, or it can be broth or milk thickened with flour (in the form of a roux) and simmered with the main ingredient, which might be chicken, broccoli, asparagus, or tomato, for instance. Both purée soups and cream soups, whether or not they contain cream, are creamy when properly cooked. Cream soups can be strained for an elegant texture; purée soups usually are not. Serve purée soups with a plain garnish, like tiny croutons or a fine dice of ham. For bisque, a type of cream soup, shells from shrimp, lobster, crab, or crayfish are cooked and puréed in the base. The base is then strained and finished with cream.

Hearty soups, sometimes classified in older cookbooks as special, regional, or ethnic soups, may combine the characteristics of more than one soup type. They usually feature an area's specialties, such as local seafood, or storeroom staples like cabbage, potatoes, or beans. Some are traditionally made to celebrate seasonal holidays. As these soups travel the globe, they are changed and adapted. Chowders are an excellent example of how one soup can vary from one region to another. The traditions of two different regions illustrate how different one chowder can be from another. New England clam chowder is based on milk and never contains tomatoes. Manhattan clam chowder, on the other hand, is brothy, flavored and colored by plenty of tomatoes, and studded with bell peppers. The two essential ingredients—clams and potatoes—are always included in both varieties of chowder, but these soups are strikingly different in all other respects.

Selecting ingredients

Choose flavorful ingredients for your soup. This is the place to use richly flavored and well-exercised cuts of meat, such as the shank or shin, or mature stewing hens. The simmering will tenderize these tougher cuts. A turkey neck gives a soup extra body and a subtle flavor. The aromatics and other ingredients you choose—onions, carrots, celery, leeks, herbs, spices, mushrooms, or tomatoes—can change a basic broth from a comfortable chicken noodle soup into a spicy Thai-inspired one.

Preparing and serving soups

Cook soups at a gentle simmer until they are flavorful, and stir them as often as necessary to keep them from scorching. Pay special attention to soups made with beans or potatoes or thickened with flour, as they scorch easily. If you are reheating a soup after storing it, be sure to bring it up to a vigorous simmer. Broth-based soups can be heated over high heat, but purée or cream soups should be placed over low heat until they soften, and stirred frequently as they heat. When making soup, sample it at every stage. But to avoid "double dipping," ladle small amounts into a cup you keep nearby. When the soup is done, or after reheating, taste and adjust the seasonings one more time before ladling it into bowls and presenting it at the table. Serve hot soups very hot, in warmed bowls or cups. Serve cold soups very cold, in chilled dishes.

Making broth

High-quality ingredients, the use of aromatics, and patience are the keys to preparing good broths.

1 Combining the ingredients

Place the ingredients—poultry, meat, fish, shellfish, and/or vegetables—in a tall stockpot. Start with cool water and slowly bring to a simmer. This gradual heating allows a more gentle extraction of flavor than does adding ingredients to hot water. The water should cover the ingredients by about 2 inches.

2 Simmering the broth

Maintain a low, gentle simmer throughout the cooking process. The French use the term *frémir,* "to tremble," to describe the way simmering broths look. Bubbles should break the surface infrequently. As the ingredients simmer, they will release into the water fat and impurities that might cloud the finished broth. These will coagulate and rise to the surface, where they should be skimmed away from time to time with a large spoon.

3 Adding the aromatics

Aromatic vegetables and herbs need only 1 hour or less to release their flavor in a broth. For quick broths, such as seafood broths, herbs are added at the start of cooking. Long-simmering broths made from meat or poultry gain the best flavor if the aromatics are added when the broth has about an hour of simmering time left.

4 Straining and cooling

Place a fine-mesh sieve or colander lined with rinsed cheesecloth over a clean pot or large bowl. (Rinsing the cheesecloth removes loose fibers, helps the cloth adhere to the sieve, and prevents the fibers from soaking up the flavorful broth.) Gently ladle the broth into the sieve or colander, disturbing the solid ingredients as little as possible. Once you have ladled out as much as you can, carefully pour the remaining broth through the sieve or colander. If using the broth right away, skim away any fat floating on the surface. To store the broth for later use, cool it in an ice bath (see page 27) to room temperature, then refrigerate for up to 3 days or freeze for up to 2 months. Note that refrigerating the broth will cause the fat to harden on the surface, making it easy to lift away and discard.

Making a spice sachet

These bundles of herbs and spices are used to add flavor to a simmering broth, soup, or stew.

1 Making and using a sachet

A basic sachet that will flavor 2½–3 qt of liquid contains 5 or 6 cracked peppercorns, 3 or 4 parsley stems, 1 sprig fresh thyme or ½ teaspoon dried thyme, and 1 bay leaf. Add or substitute other spices to complement the flavors in a specific dish: for example, use cardamom, chiles, or star anise to flavor an Asian-style soup. Place the herbs and spices on a square of cheesecloth large enough to contain them. Twist the corners of the cheesecloth together and tie securely with one end of a long piece of string. When adding to the pot, tie the other end of the string to the pot handle for easy removal later. At the end of cooking, gently pull out the bundle, untie the string from the pot handle, and discard. If you prefer, enclose the herbs and spices in a large teaball in place of the cheesecloth and hook it to the side of the pot.

Thickening with roux and slurry

Roux adds a special depth of flavor to a sauce as well as thickening power, while starch slurries give an appetizing translucent sheen.

Thickening with roux

Roux is made by cooking flour in fat. You can use butter, oil, or meat or chicken drippings. Heat the fat over medium heat and then stir in the flour until smooth and moist, with a glossy sheen. Stir frequently to prevent scorching as you cook the roux to the desired color. White roux is barely colored and has a mild flavor. Blond roux, with its golden straw color, is slightly nutty in aroma. For brown or dark roux, "cook out" the roux until it is a deep brown with a smooth texture and a strong nutty aroma. The darker the roux, the more flavor but less thickening power it has. When adding liquid to a roux, avoid extreme temperature differences. Very cold liquids harden the roux, while extremely hot liquids can splatter when combined with roux. After combining roux with a liquid, return the mixture to a full boil so the flour can properly thicken the liquid.

Thickening with slurry

A slurry is cornstarch blended with enough cold water or broth to make a paste the consistency of heavy cream. Starch and liquid are typically used in equal amounts by volume. Use only as much slurry as needed to thicken a broth. While stirring, gradually pour the slurry into the simmering broth in a thin stream, stopping when the liquid has thickened to the desired consistency.

Finishing with cream and egg liaisons

Cream or a mixture of egg yolk and cream called a liaison may be used at the end of cooking to add body and sheen to a dish.

Finishing with cream

To finish a hot soup with cream, bring the soup up to a full boil and check the consistency and seasoning. Stir warmed cream into the soup gradually and stop when you reach the flavor and color you like. For cold soups, make the soup base and chill it completely, at least 3 hours, before adding cold cream to taste.

Finishing with egg liaison

Egg yolk can be used to finish a soup or sauce, but it must be handled with care. Mixing cream with egg yolks makes the yolks less likely to curdle when hot liquid is added. In a large bowl, whisk cream and egg yolk together until evenly blended. To make the liaison, gradually add some of the hot liquid to be thickened, a ladleful at a time, to the egg mixture while whisking constantly to temper the eggs and prevent curdling. Slowly pour the tempered mixture into the pot of hot liquid while stirring constantly. Gently warm the mixture, stirring frequently, until it thickens slightly. Do not allow it to go above 185°F, or the egg yolks can still curdle. Serve the soup or sauce as soon as possible to ensure the safety and quality of the finished dish. For more information on tempering eggs, see page 272.

3 Food mill

Food mills tend to make denser purées than blenders or food processors, as no air is whipped into the mixture. They will also strain out skins, seeds, and tougher fibers as they purée. If your food mill has more than one disk, fit it with a fine disk for a velvety smooth soup, or a coarse disk for a thicker, more textured purée. For the best consistency, pass the soup through the coarse disk first, then switch to the fine disk. (If you cannot change disks on your food mill, use the mill for the first pass and a blender for the second.) Work in batches, filling the food mill no more than halfway each time, and discard the accumulated solids between batches.

4 Sieve and spoon

Rustic or home-style purées or purée soups can be relatively coarse and rely simply on pressing the cooked solids through a sieve using a wooden spoon. Work in several small batches and discard the solids frequently to keep the sieve's holes open. Using a circular motion, press firmly against the food with the rounded back of a wooden spoon. Be sure to collect the purée that clings to the outside of the sieve.

Puréeing

A variety of techniques can be used to purée soups and other preparations.

1 Immersion blender

An immersion blender permits you to purée a soup or other preparations directly in the pot. First, remove any sachets, bay leaves, bones, or other inedible ingredients. Stir the soup slowly with the blender's motor running. Keep the head completely submerged while the blades are turning to prevent splatters.

2 Blender or food processor

To use a regular standing blender or a food processor to purée, cool the soup or other preparation slightly first. Fill the blender or the work bowl of the food processor no more than halfway full to avoid making a mess or, worse, scalding yourself. Like immersion blenders, standing blenders and food processors produce a very fine, smoothly textured soup with just a small amount of air incorporated into the purée.

Chicken Broth

4 lb stewing hen parts, including
backs and necks

1 large yellow onion, diced

1 stalk celery, diced

1 carrot, diced

1 spice sachet (p. 46)

Salt

Makes 2½ quarts

Put the chicken and 3 qt water in a large pot. Add water if needed
to cover the chicken by at least 2 inches. Bring to a boil over medium
heat, skimming any foam that rises to the surface. Once at a boil,
adjust the heat to cook at a slow simmer. Cover partially and simmer
for 2 hours, skimming foam from the surface as needed. Add the
onion, celery, carrot, sachet, and 1½ tsp salt. Continue to simmer,
skimming as necessary, until the broth is flavorful, about 1 hour
more. Taste and season with salt, if needed.

Remove meaty parts and save for another use. Strain the broth and
discard the solids. Skim the fat from the surface or cool in an ice
bath, chill, and lift away the hardened fat. Store the broth in the
refrigerator for up to 5 days, or in the freezer for up to 3 months.

Some stores sell packages
of necks and backs that may
be used to prepare broth.
This broth may also be
made with the carcasses of
roasted birds. Save the
bones from 3 birds after all
the meat has been pulled
or carved away (freeze them
if you will not be making
the broth within two days).

making broth p. 45

straining and cooling p. 45

cooling in an ice bath
p. 27

VARIATIONS

Beef Broth

Replace the chicken with 4 lb bony beef cuts such as short ribs or
shank. Brown the bones and vegetables, along with ½ cup tomato
purée, in a 350°F oven for 45 minutes. Proceed as directed, increasing
the simmering time to a total of 4–4½ hours and adding 1 leek,
chopped, and ¼ cup celery leaves along with the vegetables.

Fish or Shellfish Broth

Replace the chicken with 5 lb bones from mild, lean white fish or
shrimp, crab, and/or lobster shells. Replace the carrot with a coarsely
chopped leek. Sauté until the onion and leek are translucent, then
add the bones or shells. Cover and cook over low heat until the flesh
on the bones is opaque or the shells turn bright red, 5–6 minutes.
Add the water and simmer until very flavorful, 30–45 minutes.

Vegetable Broth

Replace the chicken and vegetables with 1 onion, 1 celery stalk, 1 leek,
1 carrot, 1 parsnip, 1 cup broccoli stems, and 1 cup fennel, all thinly
sliced. Sauté until starting to release juices, before adding the water;
cover the pot and stir occasionally, 10–12 minutes. Simmer for 1 hour.

Onion Soup Gratinée

¼ cup olive oil or vegetable oil

4 yellow onions, thinly sliced

2 cloves garlic, minced

½ cup brandy

6 cups beef or chicken broth, heated

1 spice sachet, including 1 sprig fresh tarragon or ½ tsp dried

Salt and freshly ground pepper

Eight ¼-inch-thick slices French bread

1 cup shredded Gruyère cheese, or as needed

8 cups boiling water, or as needed

Makes 8 servings

Heat the oil in a soup pot over medium-low heat. Add the onions and cook without stirring until they begin to brown on the bottom. Raise the heat to medium, stir, and continue to cook, stirring occasionally, until the onions are deeply caramelized, a dark golden brown, and very soft. The total cooking time will be 30–45 minutes. If the onions begin to scorch, add a few Tbsp of water.

Add the garlic and continue to cook for an additional minute. Add the brandy and stir to deglaze the pan, scraping up any browned bits from the pan bottom. Simmer until the liquid has nearly evaporated, 2–3 minutes.

Add the broth and sachet. Bring to a simmer and cook, partially covered, for 45–60 minutes, skimming foam from the surface as needed. Remove and discard the sachet. Taste and season with salt and pepper.

At this point, the soup may be cooled in an ice bath and stored in the refrigerator to allow the flavors to develop.

When ready to serve the soup, preheat the oven to 350°F.

Ladle the soup into individual ovenproof soup crocks. Top each crock with a slice of bread and sprinkle with grated cheese, covering the bread completely and coming to the edges of the crocks.

Set the soup crocks in a large baking dish and add enough boiling water to the baking dish to reach two-thirds of the way up the sides of the crocks, making a water bath. Bake until the soup is thoroughly heated, if needed, and the cheese is lightly browned, 10–15 minutes.

Serve at once.

The secret to making a fine French onion soup is to allow plenty of time for it to develop flavor. Ideally, make the soup the day before you plan to serve it so that the flavor can mature and mellow.

making a spice sachet
p. 46

baking in a water bath
p. 271

Thai Hot-and-Sour Soup

¼ lb small shrimp, peeled, butterflied, and deveined

2 oz thin rice noodles (rice vermicelli)

8 cups fish or chicken broth

1 stalk lemongrass, cut into 2-inch pieces, smashed

¼ cup Thai fish sauce (nam pla)

2 Tbsp chile oil

1 Tbsp lemon juice

1 Tbsp lime juice, plus 2 tsp zest

½ pickled chile

Salt and freshly ground pepper

⅓ cup rinsed and drained canned straw mushrooms

¼ cup chopped fresh cilantro

Makes 8 servings

Bring a pot of water to a boil. Add the shrimp and boil until cooked through, about 3 minutes. Use a slotted spoon to transfer the shrimp to a colander, reserving the boiling water. Rinse the shrimp under cold water to stop the cooking, drain, and set aside. In the same pot of boiling water, cook the rice noodles until tender, 2–3 minutes. Drain, rinse under cold water, and drain again. Set aside.

Combine the broth with the lemongrass, fish sauce, chile oil, lemon juice, lime juice, lime zest, and pickled chile in a soup pot. Bring to a simmer and cook for 10 minutes. Use tongs to remove the lemongrass. Taste and season with salt and pepper.

Distribute the rice noodles, shrimp, mushrooms, and cilantro among heated bowls. Pour the broth over and serve.

Some of the ingredients for this soup—rice vermicelli, lemongrass, Thai fish sauce, and pickled chile—may require a trip to an Asian grocery or specialty market. All of them are crucial to the overall flavor. Once you have all your ingredients assembled, the soup goes together quickly.

preparing shrimp p. 129

zesting and juicing citrus p. 182

Amish-Style Chicken and Corn Soup

½ stewing hen (4–4½ lb), quartered

8 cups chicken or vegetable broth

¾ cup chopped yellow onion

½ cup chopped carrot

½ cup chopped celery, plus ½ cup finely diced celery

Salt and freshly ground pepper

1 tsp saffron threads, crushed

¾ cup fresh or frozen corn kernels

½ cup uncooked egg noodles

1 Tbsp chopped fresh flat-leaf parsley

Makes 8 servings

Combine the stewing hen with the broth, onion, carrot, chopped celery, 2 tsp salt, and saffron threads in a soup pot over medium heat. Bring to a simmer and cook until the chicken is cooked through and tender, about 1 hour, skimming foam from the surface as needed.

Remove the stewing hen from the broth. When cool enough to handle, discard the skin, pick the meat from the bones, and cut into neat dice.

Strain the saffron broth through a fine-mesh sieve into a clean pot; discard the solids.

Add the finely diced celery, corn, and noodles to the broth. Return the soup to a simmer and cook until the noodles are tender, about 12 minutes. Add the chicken and parsley; simmer for 2–3 minutes more, to heat the chicken completely. Taste and season with salt and pepper.

Stewing hens (or fowls) are the best choice for many soups. They are more full-flavored than fryers or broilers, so the finished soup will have a wonderfully rich flavor and body.

making broth p. 45

cutting a chicken into serving pieces p. 66

Shrimp and Andouille Gumbo

¼ cup olive oil or vegetable oil

¼ cup all-purpose flour

8 cups chicken broth

½ lb medium or large shrimp

½ lb fresh okra, stem ends trimmed, sliced ¼ inch thick

¼ lb andouille sausage, diced

2 bay leaves

½ tsp ground cayenne pepper, or to taste

Tabasco sauce

Salt and ground black pepper

2 tsp filé powder (optional)

4 cups steamed white rice

Makes 8 servings

Heat the oil in a soup pot over high heat. Reduce the heat to medium-low, add the flour, and cook, stirring frequently with a wooden spoon, to make a dark roux with an intensely nutty aroma, 10–15 minutes.

Add the broth gradually, whisking well to work out any lumps. Simmer for 15–20 minutes, stirring frequently.

Peel and devein the shrimp, dice, and add to the soup with the okra, sausage, and bay leaves. Cook until the okra is tender, about 15 minutes.

Remove and discard the bay leaves. Add the cayenne and the Tabasco to taste, then taste and season with salt and black pepper.

Remove the gumbo from the heat and add the filé powder gradually (if using). Serve ladled over the rice.

The secret of success for gumbo is to cook the roux until it is very dark, nearly the color of chocolate. You want to stop just short of burning it. Be careful; it will get extremely hot and may bubble and spatter. The dark roux adds good flavor but contributes less thickening power than a typical roux, so filé powder, made of ground sassafras root, is traditionally added to gumbo as a thickener.

thickening with roux and slurry p. 46

preparing shrimp p. 129

cooking rice and pilaf p. 206

French Lentil Soup

2 Tbsp olive oil or vegetable oil

1 yellow onion, finely diced

1 clove garlic, minced

1 leek, white and light green parts, finely diced

2 carrots, finely diced

1 stalk celery, finely diced

1 Tbsp tomato paste

7 cups chicken broth

1¾ cups French (green) lentils

¼ cup Riesling wine

2 Tbsp sherry wine vinegar

½ lemon, seeded

1 spice sachet (p. 46), including ¼ tsp caraway seeds

Salt and freshly ground pepper

Makes 8 servings

Heat the oil in a soup pot over medium heat. Add the onion and garlic and cook, stirring occasionally, until the onion is translucent, 4–6 minutes.

Add the leek, carrots, and celery and cook, stirring occasionally, until softened, 5–7 minutes.

Add the tomato paste, stir well, and cook until it darkens, about 5 minutes.

Add the broth, lentils, wine, vinegar, lemon, and sachet and bring to a simmer. Cook, uncovered, until the lentils are tender, about 40 minutes. Remove and discard the sachet and lemon half.

Taste and season with salt and pepper.

This is intended to be a brothy soup, but for a heartier, thicker soup, you can purée half of the soup and combine it with the unpuréed half. If you store any leftover soup in the refrigerator, it may become thicker. Adjust the consistency by adding more broth, then recheck the seasoning before serving. If Riesling is not available, choose another slightly sweet white wine.

cleaning leeks p. 186

dicing onions p. 180

Vegetable Soup

3 Tbsp olive oil or vegetable oil

1 yellow onion, diced

½ leek, diced

2 carrots, diced

1 stalk celery, diced

½ cup diced cabbage

⅓ cup diced turnip

8 cups vegetable broth

1 spice sachet (p. 46)

2 plum (Roma) tomatoes, peeled, seeded, and diced

½ cup diced peeled yellow or white waxy potato

½ cup lima beans

½ cup corn kernels

¼ cup chopped flat-leaf parsley

Salt and freshly ground pepper

Makes 8 servings

Heat the oil in a soup pot over medium heat. Add the onion, leek, carrots, celery, cabbage, and turnip and cook, stirring occasionally, until softened, 10–15 minutes.

Add the broth and sachet. Bring to a simmer and cook for 10 minutes.

Add the tomatoes, potato, lima beans, and corn. Continue to simmer until the potatoes are tender, 30–35 minutes.

Remove and discard the sachet. Add the parsley. Taste and season with salt and pepper.

This clear soup bursts with the flavors of fresh vegetables. It is easily varied with different combinations of vegetables, herbs, and spices. Try one of the variations below or create your own version.

making broth p. 45

preparing corn kernels p. 186

VARIATIONS

Borscht

Boil 3 beets until nearly tender, 10–15 minutes. Drain and cool. When cool enough to handle, peel and grate them (use gloves to keep your hands from turning purple). Add 1 sprig fresh marjoram or ½ tsp dried marjoram to the sachet. Proceed as directed above, adding the grated beets with the broth and simmering until all the vegetables are tender, about 30 minutes. Garnish with sour cream and fresh dill.

Zucchini Soup

Replace the oil with 2 strips bacon, minced and cooked until crisp, 2–3 minutes. Omit the carrots, celery, and cabbage. Proceed as directed above, adding about 7 cups finely diced zucchini (seed more mature zucchini) with the broth, along with ½ cup tomato purée and ¼ cup cider vinegar. Garnish with ¼ cup fresh basil chiffonade.

shredding and chiffonade p. 17

Billi Bi

1 cup dry white wine

1 Tbsp minced shallot

1 tsp saffron threads, crushed

2 lb mussels, scrubbed and debearded

4 Tbsp unsalted butter

1 yellow onion, minced

5 Tbsp all-purpose flour

5 cups fish, chicken, or vegetable broth

1 spice sachet (p. 46)

1 cup heavy cream or half-and-half

1 large egg yolk

Salt and freshly ground white pepper

Makes 6–8 servings

Combine the wine, shallot, and saffron in a pot large enough to hold the mussels. Bring to a boil over medium-high heat. Add the mussels, cover the pot tightly, and reduce the heat to medium-low. Cook the mussels for 5–6 minutes, shaking the pot occasionally. Remove the mussels from the pot as their shells open. Discard any that do not open. Separate the meat from the shells; refrigerate the meat and discard the shells. Strain the cooking liquid and reserve.

Melt the butter in a soup pot over medium heat. Add the onion and stir to coat evenly. Cover the pot and cook the onion until translucent, 3–4 minutes. Add the flour and cook, stirring frequently with a wooden spoon, to make a blond roux, about 5 minutes.

Add the mussel-cooking liquid and the broth gradually, whisking well to work out any lumps. Add the sachet and bring to a simmer. Simmer gently, stirring occasionally and skimming foam from the surface as needed, until the soup is flavorful and thickened, about 45 minutes.

Remove and discard the sachet. Strain the soup through a fine-mesh sieve or a colander lined with cheesecloth. Return the soup to the stove and bring to a simmer.

Make a liaison by whisking the cream with the egg yolk in a bowl. Reduce the heat to low, stir about 1 cup of the hot soup into the liaison, then gradually stir the heated liaison into the soup. Cook over low heat, stirring constantly, until the soup reaches a bare simmer and is thickened.

Add the mussels to the soup and simmer until they are heated through. Taste and season with salt and pepper.

There are several tales surrounding the origin of this luxurious French cream of mussel soup. The most popular story is that a chef at the famed Maxim's of Paris named it after American tin tycoon William B. ("Billy B.") Leeds, a regular customer who adored this soup.

finishing with cream and egg liaisons p. 46

cleaning mussels p. 129

New England Seafood Chowder

1¼ lb mussels, scrubbed and debearded

8 chowder clams (quahogs), scrubbed

5 peppercorns, crushed

2 fresh thyme stems, plus 1 Tbsp leaves

2 fresh flat-leaf parsley stems

½ bay leaf

2 Tbsp ground salt pork or 2 strips bacon, minced

1½ yellow onions, diced

2 stalks celery, diced

½ cup all-purpose flour

2 large yellow or white waxy potatoes, peeled and diced

¼ lb cod fillet

¼ lb sea scallops, diced

1 cup whole milk

1 cup heavy cream

Salt and freshly ground pepper

Makes 8 servings

Place the mussels and clams in a large pot with 5 cups water and the peppercorns, thyme stems, parsley stems, and bay leaf. Bring to a simmer over medium heat, cover, and steam until the shells open, 12–15 minutes. Discard any that do not open.

Remove the clams and mussels and strain the broth through a fine-mesh sieve, then through a coffee filter, reserving the cooking liquid. Set the cooking liquid aside.

Remove the clams and mussels from their shells and dice the meat. Refrigerate.

Heat a soup pot over medium heat and add the salt pork. Cook, stirring frequently, until the fat renders and the bits of meat become crisp, 6–8 minutes.

Add the onions and celery and cook, stirring occasionally, until tender, about 5 minutes.

Reduce the heat to medium-low, add the flour, and cook, stirring frequently with a wooden spoon, to make a blond roux, about 5 minutes. Stir in the thyme leaves, then add the reserved mussel-cooking liquid gradually, whisking well to work out any lumps. Simmer, stirring occasionally, for 30 minutes.

Add the potatoes and simmer until tender, about 20 minutes.

Add the cod fillet and simmer until opaque throughout, 4–6 minutes. Remove the cod, use 2 forks to flake it apart, and return to the chowder.

Add the reserved clams and mussels, the scallops, milk, and cream. Heat gently, but do not simmer, until the scallops are opaque throughout, about 3 minutes.

Taste and season with salt and pepper.

This thick, rich, creamy chowder is packed with fish and shellfish. The use of cream makes it a New England–style chowder, as opposed to a Manhattan-style chowder, which includes tomatoes but not cream. Round out the soup with a green salad, some crusty bread, and a bottle of dry white wine to make a meal, or top with a handful of crunchy oyster crackers for a classic New England supper.

making broth p. 45

cleaning mussels p. 129

Cream of Broccoli Soup

2 lb broccoli, separated into stems and florets

¼ cup olive oil or vegetable oil

1 yellow onion, chopped

1 leek, white and light green parts, chopped

1 stalk celery, chopped

¼ cup all-purpose flour

6 cups chicken or vegetable broth

½ cup heavy cream, warmed

1 tsp fresh lemon juice

Salt and freshly ground pepper

Makes 8 servings

Set aside 1 cup of the nicest-looking small broccoli florets for garnish. Coarsely chop the remaining florets and the stems.

Heat the oil in a soup pot over medium heat. Add the onion, leek, celery, and chopped broccoli. Cook, stirring frequently, until the onion is translucent, 6–8 minutes. Add the flour and cook, stirring frequently with a wooden spoon, to make a blond roux, 5 minutes.

Add the broth to the pot gradually, whisking well to work out any lumps. Bring the soup to a simmer and cook until flavorful and thickened, about 45 minutes. Stir frequently and skim as needed.

Meanwhile, bring a large pot of water to boil. Have ready a large bowl of ice water. Add the reserved broccoli florets and parboil, cooking until just tender, 3–4 minutes. Remove the florets with a slotted spoon and plunge them into the ice water. Once cool, drain and reserve.

Strain the soup, reserving both the solids and the broth. Purée the solids, adding broth as needed to facilitate puréeing.

Combine the purée with enough of the reserved broth to achieve the consistency of heavy cream. Strain the soup through a fine-mesh sieve, if desired. Return the soup to a simmer.

Remove the soup from the heat and add the cream and lemon juice. Taste and season with salt and pepper. Garnish with the reserved florets.

By plunging the just-cooked broccoli into an ice-water bath—a technique known as refreshing vegetables—you'll stop the broccoli from continuing to cook with its own residual heat. The sudden chill will also help set a vivid green color.

boiling, parboiling, or blanching p. 37

thickening with roux and slurry p. 46

VARIATIONS

Cream of Asparagus Soup

Replace the broccoli with 3 lb asparagus, ends trimmed. Reserve 16 of the best-looking asparagus tips for the garnish and coarsely chop the remaining asparagus. Proceed as directed above.

Cream of Celery Soup

Replace the broccoli with coarsely chopped celery or celeriac (celery root), peeled. Garnish with diced celery, steamed or boiled until just tender. Proceed as directed above.

Purée of Split Pea

2 strips bacon, minced

1 yellow onion, diced

1 leek, white and light green parts, diced

1 stalk celery, diced

1 carrot, diced

6 cups chicken broth

2 yellow or white waxy potatoes, peeled and diced

1 cup dried split green or yellow peas

1 smoked ham hock

1 spice sachet (p. 46), including 1 clove and 1 clove garlic

Salt and freshly ground pepper

1 cup small croutons

Makes 8 servings

Cook the bacon in a soup pot over medium-high heat until crisp and brown, 2–3 minutes. Remove the bacon with a slotted spoon; drain on absorbent towels, and set aside. Add the onion, leek, celery, and carrot; stir to evenly coat with bacon fat. Cover the pot and cook over medium-low heat, stirring occasionally, until the onion is tender and translucent, 6–8 minutes.

Add the broth, potatoes, peas, and ham hock. Bring to a simmer over medium heat and cook for 20 minutes, stirring occasionally. Add the sachet and simmer, skimming foam from the surface as needed, until the split peas are soft, about 30 minutes.

Remove and discard the sachet. Remove the ham hock and set aside to cool. When cool enough to handle, dice the ham and set aside.

Strain the soup through a sieve, reserving both the solids and the liquid. Purée the solids and return them to the soup pot. Add enough of the reserved liquid to achieve a thick soup consistency. Blend well. Stir in the diced ham and bacon and simmer for 2–3 minutes more to heat thoroughly. Taste and season with salt and pepper. Garnish with croutons.

The bacon and ham hock add a traditional smoky flavor to this thick, hearty purée of vegetables and split peas. If you prefer a meatless version, omit the bacon and ham hock, substitute vegetable broth for the chicken broth, and replace the bacon fat with vegetable oil.

puréeing p. 47

Vichyssoise

1½ Tbsp vegetable oil

3 leeks, white parts only, finely chopped

½ yellow onion, minced

5 cups chicken or vegetable broth

3 russet potatoes, peeled and diced

1 spice sachet (p. 46), including 2 whole cloves

1½ cups half-and-half, chilled

Salt and ground white pepper

¼ cup thinly sliced fresh chives

Makes 8 servings

Heat the oil in a soup pot over medium heat. Add the leeks and onion and sauté until tender and translucent, 4–5 minutes.

Add the broth, potatoes, and sachet. Bring to a simmer and cook until the potatoes are starting to fall apart, about 25 minutes. Remove and discard the sachet.

Purée the soup and return it to the pot. Place the pot in an ice bath and stir occasionally until cool, 1–1½ hours. Transfer to the refrigerator for another 2–3 hours to chill.

Just before serving, stir the half-and-half and 1 tsp salt into the soup. Taste and season with salt and pepper. Serve in chilled bowls, garnished with the chives.

This is The Culinary Institute of America's recipe for this classic warm-weather soup. First prepared by French chef Louis Diat at New York City's Ritz Carlton Hotel in 1917, the chilled potato and leek soup sprinkled with chives was inspired by a favorite hot soup made by Diat's mother.

cleaning leeks p. 186

cooling in an ice bath p. 27

Garbanzo Bean and Farro Soup

1½ cups dried garbanzo beans (chickpeas), soaked for 4–12 hours

1 spice sachet (p. 46), including 2 cloves garlic and zest of 1 orange

1 carrot, cut in half, plus ½ cup diced carrot

Salt

Ground cayenne pepper

1 cup farro (spelt)

½ yellow onion, plus 1 cup diced onion

1 sprig fresh thyme

1 bay leaf

¼ cup olive oil or vegetable oil

½ cup diced celery

1 Tbsp julienned orange zest

1 Tbsp chopped fresh rosemary

1 Tbsp coarsely chopped fresh flat-leaf parsley

Makes 6 servings

Drain the beans and combine with the sachet and 1 carrot half in a soup pot. Add water to cover by 3 inches. Bring to a boil over high heat, then reduce the heat to medium and simmer, stirring occasionally and adding water as necessary to keep the beans completely covered, until the beans are barely tender to the bite, 60–75 minutes. Add the salt and cayenne to taste and continue simmering until the beans are very tender, 30–45 minutes more. Drain, reserving the cooking liquid. Discard the carrot half and the sachet.

Meanwhile, rinse the farro in several changes of cool water. Remove any black kernels. Combine 4 cups water, the onion half, remaining carrot half, thyme, and bay leaf in a medium saucepan over high heat. Bring to a boil, reduce the heat, and simmer for 5 minutes. Add the farro and ½ tsp salt and simmer, uncovered, until the farro pops open and is soft enough to bite, but still noticeably chewy, 45–60 minutes. Drain; remove and discard the vegetables and herbs. Set aside and cover to keep warm.

Purée about two-thirds of the beans with 2½ cups of their cooking liquid until smooth. Return the purée and whole beans to the soup pot. Add more cooking liquid as needed to thin the consistency.

Heat the oil in a medium sauté pan over medium heat. Add the diced onion, diced carrot, and celery and sauté until they are tender but not brown, 5–6 minutes. Stir into the garbanzos. Return the soup to a simmer and taste and season with salt and cayenne. Ladle the soup into heated bowls and top each portion with 2 Tbsp of the farro. Scatter the orange zest over the top and garnish with rosemary and parsley.

Farro is a Tuscan wheat that is often served in combination with beans, traditionally cannellini beans. In the United States it is known as spelt and can be found in most health-food stores, or in gourmet food shops specializing in Italian products. The whole berry is used for this dish.

preparing legumes p. 206

puréeing p. 47

Chilled Red Plum Soup

2½ lb red plums, pitted and chopped (about 6 cups)

1 qt apple juice

1 spice sachet, including 1 large slice fresh gingerroot, 1 whole allspice berry, and ½ cinnamon stick

¼ cup honey

Fresh lemon juice to taste

6 Tbsp sour cream

2 Tbsp slivered almonds, toasted

Makes 8 servings

Combine the plums, apple juice, sachet, and honey in a soup pot over medium heat. Bring to a simmer and cook until the plums are tender, about 20 minutes. Remove and discard the sachet.

Purée the soup until it is very smooth. Taste and season with the lemon juice.

Return the soup to the pot. Place the pot in an ice bath and stir occasionally until cool, 1–1½ hours. Transfer to the refrigerator for another 2–3 hours to chill.

Serve the soup in chilled bowls, garnished with a dollop of the sour cream and a scattering of almonds.

Choose plums that are ripe, but not extremely soft, for this sweet and spicy soup. It makes the perfect beginning or end to a summer luncheon or outdoor dinner. If red plums are unavailable, black plums will also do well in this soup.

making a spice sachet p. 46

toasting nuts p. 26

Lobster Bisque

¼ cup vegetable oil

½–1 lb lobster shells, coarsely chopped

1 yellow onion, thinly sliced

1 leek, white part only, thinly sliced

1 stalk celery, thinly sliced

1 Tbsp minced shallot

½ cup tomato purée

1 Tbsp sweet paprika

¼ cup brandy

2 qt fish or vegetable broth

½ cup dry white wine

1 spice sachet (p. 46)

1 cup long-grain white rice

½ cup heavy cream, warmed

Salt

Ground cayenne pepper

1 cup sliced cooked lobster tail meat

Makes 8 servings

Heat the oil in a soup pot over high heat. Add the lobster shells, reduce the heat to medium, and cook, stirring occasionally, until the shells turn bright red, about 10 minutes.

Add the onion, leek, celery, and shallot. Continue to cook until the vegetables have softened, 4–6 minutes. Add the tomato purée and paprika. Cook until the purée darkens, about 3 minutes. Add the brandy and let the liquid boil away until nearly dry.

Add the broth, white wine, and sachet. Bring to a simmer and cook until well flavored, about 30 minutes.

Add the rice and continue to simmer until the rice is very soft, about 30 minutes more.

Remove and discard the sachet. Purée the bisque (including the shells), preferably in a food mill. Strain through a fine-mesh sieve.

Return the bisque to a simmer, then remove the bisque from the heat and add the warm cream. Stir well. Taste and season with salt and cayenne pepper.

Heat the lobster meat in a small amount of bisque in a medium saucepan over low heat. Divide the lobster among heated bowls. Ladle the bisque over the lobster and serve.

Much of the flavor in this soup comes from lobster shells. You will need ½–1 lb of shells to make the bisque, and it takes about 4 lb of lobster to yield ½ lb of shells. But there's no need to buy lobster just to get the shells. Instead, every time you purchase lobster for another use, save the shells in the freezer. For a luxurious finish, pour in an additional ¼ cup brandy just before serving.

preparing lobster p. 128

puréeing p. 47

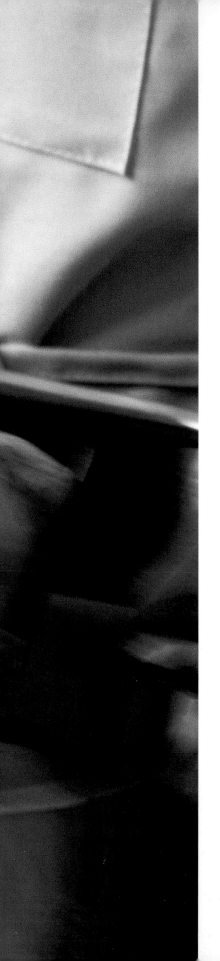

2 Poultry

Chicken and related poultry breeds are so much a part of the contemporary American diet that it is hard to believe there once was a time when the promise of "a chicken in every pot" meant prosperity, security, and comfort that was out of reach for many.

In 1999, we bought enough chicken in this country to feed 99 pounds to each one of us. By the year 2009, that figure will climb to nearly 115 pounds. Why do we cook so much chicken? Poultry is available year-round and comes to the market plumper and more tender than it did in the past. Reliable, familiar, and inexpensive, it is a great vehicle for learning about and mastering every basic cooking method, from broiling to braising. Poultry's versatility is the cook's greatest asset. As the French gastronome Jean Anthelme Brillat-Savarin wrote in the early nineteenth century, "Poultry is to the cook what canvas is to the painter."

Types of poultry

Today's chickens are descended from the Southeast Asisan jungle fowl, a bird first domesticated in India some 5,000 years ago. But chickens aren't the only birds we love to eat. Turkey, goose, duck, and even game birds that used to be available only during the fall and winter holiday season now line meat cases throughout the year. Turkey is a popular alternative to red meats because it offers delicious flavor without all the fats and cholesterol found in red meats. Water fowl, including ducks and geese, have rich and flavorful meat. They also have a layer of fat just below the skin that keeps them warm, and also keeps the meat moist and succulent during cooking. Game birds, from quail to pheasant, are raised on farms today in the same way as domestic poultry, but farm-raised game has a milder flavor than game hunted in the wild.

Selecting poultry

Selective breeding has dramatically changed the shape, texture, and flavor of birds. Modern poultry-raising practices run the gamut from huge operations with nationally recognized brand names to much smaller farms where birds are free to roam outside in a yard or pen. All birds raised for retail sale, domestic and game birds alike, must be inspected for wholesomeness and safety. Farms and processing plants are inspected regularly. Trained federal or state inspectors check the birds for any visible signs of disease after slaughter.

Although inspection is mandatory, quality grading is elective. The poultry found in your grocery store has most likely been graded "USDA A." This indicates that the bird met specific standards in the areas of meatiness, appearance, and freedom from such defects as broken bones or discoloration.

Whole birds are labeled with a specific name—broiler, fryer, roaster—determined by the bird's breed, age, sex, and weight. These distinctions are helpful in choosing a cooking method because the younger the bird, the more naturally tender it is. Mature birds, like well-exercised cuts of meat, need longer, gentler cooking techniques to turn out tender and flavorful. Poultry is often disjointed into parts before it is packaged.

When you buy poultry, take the time to read the label or talk to the butcher. "Fresh" means that the bird was never chilled below 26°F. If you see the word "Natural" on a package, you should also see a statement explaining exactly what this means: perhaps "no added coloring or artificial ingredients" or "minimally processed." Note, however, that hormones are not a concern, since hormones are prohibited in the raising of poultry.

Many chefs prefer organic or free-range poultry for a variety of reasons, including health, nutrition, and, perhaps most important, flavor. To qualify their birds as free-range or free-roaming, producers must demonstrate to the USDA that birds have access to the outside. Birds bearing the organic symbol or the word "Organic" are raised using organic management techniques from the second day of life and are certified by an entity such as the National Organic Program (NOP), which meets USDA-approved criteria and has a system for ensuring that those standards are met. And while free-range does not mean that birds are organically raised, all organically raised birds must be allowed access to the outdoors.

Preparing and serving poultry

There is a potential for food-borne illness whenever you work with poultry. To minimize the risk, as well as to keep the food's quality as high as possible, use the following procedures: Keep raw poultry refrigerated, rewrapping it if necessary. Use a dish or pan to catch any juices that might leak from the bird. Wash your hands thoroughly before, during, and after any cooking sessions with chicken. Be sure to clean the cutting board and any tools or containers that come in contact with raw poultry with hot, soapy water before using them to cut or hold other foods. Cook poultry to the correct doneness temperature to be certain that any potentially harmful bacteria are killed. Thaw frozen poultry safely: overnight in the refrigerator, under cold running water, or in the microwave just before you are ready to cook it.

The tender flesh of poultry responds well to roasting, grilling, broiling, sautéing, frying, poaching, braising, or stewing. Each cuisine has a few favorite flavor combinations that complement poultry. Classic dishes from a European tradition may add herbs, cream, mustard, or wine. Asian stir-frys might pair spicy and aromatic ingredients like ginger and garlic, curry pastes, or chiles with chicken. Pungent mole sauces from Mexico marry chocolate and nuts with poultry for a great depth of flavor. Poultry of all types truly offers a marvelous canvas for the creative cook.

Best cooking methods for poultry

TYPE OF POULTRY	SIZE OR CUT	WEIGHT	BEST COOKING METHODS
Capon		4–8 lb	Roasting, *poêléing*
Cornish game hen		¾–2 lb	Roasting, *poêléing*, grilling, broiling, poaching
Chicken, whole			
	Broiler	1½–2 lb	Broiling, grilling, roasting, stewing
	Roaster	2½–3½ lb	Roasting, braising, stewing, simmering, poaching
	Stewing hen	3½–6 lb	Poaching, stewing, braising, making broths
Chicken pieces, white meat			
	Bone-in breast, with skin	6–10 oz	Baking, grilling, broiling, sautéing, poaching
	Boneless, skinless breast	4–8 oz	Sautéing, pan-frying, grilling, broiling, baking, stir-frying, poaching, shallow-poaching
Chicken pieces, dark meat			
	Bone-in thigh	4–8 oz	Grilling, broiling, baking, braising, stewing, sautéing, pan-frying
	Bone-in drumstick	4–8 oz	Grilling, broiling, baking, braising, stewing, sautéing, pan-frying
	Bone-in leg	8–16 oz	Grilling, broiling, baking, braising, stewing
	Wings	2–4 oz	Baking, pan-frying, deep-frying
Duckling			
	Broiler or fryer	2–4 lb	Roasting, broiling, braising
	Roaster	4–6 lb	Roasting, stewing, braising
	Boneless breast	10–14 oz	Sautéing, grilling, broiling
	Leg	6–8 oz	Roasting, baking, braising
Turkey			
	Young hen or tom	8–22 lb	Roasting, poaching, braising (parts), grilling (parts)
	Yearling turkey	10–30 lb	Roasting

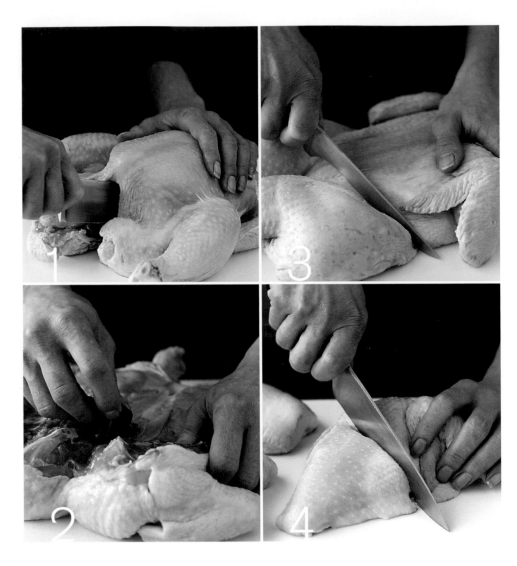

2 Removing the keel bone

Spread the bird open, skin side down. Use a boning knife to make a small cut just through the white cartilage located at the center of the breast at the top of the dark, hard, and flat keel bone. Grasp the bone firmly and pull it, along with the attached white cartilage, away from the breast meat. If needed, use the knife to remove any small pieces of cartilage or bone remaining on the breast meat. Cut the chicken into halves down the center of the breast.

3 Cutting a bird into quarters

Separate the leg and thigh from the breast and wing by cutting through the skin where it stretches between the top of the thigh and the bottom edge of the breast, exposing the joint, then cut through the joint. You now have 4 large pieces.

4 Cutting a bird into eighths

If necessary, cut a quartered bird into smaller serving pieces. Place the legs skin side down. Look for a layer of fat over the joint connecting the drumstick and thigh. Slice through the joint on the drumstick side of this layer (wiggle the leg to help locate the joint). Next, cut each of the half-breast portions into 2 pieces. Make a cut through the breast and the bones with a firm downward slicing motion. To produce pieces with equal amounts of meat, cut the breast not at the exact midpoint, but allot one-third of the breast to the portion with the wing attached and two-thirds of the breast to the other portion.

Cutting a chicken into serving pieces

This technique may be applied to ducks, pheasant, turkey, and quail.

1 Cutting out the backbone

Use heavy kitchen shears, a stiff-bladed boning knife, or a chef's knife to cut along each side of the backbone from the tail to the neck opening. If you are using a knife, insert the blade into the bird's cavity from the tail end while the bird is breast side up and cut through the rib cage with firm, steady motions. While cutting down along the second side of the backbone, you can pull the tail end of the bird upward slightly to make it easier to cut. Keep your blade close to the backbone, use as few cuts as possible, and avoid slashing the breast meat from inside the cavity for a neat appearance. Save the backbone for making broth.

Butterflying

Butterflying evens out chicken breasts and other boneless cuts for uniform cooking and for stuffing.

1 Butterflying a chicken breast

By carefully cutting a boneless chicken breast or other boneless cut nearly in half horizontally and then opening it like a book or a butterfly, you create a cut that is thin enough to cook rapidly at high heat or to roll around a filling. Place the breast flat on a work surface. Place your guiding hand flat on the breast to keep it stable and hold your knife blade parallel to the work surface. Making long, shallow cuts into the curved side of the breast, cut almost through to the other side, stopping ½–1 inch short. This intact portion creates the "hinge" that allows you to open the breast into a flat, thin piece. After butterflying the breast, you can place it between 2 sheets of plastic wrap or parchment paper and pound it lightly with a mallet to an even thickness.

Boning chicken

Boneless breasts and thighs can be sautéed or pan-fried quickly or stuffed with a filling.

1 Boning a chicken breast

Place the breast skin side down, wing end pointing away from you. Insert the point of a boning knife carefully under the tip of the long, thin bone that extends down the breast meat. Carefully cut this bone away from the breast meat, and then guide your blade along the contour of rib bones to remove the entire rib cage. Make small, shallow cuts, pressing the knife against the bones to avoid cutting into the meat. To remove the tough, white tendon that runs the length of the breast, hold the tendon taut with one hand while gently scraping the meat from it with your knife. Trim away excess fat at the edges of the breast. (If desired, remove the skin before boning by grasping it firmly and pulling it away from the meat. Use the tip of your knife to cut the skin away at points where it is attached to the meat.)

2 Boning a chicken thigh

Place the thigh skin side down. With a boning or paring knife, make an incision through the meat along the entire length of the thigh bone. While you lift the bone up, carefully scrape the meat away from it. Trim away excess fat and tendon. (If desired, remove the skin before boning by grasping it firmly and pulling away from the meat.)

Marinating

Soaking meat, poultry, or fish in a marinade adds moisture and flavor before and during cooking.

1 Soaking in marinade

Marinades vary greatly, but they are generally a combination of oil, acid, and aromatics that add flavor as well as moisture. Combine the marinade and meat in a resealable plastic bag or shallow container. Turn the meat to coat it evenly, cover, and marinate it in the refrigerator for 30 minutes to overnight, depending on the size of the pieces and the level of acidity in the marinade. During longer marinating times, turn the meat once or twice. If a recipe calls for using part of the marinade in an accompanying sauce, reserve some of it before adding the meat or boil the marinade for several minutes after removing raw meat.

Dredging and breading

These basic coating techniques create crisp crusts on fried foods.

1 Dredging in flour

Blot the food to be dredged dry with absorbent towels. To dredge, place flour on a plate, in a shallow bowl, or in a plastic bag. Working with 1 piece of food at a time, drag each in the flour, turning to coat them completely. Shake off any excess flour. Note that allowing food to sit for any length of time after dredging may cause the coating to absorb moisture and become gummy.

2 Dipping in egg wash

To bread food, after dredging the items in flour, follow with coatings of egg wash and then bread crumbs. Egg wash is a simple mixture of eggs beaten with milk or water. For the best results, place the flour, egg wash, and bread crumbs in separate shallow bowls in a row. Dredge the food, then transfer it to the egg wash. Turn the food to coat it with egg wash evenly on all sides.

3 Coating in bread crumbs

Transfer the food to the bowl or plate of bread crumbs. Sprinkle or pat the crumbs into an even coating on the food. Shake off any excess.

Stuffing poultry

Stuff aromatics inside a whole bird or under its skin.

1 Flavoring with aromatics

Add flavor and moisture to a roasted bird and its pan drippings by stuffing its cavity with aromatic or flavorful ingredients, such as onion, garlic cloves, fresh herbs, citrus, apples, or mushrooms. Choose aromatic ingredients that suit the other flavorings in your dish, rinse and trim them as necessary, then pack them loosely into the cavity. Another way to stuff a bird with aromatics is to tuck sprigs of a fresh herb, sage leaves, or garlic slivers under the skin. Loosen the skin over the breast or thigh with your fingers, and slide the herb or garlic in place. Or, try an herb paste, like pesto, or a flavored butter spread in an even layer between the meat and the skin.

Trussing poultry

Tying a bird gives it a smooth, compact shape and helps it cook more evenly. It is a common first step in roasting recipes.

1 Looping string around the legs

Place the bird to be trussed breast side up on a work surface. Cut a piece of kitchen string long enough to wrap around the bird twice lengthwise. Pass the string under both drumsticks, then loop the string around the end of each drumstick and cross it to make an X between the legs.

2 Pulling in the legs

Pull the string to draw the legs together and down toward the tail. Next, pass both ends of the string tightly under the drumsticks to draw them close to the bird's body.

3 Tucking in the wings

Pull the string over the joints that connect the drumsticks to the thighs. Continue pulling the string along the side of the bird's body and over the wings, tucking the wings in neatly. Turn the bird over onto its breast and tie the ends of the string securely underneath the backbone at the neck opening. Cut off any excess length of string.

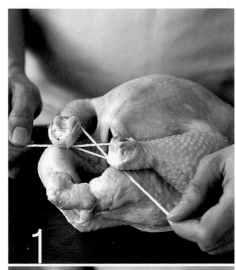

Testing for doneness

Several cues indicate doneness in poultry.

Temperature and other tests

Temperature is the best way to determine doneness in poultry as well as meat. See the chart below for doneness temperatures of specific poultry parts. To test the temperature, insert an instant-read meat thermometer in the thickest part of the flesh. Keep the tip of the thermometer away from the bird's bones, which can skew the reading. In bigger birds, residual heat continues to cook the meat after it is removed from the heat. The internal temperature of a whole turkey or goose may rise another 10°F on average as it rests, so the bird may be removed from the oven before the final temperature is reached.

Other, less accurate tests of doneness in poultry are checking that legs move easily in their sockets; checking that juices run clear when a thigh is pierced; checking that breast meat is firm and opaque throughout; and checking that the meat of legs, thighs, and wings releases easily from the bone.

Resting

This final but essential step allows a bird's juices to be reabsorbed evenly throughout the meat rather than drain onto the carving board.

Sitting before serving

As foods roast, their juices become concentrated at the center. Letting whole poultry rest before serving gives the juices time to redistribute evenly throughout the bird and firms the meat for better slicing. Resting also allows the temperature of the meat to equalize, thus improving its texture, aroma, and flavor. After you remove the bird from the oven, leave it in a warm place. Allow a resting time of 5 minutes for small birds such as Cornish game hens, up to 15 minutes for a chicken, and 20–30 minutes for a turkey.

Safety

Working with poultry calls for a few basic precautionary measures.

Preventing cross-contamination

When working with any type of poultry, keep all tools and work surfaces clean to avoid cross-contamination of other foods with bacteria commonly found in poultry. Wash cutting boards and knives thoroughly with hot, soapy water before and after you use them to cut poultry. Rinse poultry with cold water and pat dry with absorbent towels before cooking. Store uncooked birds in leakproof containers in the refrigerator, placing them below other foods to prevent their juices from dripping onto other ingredients. Stuff birds just before cooking, and remove the stuffing directly afterward. Thaw frozen birds in the refrigerator.

Doneness temperatures for poultry

	INTERNAL TEMPERATURE	VISUAL CUES
Whole birds	180°F in thigh (170°F before resting for large birds)	Legs will move easily in sockets. When the thigh is pierced, juices will run clear. Juices in a bird's cavity will no longer have a pink hue.
Breasts	170°F	Meat becomes opaque and firm throughout.
Legs, thighs, and wings	180°F	Meat releases easily from the bone.
Stuffing	165°F	Check the temperature of stuffing cooked inside a whole bird.

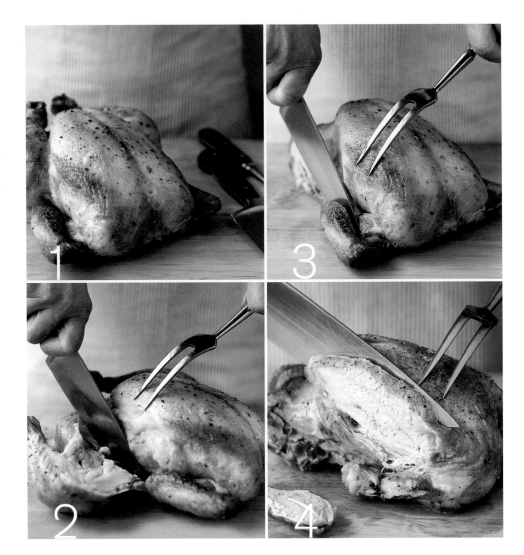

2 Removing the legs

As much as possible, press the flat of the fork's tines against the bird instead of piercing the skin or meat, which will let juices escape. Remove the legs first, to give yourself more room for slicing the breast. Cut through the skin between the thigh and the breast. Pull the thigh away from the body, wiggling it to locate the hip joint, and cut through the joint. Repeat with the other leg. If desired, separate the drumsticks from the thighs by cutting through the leg joint, which may be located by wiggling the drumstick. If desired, slice the meat from large drumsticks and thighs by cutting parallel to the leg bones.

3 Removing the wings

Cut the wings off at their second joint if this was not done before cooking. Leaving the upper part of the wing intact will help stabilize the bird as you carve the breasts.

4 Carving the breast

Make a horizontal cut just above the wing to separate the breast meat from the shoulder. Cut large, thin vertical slices of meat from the breast, carving one side of the bird completely before beginning to carve the other side. Arrange the sliced meat on the platter, then serve.

Leftover meat and stuffing should be removed from the carcass before storing.

Carving

When special meals call for cutting and serving the whole bird at the table, following these steps will make carving simple.

1 Preparing to carve

After roasting a bird and letting it rest, transfer the bird to a cutting or carving board and place it breast side up. (A carving board is a cutting board with an indentation that captures juices released during carving.)

You can also carve on a platter, but make sure the platter's edges are not so high as to obstruct the blade of your knife. Have ready a separate serving platter or a stack of dinner plates where you can arrange the meat as you carve. A carving fork or kitchen fork will help you steady the bird as you cut. Cut away the trussing string before you begin.

Chicken Paillards with Orange-Thyme Butter

Orange-Thyme Butter

4 Tbsp unsalted butter, softened

2 Tbsp ground almonds

1 Tbsp fresh orange juice

1 tsp fresh thyme leaves

½ tsp grated orange zest

¼ tsp salt

⅛ tsp freshly ground pepper

4 boneless, skinless chicken breast halves (7–8 oz each)

Vegetable oil for brushing

Makes 4 servings

For the orange-thyme butter, blend the ingredients in a small bowl. Transfer onto a piece of plastic wrap. Roll into a 1-inch-diameter cylinder and secure the ends by twisting. Chill until firm, about 2 hours.

Trim the chicken breasts of excess fat. Pull away the tenderloin from the underside of each breast and reserve for another use. Make a cut through the thickest part of the breast to butterfly it. Open each breast between sheets of parchment or plastic wrap and pound it to an even ¼-inch thickness to make a *paillard*.

Prepare a grill for a hot fire. Season the *paillards* with salt and pepper and brush lightly with oil. Grill on the first side until marked, 1–2 minutes. Turn and grill on the second side until the edges of the *paillards* are white and the surfaces appear moist, 1–2 minutes more. Top each *paillard* with a slice of the compound butter and serve.

Boneless chicken breasts, like boneless pork or veal, can be pounded into thin, even cutlets—sometimes called *paillards*—to ensure rapid cooking by grilling or sautéing. Adjust the weight of the mallet and strength of the blow to match the meat. Chicken, for example, requires a more delicate touch than pork. Be careful not to tear or overstretch the meat while pounding it.

grilling and broiling p. 28

butterflying p. 67

Grilled Chicken with Barbecue Marinade

Barbecue Marinade

½ cup vegetable oil

2 Tbsp cider vinegar

1 Tbsp Worcestershire sauce

1 tsp *each* brown sugar and dry mustard

2 cloves garlic, minced

½ tsp Tabasco sauce

½ tsp *each* garlic powder and onion powder

2 Tbsp bourbon (optional)

1 or 2 dried red chiles, crushed

1 tsp tomato paste

2 chickens (2½–3 lb each), cut into eighths and trimmed

Salt and freshly ground pepper

Fresh lemon juice for drizzling

Makes 6 servings

For the marinade, combine all the ingredients in a medium bowl. Reserve half of the marinade for basting.

Season the chicken with salt and pepper. Put in a resealable plastic bag and pour in half of the marinade. Close the bag, squeeze to distribute the marinade, and place in the refrigerator for 2–12 hours. Periodically turn to keep the chicken evenly coated with marinade.

Prepare a grill for a medium fire with a cooler zone. Remove the chicken from the marinade and grill directly over the fire on the first side until well browned, 6–8 minutes. Turn the pieces over, place over the cooler zone, and cover the grill. Cook the chicken breast halves until an instant-read thermometer registers 170°F, 12–14 minutes more. Cook the thighs and drumsticks until they register 180°F, 15–18 minutes. Brush the chicken periodically with some of the reserved marinade to moisten and flavor it. To test for doneness, insert a fork in the thickest part of the chicken piece and press lightly; the juices should run clear.

Remove the chicken to a platter and let rest for 5–10 minutes before serving. Drizzle with a few drops of fresh lemon juice and serve.

Creating hot and cool zones on the grill is a real necessity when cooking chicken on the bone. After browning the chicken pieces over hot coals, shift them to a cooler area of the grill. This will allow the pieces to cook all the way through without burning the skin and drying out the meat.

grilling and broiling p. 28

cutting a chicken into serving pieces p. 66

testing for doneness p. 70

Plum-Glazed Grilled Chicken

Plum Glaze

¼ cup **Chinese rice wine or dry sherry wine**

¼ cup **soy sauce**

¼ cup **plum sauce**

3 Tbsp **rice wine vinegar**

3 Tbsp **honey**

1 tsp **salt**

½ tsp **freshly ground pepper**

2 chickens (2½–3 lb each), cut into eighths and trimmed

Makes 6 servings

For the glaze, combine the rice wine, soy sauce, plum sauce, ¼ cup water, the vinegar, honey, salt, and pepper in a small saucepan. Bring to a boil over medium heat. Thin the glaze with water if needed.

Prepare a grill for a medium fire with a cooler zone. Grill the chicken directly over the fire on the first side until well browned, 6–8 minutes. Place the chicken over the cooler zone, brush with glaze, and cover the grill. Cook chicken breast halves until an instant-read thermometer registers 170°F, 12–14 minutes more. Cook thighs and drumsticks until they register 180°F, 15–18 minutes. Brush the chicken periodically with the glaze and turn. To test for doneness, pierce a thigh and press lightly; the juices should run clear. Remove the chicken to a platter and let rest for 5–10 minutes, then serve.

Look for bottled plum sauce in the Asian foods section of the supermarket.

grilling and broiling p. 28

cutting a chicken into serving pieces p. 66

Chicken Thighs with Duxelles Stuffing

8 **chicken thighs** (3–4 oz each), boned

3 Tbsp **unsalted butter** (divided use)

⅓ cup **minced shallot**

3 cups **finely diced white mushrooms**

2 tsp **fresh lemon juice**

Salt and freshly ground pepper

½ cup **heavy cream**

3 Tbsp **minced fresh flat-leaf parsley**

2 Tbsp **fresh bread crumbs**

Makes 4 servings

Place each boneless thigh between sheets of parchment paper and pound to an even ¼-inch thickness. Place in the refrigerator to chill.

Heat 1 Tbsp of the butter in a large skillet over medium heat. Add the shallot and sauté until translucent, 5–6 minutes. Add the mushrooms and sauté until dry, 10–15 minutes, to create a duxelles. Taste and season with the lemon juice, salt, and pepper. Add the cream and simmer until thickened, 2–3 minutes. Add the parsley and bread crumbs and combine well. Set aside.

Preheat the oven to 350°F. Place 1½ Tbsp of the duxelles in the center of each chicken thigh. Wrap the thigh meat around the duxelles and tie with kitchen string to secure it. Melt the remaining 2 Tbsp butter in a small pan and brush it on the thighs. Season the chicken with 1 tsp salt and ½ tsp pepper.

Place the chicken thighs on a rack in a flameproof roasting pan. Bake, basting from time to time, until a thermometer inserted in the thickest part of the meat registers 180°F, 35–40 minutes. Turn on the broiler and position the thighs 2–3 inches from the heat source. Brown until well colored, about 2 minutes. Remove the chicken to a platter and let rest for 5 minutes before serving.

Duxelles is the French term for a combination of finely diced shallots and mushrooms, lightly sautéed in butter and often used as a base for stuffings. Cooking the mixture just until the mushrooms' liquid has just evaporated concentrates the flavors and keeps the stuffing from becoming soggy.

roasting and baking p. 30

boning chicken p. 67

making bread crumbs p. 26

Roast Chicken with Pan Gravy

1 roasting chicken (3–3½ lb)

Salt and freshly ground pepper

2 sprigs fresh thyme

2 sprigs fresh rosemary

¼ cup vegetable oil or 4 Tbsp unsalted butter, softened

½ cup diced yellow onion

¼ cup diced carrot

¼ cup diced celery

1 Tbsp all-purpose flour

1½ cups chicken broth

Makes 4 servings

Preheat the oven to 400°F. Season the chicken with salt and pepper and place the herbs in the cavity. Rub the skin with the oil and truss the chicken. Place, breast side up, on a rack in a flameproof roasting pan. Roast, basting occasionally with the accumulated pan juices or oil, for 40 minutes.

Remove the pan from the oven, and lift out the bird. Scatter the onion, carrot, and celery on the bottom of the pan and replace the bird. Continue to roast, basting occasionally, until an instant-read thermometer inserted in the thickest part of the thigh registers 170°F, 30–40 minutes more.

Remove the chicken and rack from the roasting pan and let the chicken rest for 15 minutes before carving.

Meanwhile, place the roasting pan on the stove top over medium-high and cook the vegetables until browned, about 5 minutes. Pour off all but 2 Tbsp of the fat. Add the flour and cook, stirring frequently with a wooden spoon, to make a blond roux, about 5 minutes. Whisk in the broth until completely smooth. Simmer the gravy until it reaches a saucelike consistency, 10–12 minutes. Taste and adjust the seasoning with salt and pepper. Strain the gravy through a fine-mesh sieve.

Carve the chicken and serve with the pan gravy.

Depending on how many diners you have, the leftover meat from this roasted chicken can be used to make a second meal of chicken salad, risotto, or pot pie. Keep the leftover bones to add to homemade broth. When making the pan gravy, add the wing tips into the pan along with the vegetables for a flavor boost.

trussing poultry p. 69

making a pan sauce p. 98

resting p. 70

VARIATION

Lemongrass Chicken with Pan Gravy

Make a paste by mincing the soft inner parts of 4 lemongrass stalks and combining in a food processor with 3 mashed garlic cloves, 1 sliced shallot, 4 seeded hot chiles, 1 Tbsp sugar, and ½ tsp salt. Add 4–5 Tbsp Thai fish sauce *(nam pla)*. Rub half of the paste underneath the skin of the breast and thighs of the chicken. Rub the remaining paste over the exterior of the chicken. Proceed as directed, omitting the herbs. After 30 minutes, occasionally baste the chicken with a mixture of 2 Tbsp peanut oil, 1 tsp fresh lime juice, ¼ tsp salt, and a few grindings of pepper, plus any accumulated pan juices.

Roast Goose with Apple-Prune Sauce

1 goose (9–11 lb), neck and giblets reserved

Salt and freshly ground pepper

1 Golden Delicious apple, peeled, cored, and quartered

8 pitted prunes

1 sprig fresh rosemary

1 yellow onion, coarsely chopped

1 stalk celery, coarsely chopped

1 small carrot, coarsely chopped

Makes 8–10 servings

Preheat the oven to 350°F.

Cut the wings from the goose and cut into 2-inch pieces. Cut the neck into 2-inch pieces. Combine with the gizzard and heart. Set aside, and reserve the liver separately.

Prick the skin of the goose all over with a kitchen fork. Season with salt and pepper. Put the apple, prunes, and rosemary in the body cavity of the goose. Truss the goose (see page 69) and place it on its side on a rack in a flameproof roasting pan.

Roast for 30 minutes, then turn the goose over on its other side and roast for 30 minutes more. Remove the goose on its rack from the pan and pour off the excess fat, reserving 2 Tbsp.

Return the goose to the pan, breast side up, pricking the skin again. Reduce the oven temperature to 325°F and continue to roast until a meat thermometer inserted in the thickest part of the thigh registers 170°F, about 1½ hours more.

While the goose is roasting, heat the reserved 2 Tbsp fat in a heavy medium saucepan over medium heat. Add the reserved goose wings, neck, gizzard, and heart, and sear, about 2 minutes. Add the onion, celery, and carrot and cook, stirring often, until browned, about 10 minutes. Add water to cover by an inch and bring to a boil. Reduce the heat and simmer, uncovered, until the broth is very flavorful, about 45 minutes. Add the liver and simmer until cooked through, 15 minutes more. Strain the broth and discard the solids. This should yield 2½–3 cups broth.

Remove the goose from the roasting pan, cover to keep warm, and let rest. Pour off the fat from the roasting pan. Add the broth and stir to deglaze the pan. Strain and set aside to cool slightly.

Remove the apples and prunes from the goose and place in a blender. Remove and discard the rosemary. Add a little of the broth to the apples and purée, adding more broth as needed to ease the puréeing. Combine the purée with enough broth to give it a good sauce consistency; you should have 2–2½ cups. Put in a saucepan and return to a boil over high heat. Reduce the heat and simmer until flavorful, 5 minutes. Taste and season with salt and pepper.

Carve the goose and serve with the sauce.

Richer in flavor than chicken or turkey, goose renders a fair amount of fat during the roasting process. Carefully pricking the skin with a sharp fork will help the excess fat drain out as the bird cooks, ensuring crisp skin and moist meat. To turn the bird safely, remove the roasting pan from the oven first. Then, use tongs or kitchen forks to maneuver the bird as you roll it over.

carving p. 71

testing for doneness p. 70

Roast Turkey with Pan Gravy

1 turkey (about 15 lb)

1 apple, quartered

1 bay leaf

1 large sprig fresh thyme

½ bunch fresh flat-leaf parsley

1–2 Tbsp fresh lemon juice

Salt and freshly ground pepper

¾ cup diced yellow onion

½ cup diced carrot

½ cup diced celery

5 cups chicken broth
(divided use)

Cornstarch slurry: ⅓ cup cornstarch blended with ⅓ cup cold water or chicken broth

Makes 10 servings

Preheat the oven to 450°F. Set a roasting rack in a large flameproof roasting pan.

Stuff the turkey with the apple, bay leaf, thyme, and parsley. Rub the lemon juice over the entire bird and season with salt and pepper. Place the turkey breast side up on the rack in the roasting pan, transfer to the oven, and immediately reduce the oven temperature to 350°F. Roast for 3 hours, basting occasionally with accumulated pan drippings. Remove from the oven. Transfer the turkey, on its rack, to a baking sheet. Degrease the pan drippings by skimming away any excess fat from the surface. Return the turkey and any juices that have accumulated on the sheet to the roasting pan and return to the oven. Roast until an instant-read thermometer inserted in the thickest part of the turkey's thigh registers 180°F, 30–60 minutes more. Remove the turkey and the rack from the roasting pan, cover the bird, and let rest.

While the turkey is resting, combine the pan drippings, onion, carrot, and celery in a saucepan. Add ½ cup of the broth to the roasting pan and stir to deglaze the pan, scraping up any browned bits from the pan bottom. Add to the saucepan along with the remaining broth. Simmer over medium heat until slightly reduced and flavorful, skimming away any fat that rises to the surface, 20–25 minutes.

Gradually add the cornstarch slurry to the simmering broth, whisking constantly, until the gravy has a good consistency. Simmer 2 minutes more, strain, taste, and season with salt and pepper.

Remove and discard the apple, bay leaf, thyme, and parsley. Carve the turkey and serve with the gravy.

The rule of thumb for turkey roasting is to allow about 20 minutes per pound; use this to calculate the approximate roasting time for birds larger than the one called for in this recipe.

If desired, serve with Apple-Sage Dressing (p. 219).

roasting and baking
p. 30

making gravy p. 98

Capon with Tomatoes and Artichokes

1 capon (about 7 lb)

Salt and freshly ground pepper

2 or 3 whole fresh chives, plus 2 Tbsp chopped

2 or 3 fresh flat-leaf parsley stems, plus 2 Tbsp chopped leaves

2 or 3 tarragon stems, plus 2 Tbsp chopped leaves

4 Tbsp unsalted butter, plus softened butter as needed for coating

2 strips thick-sliced bacon, diced

¾ cup diced yellow onion

½ cup diced carrot

½ cup diced celery

4 fresh artichoke hearts or ½ lb rinsed canned

2 cups chicken broth

2 tomatoes, peeled, seeded, and chopped

Makes 8 servings

Preheat the oven to 300°F.

Season the capon with salt and pepper and stuff the cavity with the herbs. Set aside.

Heat the 4 Tbsp butter in a Dutch oven over medium heat. Add the bacon and cook until some of the fat renders and the bacon is crisp, 2–3 minutes. Add the onion, carrot, and celery and cook until the onion is light golden brown, 10–12 minutes.

Remove the pot from the heat. Place the capon on top of the vegetables and rub with softened butter.

Cover the pot and place in the oven. *Poêlé*, basting the capon every 30 minutes with pan drippings or additional butter, and removing the lid during the last 30 minutes of cooking time to allow the capon to brown, until a thermometer inserted in the thickest part of the thigh registers 170°F, 4–4½ hours. If using fresh artichoke hearts, add them to the pot after 3 hours. Remove the capon and let rest while finishing the sauce.

Place the pot over high heat and bring the liquid to a boil. Reduce slightly. Skim away any excess fat that rises to the surface. Add the broth and bring to a boil. Degrease the sauce again thoroughly. Reduce the heat slightly and simmer until reduced and thickened to a saucelike consistency, about 10 minutes.

Add the tomatoes, artichoke hearts (if using canned), and chopped herbs. Simmer just until the tomatoes are heated through. Taste and season with salt and pepper.

Carve the capon and serve with the sauce.

A capon is a neutered young male chicken, usually about twice the size of a regular fryer. Here, the bird is cooked by *poêléing*, or butter-roasting. Rubbed with butter and nestled into a bed of diced aromatic vegetables flavored with bacon (known as a *matignon*), the capon cooks in a covered pot that traps all the juicy flavor inside the bird. To *poêlé* properly, the bird should fit snugly into the pot, so there's no need to truss.

peeling and seeding tomatoes p. 184

trimming artichokes p. 185

Duck Breast with Golden Raisin and Orange Sauce

4 duck breast halves
(8–10 oz each)

Salt and freshly ground pepper

2 Tbsp golden raisins

¾ cup brandy

2 Tbsp sugar

3 Tbsp fresh orange juice
(divided use)

¼ cup cider vinegar

1 Tbsp currant jelly

2 cups chicken broth

2 tsp grated orange zest

Makes 4 servings

Trim the duck breasts of excess fat and season with salt and pepper. Set aside.

Combine the raisins with the brandy and warm in a microwave oven for 40 seconds at full power. Or, combine in a small saucepan and warm over low heat. Allow the raisins to plump for about 10 minutes.

Meanwhile, combine the sugar and 1 Tbsp of the orange juice in a heavy, nonreactive sauté pan and cook over medium heat without stirring. Once the sugar has begun to melt, stir occasionally until the sugar is completely melted and the mixture is golden brown, about 8 minutes. Immediately add the vinegar and continue to cook until reduced by half, 2–3 minutes more.

Add the remaining 2 Tbsp orange juice to the reduced sugar mixture. Add the raisins, along with any unabsorbed brandy, and the currant jelly. Set aside.

Heat an ovenproof sauté pan over high heat. Add the duck breasts, skin side down. Reduce the heat to medium-low and cook until the skin is nicely browned and crisp, about 15 minutes. Turn the breasts and cook 10 minutes more for medium. Transfer the duck breasts from the pan to warmed plates and cover to keep warm while completing the sauce.

Pour off the fat from the sauté pan and return to medium heat. Add the broth and stir to deglaze the pan, scraping up any browned bits from the pan bottom. Simmer rapidly until the broth is reduced by half, 4–5 minutes. Add the raisin and orange sauce and stir. Taste and season with salt and pepper.

Garnish each breast with the orange zest and serve with the raisin and orange sauce.

Duck has a thick layer of fat under its skin that helps keep this aquatic bird warm. Most recipes for duck involve a step designed to render away much of this fat, leaving the skin deliciously crisp. Here, the breasts are slowly cooked skin side down for a good 15 minutes to let the fat melt away.

rehydrating and plumping
p. 182

zesting and juicing citrus
p. 182

Chicken Breast Fillet with Fines Herbes Sauce

4 boneless, skinless chicken breast halves (7–8 oz each)

Salt and freshly ground pepper

All-purpose flour for dredging

2 Tbsp vegetable oil

2 tsp minced shallot

½ cup dry white wine

½ cup chicken broth

¼ cup heavy cream

Cornstarch slurry: 1 tsp cornstarch blended with 1 tsp cold water (optional)

Fines herbes: 1 tsp *each* minced fresh tarragon, flat-leaf parsley, chives, and chervil

Makes 4 servings

Season the chicken breasts with salt and pepper. Dredge in the flour.

Heat the oil in a large sauté pan over medium-high heat and sauté the chicken on the first side until light golden, about 5 minutes. Turn and continue to sauté until opaque throughout, 7–8 minutes more. Transfer to warmed plates and cover to keep warm while completing the sauce.

Pour off all but 1 Tbsp oil from the pan and place over medium-high heat. Add the shallot and sauté until translucent, 1–2 minutes.

Add the wine and stir to deglaze the pan, scraping up any browned bits from the pan bottom. Let the liquid reduce until it is nearly cooked away. Add the broth, simmer briefly, then add the cream and simmer until reduced to a saucelike consistency and flavorful, about 5 minutes. If needed, add just enough of the cornstarch slurry while stirring to thicken the sauce slightly. Add the *fines herbes,* taste, and season with salt and pepper. Serve the sauce over the chicken.

A classic French flavoring combination of finely minced fresh herbs, *fines herbes* brings together the oniony bite of chives and slightly musky anise scent of tarragon with the forthright grassiness of parsley and the delicate sweetness of chervil. If fresh chervil proves difficult to find, it may be omitted.

sautéing and stir-frying p. 32

dredging and breading p. 68

thickening with roux and slurry p. 46

VARIATIONS

Chicken with Leek and Mustard Seed Sauce

Omit the *fines herbes.* After deglazing the pan with the wine, add 1 Tbsp thinly sliced leek (white and light green parts) and 2 tsp mustard seeds along with the broth and simmer until the leek is tender, about 3 minutes. Add the cream and proceed as directed.

Chicken with Moroccan Hot and Sweet Tomato Sauce

Omit the *fines herbes.* Replace the shallot with 1 tsp minced garlic, ½ tsp ground cinnamon, ½ tsp ground ginger, and 1 pinch ground cayenne. Sauté just until aromatic, 30 seconds, before deglazing the pan with the white wine and reducing the broth as directed. Finish the sauce by adding about 1 cup diced, peeled, and seeded tomato and 2 Tbsp minced fresh cilantro. Simmer until hot and flavorful and, if needed, thicken with cornstarch slurry as directed above. Scatter toasted sesame seeds over the chicken just before serving it.

peeling and seeding tomatoes p. 184

Southern Fried Chicken with Country Gravy

1 fryer chicken (2½–3½ lb)

Salt and freshly ground pepper

1 cup buttermilk

1 Tbsp mustard

2 tsp chopped fresh tarragon

2 tsp all-purpose flour, plus
more for dredging

Vegetable oil for pan-frying

1 cup whole milk, warmed

Makes 4 servings

Cut the chicken into serving pieces. Trim the pieces of excess fat and season well with salt and pepper.

Whisk together the buttermilk, mustard, and tarragon in a large bowl to make a marinade. Put the marinade and chicken pieces in a resealable plastic bag, close, and squeeze until coated evenly. Place in the refrigerator and marinate for at least 4 hours and up to 12 hours, turning occasionally.

Preheat the oven to 300°F.

Remove the chicken from the marinade, allowing any excess to drip off. Dredge in the flour.

Pour the oil into a skillet to a depth of ½ inch. Heat over medium heat until it registers 350°F on a deep-frying thermometer. Add the legs and thighs to the hot oil, in batches as needed. Pan-fry until golden brown on the first side, 6–7 minutes, then turn and fry on the second side until golden, 7–8 minutes more. Place on a rack in a baking pan and put in the oven. Use a slotted spoon to remove browned bits from the oil and let the oil return to 350°F. Continue frying the breast pieces in the same way, then add to the pan in the oven. Bake until the chicken is opaque throughout and an instant-read thermometer inserted into the thickest parts registers 180°F for thigh and leg portions, about 25 minutes, and 170°F for breast portions, about 10 minutes.

Meanwhile, make the gravy. Use the slotted spoon to remove any browned bits from the oil in the pan and pour off all but 2–3 tsp. Add the 2 tsp flour and cook, stirring frequently with a wooden spoon, to make a blond roux, 2 minutes. Add the milk to the roux, stirring well to remove all lumps. Cook over low heat, stirring and skimming as necessary, until thickened to a saucelike consistency, 5–10 minutes. Taste and season with salt and pepper. Strain the gravy and serve with the chicken.

The presence of buttermilk in the marinade adds a special velvety tenderness to this classic Southern fried chicken. (The secret is the acid in the buttermilk, which helps tenderize the chicken.) Using milk to make the pan gravy creamy and extra-smooth is another special Southern touch. To preserve the chicken's crunchy crust, serve the gravy alongside on mashed potatoes or hot buttermilk biscuits.

cutting a chicken into serving pieces p. 66

pan-frying p. 34

dredging and breading p. 68

Ham and Mushroom–Stuffed Chicken Roulades

Ham and Mushroom Stuffing

2 Tbsp unsalted butter

¼ cup minced yellow onion

2 cups coarsely chopped white mushrooms

2–3 Tbsp dry white wine

¼ cup minced ham

1–2 tsp minced fresh flat-leaf parsley

1–2 Tbsp fresh bread crumbs

Salt and freshly ground black pepper

4 boneless, skinless chicken breast halves (7–8 oz each)

All-purpose flour for dredging

Egg wash: 1 large egg whisked with 2 Tbsp cold milk or water

1 cup dried bread crumbs

Cream Sauce

2 Tbsp unsalted butter

2 Tbsp all-purpose flour

1¾ cup chicken broth

½ cup heavy cream

¼ tsp freshly ground white pepper

Vegetable oil for pan-frying

Makes 4 servings

For the stuffing, melt the butter in a sauté pan over medium heat. Add the onion and sauté until translucent, about 5 minutes. Add the mushrooms and wine and cook until all the liquid has been absorbed, about 5 minutes. Add the ham, combine well, and remove from the heat. Fold in the parsley and bread crumbs. Cool the mixture slightly, taste, and season with salt and pepper.

Trim the chicken breasts of excess fat. Make a cut through the thickest part of each breast to butterfly it. Open each breast between sheets of parchment or plastic wrap and pound it to an even ¼-inch thickness. Blot dry and season with salt and black pepper.

Top each breast with an equal portion of the stuffing and, starting from a long end, roll the breast around the stuffing. Dredge in the flour, dip in the egg wash, and roll in the bread crumbs.

For the sauce, melt the butter in a saucepan over medium heat. Add the flour and cook, stirring frequently with a wooden spoon, to make a blond roux, 5 minutes. Add the broth gradually, whisking well to work out any lumps. Return to a simmer and add the cream. Season with ½ tsp salt and the white pepper. Simmer over low heat until flavorful, 15–20 minutes. Set aside and keep warm.

Pour the oil into a skillet to a depth of about ¼ inch. Heat over medium heat until it registers 350°F on a deep-frying thermometer. Place the rolled breasts in the hot oil, seam side down, and pan-fry on the first side until golden brown and crisp, about 2 minutes. Turn and fry on all sides until the crust is golden brown and an instant-read thermometer inserted into the thickest part of a roll registers 170°F, 6–7 minutes more. (If the crust is browned but the chicken is not cooked through, finish cooking in a 350°F oven to avoid burning the crust.)

Lift out the chicken with a slotted spoon and drain briefly on absorbent towels. Return the sauce to a simmer and taste and adjust the seasoning with salt and white pepper. Slice and serve the roulades with the sauce.

You can use any type of good-quality ham in this stuffing. Smithfield-style country hams, Italian prosciutto, or Spanish serrano hams are all good choices for a special flavor in this classic dish.

pan-frying p. 34

butterflying p. 67

making bread crumbs p. 26

Poached Chicken Florentine

4 Tbsp unsalted butter
(divided use)

2 Tbsp minced shallot

4 boneless, skinless chicken
breast halves (7–8 oz each)

1 cup chicken broth

½ cup dry white wine

¼ cup sour cream

5 cups chopped spinach

Salt and freshly ground pepper

½ cup grated Parmesan

Makes 4 servings

Preheat the oven to 350°F. Choose a large skillet and cut a parchment paper round to fit just within the top of the pan.

Rub the skillet with 2 Tbsp of the butter. Sprinkle the shallot evenly over the bottom of the pan. Add the chicken breasts, broth, and wine and bring to a simmer over low heat.

Cover the pan with the parchment and place in the oven. Poach until an instant-read thermometer inserted in a breast registers 165°F, about 15 minutes. Remove the pan from the oven and preheat the broiler.

Transfer the chicken breasts to a warmed plate and cover to keep warm. Strain the poaching liquid into a saucepan and place over medium heat. Bring to a simmer and cook until the sauce becomes syrupy and reduces to about ¼ cup, 8–10 minutes. Whisk 3 Tbsp of the poaching liquid with the sour cream in a bowl to make a glaze.

Heat the remaining 2 Tbsp butter in a large skillet. Sauté the spinach until wilted and bright green, about 2 minutes. Season with salt and pepper.

Place the spinach in an even layer in the bottom of a flameproof 8-inch square baking pan. Place the chicken on top of the spinach. Spoon 2 Tbsp of the glaze over each chicken breast half. Sprinkle the Parmesan over the glaze.

Broil lightly to brown the cheese. Serve at once.

When Caterina de' Medici left Florence for France in 1533 to marry the Duc d'Orléans (later King Henry II), she brought her Italian cooks with her. Caterina introduced to the French court spinach, among other delicacies, and ever since then, any dish dubbed "Florentine" is sure to include spinach.

poaching p. 39

preparing spinach and
leafy greens p. 184

Aromatic Chicken Braise

4 chicken drumsticks

4 chicken thighs

Salt and freshly ground
black pepper

3 Tbsp peanut oil

1 Tbsp minced gingerroot

2 cloves garlic, minced

¼ cup minced green onion,
white and green parts
(divided use)

1 one-inch-square piece orange
zest, plus 1 tsp julienned
orange zest

1 cinnamon stick

½ tsp dried red pepper flakes

½ tsp Szechwan peppercorns

1½ cups chicken broth
(divided use)

3 Tbsp dark soy sauce

3 Tbsp Chinese rice wine or dry
sherry wine

2 tsp sugar

4 cups steamed white rice

Makes 4 servings

Trim the chicken pieces of excess fat and skin, and season with salt and black pepper. Set aside.

Heat the oil in a wok over high heat. Add the ginger, garlic, 2 Tbsp of the green onion, the square of orange zest, the cinnamon stick, red pepper flakes, and Szechwan peppercorns. Stir-fry until aromatic, about 2 minutes.

Add the chicken pieces to the mixture and stir-fry until light golden brown on all sides, 4–5 minutes.

Add ½ cup of the chicken broth, the soy sauce, wine, and sugar and stir to combine. Bring to simmer and reduce the heat to maintain a bare simmer. Cover and cook gently until the chicken is opaque in the center but still tender, 25–30 minutes.

Transfer the chicken to a platter with a slotted spoon, cover to keep warm, and return the wok to high heat. Add the remaining chicken broth. Bring the liquid to a boil and cook until reduced and slightly thickened, 2–3 minutes. Taste and season with salt and black pepper.

Return the chicken to the sauce along with any juices it has released on the platter. Heat thoroughly in the sauce and turn to coat evenly, about 2 minutes.

Remove the cinnamon stick and the zest square. Serve the chicken and sauce at once over a bed of rice, garnished with the remaining green onion and the orange zest.

Dark soy sauce, available in Asian grocery stores or the ethnic aisle of supermarkets, is darker, thicker, and more strongly flavored than regular soy sauce. It's often using to make dipping sauces. Light soy sauce, by contrast, is paler and milder in flavor and can be substituted here if you prefer.

braising and stewing
p. 40

cooking rice and pilaf
p. 206

Mole Poblano de Pollo

3 Tbsp olive oil

4 bone-in chicken breast halves

1 yellow onion, finely diced

1 green bell pepper, finely diced

1 jalapeño, finely chopped

¼ cup blanched almonds, chopped

3 cloves garlic, smashed

2 Tbsp chili powder

1 tsp grated gingerroot

½ tsp minced fresh thyme leaves

¼ tsp aniseed

¼ tsp ground cinnamon

3 tomatoes, peeled, seeded, and chopped

1 cup chicken broth, plus more as needed

3 Tbsp almond butter

2 oz Mexican chocolate, chopped

Salt and freshly ground pepper

2 Tbsp toasted sesame seeds

Makes 4 servings

Preheat the oven to 350°F.

Heat the oil in a large Dutch oven over medium-high heat. Sear the chicken until browned on all sides. Remove and set aside.

Add the onion to the hot pan and brown it slightly, 10–12 minutes.

Add the bell pepper, jalapeño, almonds, and garlic to the pan and sauté until aromatic, 3–4 minutes.

Add the chili powder, ginger, thyme, aniseed, and cinnamon and sauté briefly until aromatic, about 30 seconds, being careful not to burn the mixture. Add the tomatoes.

Pour in 1 cup of the broth and stir to deglaze the pan, scraping up any browned bits from the pan bottom. Whisk in the almond butter, return the chicken to the pan, and bring to a boil. Cover the pan and transfer to the oven. Braise the chicken until tender, about 1 hour. Add a little more broth as needed throughout the cooking time to keep the level constant.

Remove the chicken from the pot and cover to keep warm. Add the chocolate to the sauce, stirring until melted. Taste and season with salt and pepper.

Return the chicken to the sauce and turn to coat evenly. Bring the mixture to a simmer over medium heat to heat the chicken through, then serve at once. Garnish with the sesame seeds.

While chocolate may be the best-known ingredient in mole sauce, it's really just a grace note in this rich harmony of spices, chiles, nuts, and seeds. In Oaxaca, in southeastern Mexico, you'd find dozens of different kinds of moles; in the indigenous Nahuatl language, *molli* means "concoction." Look for flat cakes of Mexican chocolate, flavored with sugar, cinnamon, and finely ground almonds, in the ethnic foods section of large supermarkets or in groceries specializing in Latin American foods.

braising and stewing p. 40

preparing bell peppers and chiles p. 183

Poule au Pot

1 broiler chicken (about 3 lb)

8 cups chicken broth, plus more as needed

1 spice sachet (p. 46)

Salt and freshly ground pepper

¾ cup coarsely diced carrot

¾ cup coarsely diced parsnip

¾ cup coarsely diced peeled celeriac (celery root)

1½ cup coarsely diced Yukon gold potato

¾ cup coarsely diced leek, white part only

3 Tbsp minced fresh chives

Makes 4 servings

Cut the chicken into quarters, reserving the backbone, wing tips, neck, heart, and gizzard. Save the liver for another use.

Bring the broth to a simmer in a soup pot over medium heat. Add the chicken quarters and other parts, sachet, and 1½ tsp salt. Simmer over low heat until the broth is flavorful, about 45 minutes.

Using tongs, remove and discard the backbone, wing tips, gizzard, heart, neck, and sachet. Skim the broth to remove any excess fat from the surface. Add more broth if needed to cover the chicken by 2 inches.

Add the vegetables to the pot in stages so that they all finish cooking at the same time: add the carrot and parsnip and simmer for 5 minutes; add the celeriac and simmer for 5 minutes; add the potato and simmer for 7 minutes; add the leek and simmer for 2–3 minutes. Continue to simmer, skimming as needed, until the chicken is fork-tender and all of the vegetables are tender. Taste and adjust the seasoning with salt and pepper.

Remove the chicken from the pot. Cut the drumsticks from the thighs and cut the breast pieces in half on the diagonal.

Arrange the chicken in soup bowls, placing in each a breast portion and either a drumstick or thigh. Ladle in some vegetables and broth, and garnish with the chives before serving.

In preparing your chicken, make sure to remove and save the chicken livers for another recipe; the livers are omitted here because they can give a bitter flavor and cloudy appearance to the finished dish.

braising and stewing
p. 40

cutting a chicken into serving pieces p. 66

Thai Red Curry Chicken

3 Tbsp vegetable oil

1 cup diced Spanish onion

3 cloves garlic, minced

1 Tbsp prepared red curry paste

Salt and freshly ground white pepper

3 boneless, skinless chicken breast halves (7–8 oz each), cut into large cubes

6 small red potatoes, scrubbed, each cut into 6 pieces

1½ cups chicken broth

¼ cup shredded dried coconut

½ cup coconut milk

2 Tbsp brown sugar

1 tsp grated lemon zest

Cornstarch slurry: 1 Tbsp cornstarch blended with 4 tsp cold water or chicken broth (optional)

1 Tbsp coarsely chopped fresh basil

1 Tbsp coarsely chopped fresh mint

4 cups steamed white rice

4 green onions, white and green parts, sliced on the bias

Makes 4 servings

Heat the oil in a large sauté pan over medium heat. Add the onion and sauté until translucent, 5–7 minutes. Add the garlic and cook until aromatic, about 2 minutes.

Add the red curry paste, 1 tsp salt, and ½ tsp white pepper. Stir to coat the onions and garlic evenly with the curry paste. Add the chicken and potatoes and stir to coat evenly with the curry paste. Add the broth and bring to a simmer. Simmer until the potatoes are tender, 15–20 minutes.

Meanwhile, toast the shredded coconut. Preheat the oven to 350°F. Spread the coconut on a baking sheet and bake until golden, about 5 minutes. Transfer to a bowl and set aside.

Using a slotted spoon, transfer the chicken and potatoes to a warmed platter and cover to keep warm while completing the sauce.

Add the coconut milk, brown sugar, and lemon zest to the pan the chicken was in and bring to a simmer, stirring constantly. Taste and season the sauce with salt and pepper. If needed, add just enough of the cornstarch slurry while stirring to thicken the sauce slightly.

Add the basil and mint. Return the chicken and the potatoes to the pan and stir to coat them thoroughly with the sauce.

Serve the curry over a bed of rice. Garnish each plate with about 2 Tbsp green onion and 1 Tbsp toasted coconut.

Thai red curry paste, a mixture of hot red chiles, garlic, lemongrass, galangal (a gingerlike rhizome), and salt, adds a robust glow to this creamy stew of chicken, coconut milk, and fresh herbs. Green curry paste, made with fresh green chiles, lemongrass, and kaffir lime leaves, has a milder, more tangy flavor and is often paired with vegetables or fish. Prepared curry pastes can be found in jars in the Asian foods section of many supermarkets or in specialty food shops and Asian markets.

thickening with roux and slurry p. 46

zesting and juicing citrus p. 182

cooking rice and pilaf p. 206

3 Meat

Often, a meal's crowning glory is a perfect cut of meat: rosy slices of roast beef or lamb, sizzling hot steaks marked by the grill's flame, cutlets with a golden brown coating, or braised meat that melts in your mouth.

Beef, pork, lamb, veal, and game demand good technique from the cook. They also require a certain level of adaptability. The more you prepare meats using your favorite techniques, the less wedded to recipes and more open to opportunity your cooking can become. Most recipes specify the use of a particular cut of meat, but some basic knowledge about how meats are butchered can help you spot a different cut that will work just as well, or perhaps even better.

Types of meat

Beef is the most popular meat served in the United States. The beef produced here has a vivid cherry to ruby red color; the intensity and shade of red varies depending upon the cow's breed, age, and diet. Special types of beef include Japanese Kobe, French Limousin, Brae, Certified Angus, organic, and aged.

Veal has a delicate texture and is a light pink to pinkish gray. The meat's delicate flavor deepens as the calf ages and its diet changes. True veal comes from calves no more than 3 months old. Milk-fed or nature-fed veal comes from unweaned calves that never receive grain, grass, or adult feed.

Today's pork has a relatively mild flavor. Its color ranges from a pinkish tan to a deep red. In addition to being cut into fresh pork cutlets, roasts, and chops, pork is often cured, brined, or smoked to produce bacon and ham.

Lamb comes from young sheep up to 1 year old; older animals must be labeled "mutton." Traditionally, lambs were slaughtered during the spring, but since the animals can now be raised throughout the seasons, good-quality lamb is available year-round. Neither genuine spring lamb, which still comes to market from March to October, nor hothouse lamb, raised at other times of year, has fed on anything but milk.

Although many think "venison" refers only to deer, the word is also used as a general term for game, including moose, elk, caribou, antelope, bison, and wild boar. In addition to these larger animals, rabbits and hare are also considered game. The game available in markets nowadays is farm raised and inspected using the same procedures as for other meats. True wild game is not inspected and may not be sold through retail outlets, although it can be hunted according to state laws.

Selecting meat

The United States Department of Agriculture has been charged with overseeing the inspection of meats since 1906. Over the years, inspection standards have evolved to keep pace with changes to methods for raising and butchering meats. Graders consider the age of the animal, the shape of the cut, the amount of meat, the amount and location of the fat, the color of the meat and fat, and other factors. These standards vary from species to species. Beef is unique in that its cuts can be graded based upon the presence of marbling, the intramuscular fat you can see as small veins. The beef, veal, and lamb sold in most markets have received a rating of "USDA Choice." Only a small percentage of meat is graded "Prime"; it commands a much higher price and is usually available only from butcher shops or in upscale restaurants. There are two grades awarded to pork; "Acceptable" pork is suitable for retail sale. You are far less likely to see this grade on pork than the grades assigned by processors and packers, however.

Beef and pork can also be certified. This means that they have met specific criteria of quality, including, in some cases, the breed of animal: for example, Certified Angus refers to a particular cattle breed. Meats can also be certified organic if the animal was raised using organic management techniques from the second day of life. Meats labeled "Natural" should include information about what that means, such as "no steroids" or "no genetically modified organisms." "Grass-fed" animals are allowed access to pasture land.

Choosing a cut

There are literally hundreds of names for the retail cuts of meat found in stores or restaurants, but if you learn the essential characteristics of the primal cuts of meat—the initial large cuts made by the butcher, or the part of the animal each cut comes from—you can read the labels on packages of meat with a greater understanding.

There are usually no more than seven basic primal cuts, depending on the type of meat. The smaller the animal, the fewer and smaller the primal cuts. Although these cuts may have different names from one animal to another, they are similar in terms of the meat's characteristics. The name of the primal cut is often included on the meat's label, as part of or in addition to the name of the retail cut. Knowing the primal cut can help you to determine whether the cut in your hand is best for stewing or sautéing, to substitute one cut for another, or to find a good recipe for an unfamiliar cut.

Shoulder cuts (also known as the chuck or arm) contain some of an animal's most exercised, and therefore toughest, muscles. Long, slow cooking—braising or stewing— brings out the flavor of these cuts while also tenderizing the meat.

The rib and loin contain many of the most tender roasts and steaks, including the prized tenderloin. Tenderloin cuts may be called filet, châteaubriand, tournedos, or medallions. Rib and loin cuts are well suited to quick dry-heat cooking methods such as sautéing, roasting, grilling, and broiling.

The round (also labeled leg, haunch, or ham) is cut into roasts or steaks. As with the chuck, exercise can give these meats a tendency toward toughness, especially in older animals. Leg cuts of veal, lamb, and pork, all from smaller animals, are often tender enough to roast. Even in the case of beef, certain cuts (often referred to as "top round") are sufficiently tender to cook by roasting or other dry-heat methods. Other cuts from the round need moist-heat stewing, braising, or pot-roasting to bring out their best flavor and texture.

Flank, skirt, and hangar steaks, sometimes known as "butcher's cuts," come from the very edge of the rib and loin portions of the animal. Enough intramuscular fat is present to ensure that the meat stays tender even when grilled or roasted, as long as it is not overcooked. The meat has long, coarse fibers that should be sliced carefully across the grain. The "tri-tip" steak or roast is another such cut.

Beef brisket, a cut from near the rib section, is available fresh and corned. Fresh brisket is often favored for pot roasts and other braises. It responds well to slow cooking in a sauce. Corned beef has been brined and cured with spices. Veal and lamb breasts are similar to beef brisket, both in terms of how the meat is cut and how it behaves when cooked.

The shank, or lower leg, is obviously the most exercised muscle on any animal. Many cuisines have developed long-cooked and richly flavored presentations for shank; the prototypical shank recipe, using veal shanks, is osso buco.

Ribs, whether they are beef or pork, are cut away from the primal rib. These cuts have more bone than meat and plenty of fat. They need long, slow cooking to become tender.

When purchasing meat, take time to look it over carefully. The packaging should be intact and there shouldn't be excessive moisture in the package. Although the federal government does not yet require stores to include "sell by" dates, nutrition information, or safe handling information, many stores provide that information on the label. The meat should look cleanly cut, fresh, and moist.

Preparing meat

Once home, extend the shelf life of fresh meats and game by wrapping them in coated paper (either butcher's paper or freezer wrap) or plastic wrap. Use a separate drawer to hold uncooked meats, or put them in a pan to prevent juices from dripping onto other foods. Properly wrapped and refrigerated meats last for 3 to 5 days without a noticeable loss of quality. For longer storage, wrap meats first in plastic, then in freezer paper. Be sure to label and date packages destined for the freezer. Thaw them in the refrigerator to retain the most flavor and moisture.

Wash your hands thoroughly before, after, and as needed while you work with uncooked meat. Pathogens are easily transferred to food from hands, tools, and cutting surfaces, after you work with meat and before you cut anything else, wash your cutting board and knives with hot, soapy water.

Many of the recipes in this chapter demonstrate how easy it is to substitute one meat for another, as long as they respond well to the same kind of cooking. You don't need to memorize meat charts to be successful at swapping. Even if you did, you might overlook the very cut you're looking for, displayed in plain sight in the butcher's case but hiding behind an unfamiliar name. A boneless top loin steak might be labeled strip steak, Kansas City steak, New York strip steak, hotel cut strip steak, ambassador steak, or club sirloin steak, depending on where you are shopping. The best recourse is to find a reliable market or butcher and ask questions, just the way that professional chefs depend on specialists to learn more about an unfamiliar cut, or about new ways to present familiar ones.

Best cooking methods for cuts of meat

MEAT	CUT	WEIGHT RANGES	BEST COOKING METHODS
Beef			
	Rib roast	14–16 lb	Roasting
	Brisket	10–12 lb	Braising
	Chuck	15–16 lb	Roasting, braising
	Round	top round, 17–19 lb; eye round, 2–3 lb; bottom round (also called gooseneck or inside), 18–20 lb	Stewing, braising, roasting
	Loin	bone-in, 10–12 lb; boneless, 8–9 lb	Sautéing, pan-frying, broiling, grilling
	Tenderloin	4–5 lb	Sautéing, pan-frying, broiling, grilling
	Flank steak	2–2½ lb	Baking, broiling, pan-frying, braising, sautéing
	Ground beef	as required	Braising, sautéing, pan-frying, grilling
Veal			
	Shoulder	boneless, 4 lb	Braising, roasting, pan-frying
	Breast	5 lb	Braising, stewing
	Loin	bone-in, 8 lb; boneless, 3 lb	Braising, roasting, pan-frying, broiling, grilling
	Tenderloin	1–1½ lb	Roasting, pan-frying, broiling, grilling
	Leg	boneless, 8 lb; top round, boneless, 6 lb	Roasting, sautéing, pan-frying, braising
	Shank	1½–2 lb	Braising, simmering
Pork			
	Fresh ham	bone-in, 17 lb; boneless, 8 lb	Roasting, braising, simmering, broiling, pan-frying
	Shoulder	bone-in, 16 lb; boneless picnic, 8–10 lb	Roasting, braising, simmering, broiling, pan-frying
	Loin	bone-in, 14–16 lb; boneless, 8–10 lb	Roasting, braising, pan-frying
	Loin, chops	3–8 oz	Roasting, braising, pan-frying, sautéing, broiling, grilling
	Loin, ribs	5–8 oz	Roasting, braising, pan-frying, sautéing, broiling, grilling
	Tenderloin	1–1½ lb	Roasting, braising, grilling, pan-frying, sautéing
	Spareribs	2½–3½ lb	Braising, smoking, broiling, grilling
Lamb			
	Rack	2–3 lb	Roasting, grilling, broiling, pan-frying
	Shoulder	bone-in, 12–14 lb; boneless, 6–7 lb	Roasting, grilling, broiling, pan-frying
	Loin	bone-in, 3–5 lb; boneless, 2–3 lb	Roasting, braising, grilling, broiling, pan-frying, sautéing
	Leg	bone-in, 9–12 lb; boneless, 6–8 lb	Roasting, braising
	Shanks	1–2 lb	Braising, simmering

Tying a roast

Tying a roast into a neat, compact shape helps it cook more evenly and holds in stuffings or fillings.

1 Making a compact shape

Cut several lengths of string long enough to wrap completely around the meat twice, in order to have enough string to tie knots. A butcher's knot is quick to make, simple to tighten, and very secure. Pass one length of string around the meat. Create a slip knot by crossing the ends and looping one end around your index finger, back under itself, and then through the loop where your finger was. Pull both ends of the string to tighten it until it presses firmly against the meat. Make a loop again with one of the ends and pull the other end through the loop. Pull both ends of the string to tighten securely. Trim the string near the knot for a neat appearance. Repeat, tying lengths of string at even intervals until the entire piece of meat is firmly tied.

Trimming meat

Cutting away excess fat and gristle before cooking results in a finished dish with better texture.

1 Trimming fat and gristle

Some cuts of meat, such as rack of lamb or whole beef tenderloin, have a thick layer of fat enclosing the major muscles. These layers can often be removed by gripping a corner of the fat layer and peeling it back firmly. Otherwise, use a sharp knife and smooth strokes to cut away the fat evenly, following the meat's grain as much as possible. Angle the knife's blade slightly away from the meat as you cut to avoid cutting into the meat. Look for pockets of gristle, a general term for cartilage and tough tissue, and use the tip of your knife to cut them away, removing as little meat as possible. You may decide to leave a thin layer of fat over large roasts that cook for a long period. In this case, shave off all but a ¼-inch-thick layer of fat.

2 Removing silverskin

Silverskin is a tough membrane surrounding loins, tenderloins, and leg roasts, named for its silvery, translucent appearance. As it cooks, it shrinks more rapidly than the meat does, making the meat buckle and cook unevenly. Work the tip of a boning knife, sharp edge facing away from you, under the silverskin to loosen a flap. Grip the flap and hold it taut at a low angle over the meat. Glide the knife just underneath the membrane, using a smooth stroke and angling the blade away from the meat. You may need to remove the membrane in several narrow strips.

Making gravy

After roasting meat, add flour and broth to the pan drippings to make a gravy.

1 Cooking down the drippings

If you plan to prepare a gravy from a roast, choose a heavy, flameproof roasting pan. Add diced aromatic vegetables to the pan during the last 30 minutes of roasting, enough time to brown them and develop their flavor without burning. (Any burnt bits in the bottom of the pan will give the sauce a bitter flavor.) When the meat is done, transfer to a platter to rest, tenting it loosely with foil to keep warm. Place the roasting pan over medium heat. Heat the drippings until the juices have cooked down on the bottom of the pan and the fat is transparent.

2 Adding flour

To make a gravy, after cooking down the drippings, leave enough fat in the pan to prepare a roux (see page 46). If the roasted meat was a particularly lean cut, you may need to add some oil or butter. Sprinkle flour into the pan and cook over medium-high heat for a few minutes, stirring frequently, to make the roux.

3 Adding broth

After cooking the roux, gradually add broth to the pan, whisking well to work out any lumps. Simmer the gravy until thickened and well developed in flavor. If desired, strain through a fine-mesh sieve. To keep a skin from forming, coat the surface with a thin layer of melted butter or place a piece of parchment or waxed paper directly on the surface.

Making a pan sauce

Making a pan sauce is similar to making gravy, but a little quicker and simpler.

Making a *jus* or *jus lié*

To make a *jus* (an unthickened pan sauce) or *jus lié* (a pan sauce thickened with cornstarch) after roasting or sautéing meat, pour or spoon off as much fat as possible, then add broth as well as other liquids such as wine or the juices that are released from the meat as it rests. Stir and scrape the pan with a wooden spoon to deglaze the pan and release the flavorful drippings. Simmer until reduced and very flavorful, adding herbs and spices as desired. Simply strain the sauce and skim away the surface fat to make a *jus;* for a *jus lié,* gradually add enough cornstarch slurry (see page 46) to thicken the broth to a saucelike consistency.

Testing for doneness

Use all your senses to test meat during cooking.

The cooking time quoted in a recipe can help you plan when to start cooking but by itself is not an accurate way to determine a meat's doneness. Temperature is the most accurate method for judging the doneness of meat. Use an instant-read thermometer or a meat thermometer that stays in the meat while it cooks. The chart at right gives temperatures for various meats cooked to various degrees of doneness. Except for rare beef and lamb, these temperatures conform to the USDA's recommendations, but you may choose to adjust them to suit your taste.

While temperature is a key indicator of doneness, experienced cooks rely on all their senses to evaluate meats as they cook and to judge doneness, as well as using thermometers. Appearance is one factor, used to help determine doneness as well as to make any necessary temperature adjustments. Smell is another; the smell of cooked meats is savory and rich. Touching meats to gauge their doneness is another time-honored test. Press meats with your fingertip as they cook and notice how the meat changes from soft and yielding to firm through varying degrees of doneness. If they are too small to actually press, cut into a piece. Braised or simmered meats are often considered done when they are fork tender; that is, when a fork slides easily into and out of the cooked meat. Assess how the meat tastes once it is finished cooking and make notes to help you remember for the next time.

Doneness temperatures for meat

TYPE OF MEAT	DESIRED DEGREE OF DONENESS	INTERNAL TEMPERATURE	VISUAL CUES
Ground meat	Medium	160°F	Center meat is no longer pink
Beef and lamb			
	Rare	135°F (after resting for large cuts)	Interior is red and shiny
	Medium-rare	145°F (after resting for large cuts)	Rosy pink interior, juicy
	Medium	160°F (after resting for large cuts)	Pink only at center, pale pink juices
	Well done	170°F (after resting for large cuts)	Evenly brown throughout, no traces of red or pink, moist but no juices
Veal			
	Medium-rare	145°F (after resting for large cuts)	Rosy pink interior, juicy
	Medium	160°F (after resting for large cuts)	Pink only at center, pale pink juices
	Well done	170°F (after resting for large cuts)	Evenly brown throughout, no traces of red or pink, moist but no juices
Pork			
	Medium	160°F (after resting for large cuts)	Pink only at center, slight give, juices with faint blush
	Well done	170°F (after resting for large cuts)	Opaque throughout, slight give, juices clear

Frenching rack of lamb

For an attractive presentation, clean the rib bones of all the meat and membrane.

1 Cleaning the rib bones

A stiff-bladed boning knife is the best tool for frenching, but you can also use a sharp, sturdy paring knife. Place the rack on a working surface with the long, curving rib bones pointing down and the smooth fat layer facing up. About 1 inch up from the meat, make a single straight cut through the fat layer across all the ribs, cutting down to the bone. Set the rack on one end and insert the tip of the blade between each bone, piercing the membrane, using the initial cut as a guide. Score the thin membrane in a line down the center of each rib. Press the bones through this cut in the membrane. Lay the rack with its bones facing down again, and make an even cut to remove the meat pulled away from the rib bones completely. Trim the fat layer that covers the meat to an even ¼ inch.

Carving leg of lamb

The same basic steps used to carve a leg of lamb apply to a ham or venison leg.

1 Cutting across the grain

Before you start carving, cut a small piece from the opposite side of the leg to create a flat surface to rest on the platter or cutting board. This will form a base to help steady the leg as you carve it. Hold the shank bone firmly in one hand with a clean cloth or napkin. Cut out a narrow wedge of meat down to the bone, near the shank end, to give yourself room for carving slices. Leave a 1- to 2-inch-thick piece of meat intact at the shank bone to shield your hand as you hold the leg. Begin carving large, even slices by making parallel cuts from the shank end down to the bone. Always cut against the grain of the meat, to keep the meat fibers short and the slices as tender as possible.

2 Removing the slices

Initially, make the cuts almost perpendicular to the bone, then turn the knife parallel to the bone to free the slices. When the slices become very large, begin to cut the meat at a slight angle, first from the left side, then from the right side, alternating until the leg is entirely carved. If you begin to see long fibers in the slices you cut, reposition the knife to cut at a sharper angle or at another side of the leg. To keep the meat warm throughout a meal, carve only half of it, then drape with foil and return it to a very low oven. Carve the rest of the leg as needed.

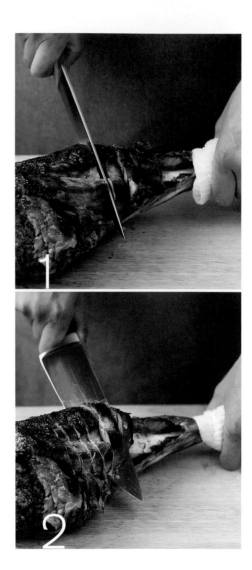

Grilled Steak with Jalapeño-Cilantro Butter

Jalapeño-Cilantro Butter

4 Tbsp unsalted butter, softened

2 Tbsp minced fresh cilantro

1 Tbsp finely minced jalapeño

Grated zest of ½ lime

Salt and freshly ground pepper

4 strip steaks (about 8 oz each)

Vegetable oil for brushing

Makes 4 servings

For the jalapeño-cilantro butter, blend the butter with the cilantro, jalapeño, lime zest, ¼ tsp salt, and ¼ tsp pepper. Taste adjust the seasoning. Transfer the butter onto a piece of plastic wrap. Roll into a 1-inch-diameter cylinder and secure the ends by twisting. Chill until firm, about 2 hours.

Prepare a grill for a hot fire with a cooler zone. Season the steaks with salt and pepper and brush them lightly with oil.

Grill the steaks on the first side until marked, about 3 minutes. Turn the steaks over and continue cooking until the meat registers 145° for medium-rare, 3–4 minutes more. If you prefer beef done medium, move the steaks to the cooler grill zone and cook for 5–6 minutes more.

Top each steak with a slice of the flavored butter and serve at once.

Easily made ahead and refrigerated until needed, flavored, or "compound," butters like the one used here are a quick way to dress up a simple grilled steak or chop. Use them with all types of meats, fish, and vegetables, varying the flavoring to suit the dish and your taste.

grilling and broiling p. 28

testing for doneness p. 99

VARIATIONS

Veal Chops with Rosemary-Mustard Butter

Substitute four 6-oz veal loin chops for the steaks. For the compound butter, replace the cilantro, jalapeño, and lime zest with 1 tsp chopped fresh rosemary or ¼ tsp crumbled dried rosemary and 2 Tbsp Dijon or other mustard. Proceed as directed, cooking the veal chops on the hotter portion of the grill just long enough to develop a good color, then sliding them into a medium or cooler zone to finish cooking, for a total of 10–12 minutes for medium.

Lamb Chops with Sun-Dried Tomato and Oregano Butter

Substitute ½-inch-thick lamb loin or rib chops (2–3 chops per person) for the steaks. For the compound butter, replace the cilantro, jalapeño, and lime zest with 2 Tbsp finely minced sun-dried tomatoes, 2 Tbsp minced fresh oregano, 2 tsp fresh lemon juice, and 2 Tbsp dry white wine. Proceed as directed, turning the chops 2 or 3 times as they grill, 6–8 minutes total for medium-rare. If you prefer lamb medium or well done, move the chops to a cooler zone and cook for 4–5 minutes more.

Beef Satay with Peanut Sauce

1½ lb beef flank steak

½ cup minced yellow onion

⅓ cup ketchup

¼ cup soy sauce

¼ cup dark sesame oil

3 Tbsp brown sugar

6 cloves garlic, minced

4 tsp minced jalapeño

Juice of ½ lime, plus wedges for garnish

1 Tbsp chili paste

2 tsp minced gingerroot

2 tsp salt

½ cup smooth peanut butter

Makes 6–8 appetizer servings

Split the steak lengthwise and cut against the grain into thin strips. Whisk the onion, ketchup, soy sauce, sesame oil, brown sugar, garlic, jalapeño, lime juice, chili paste, ginger, and salt with 1 cup water in a glass bowl. Pour into a resealable plastic bag and add the steak. Close, squeeze several times to distribute the marinade, and refrigerate for 1–12 hours.

Remove the beef from the marinade and thread lengthwise onto 16 skewers. Pour the marinade into a small saucepan and reserve.

Prepare a grill for a hot fire. Grill the beef on the first side until browned, about 2 minutes. Turn over and grill to the desired doneness, about 2 minutes more for medium-rare.

Bring the marinade to a full boil. Add the peanut butter and stir until smooth, thinning with water as necessary to give it a saucelike consistency. Serve the beef satay with the sauce, garnished with the lime wedges.

Originating in Indonesia, (where *satay* means "skewer"), this dish of skewered, quickly grilled meat served with a savory peanut dipping sauce has become a popular party dish. If you don't have metal skewers, look for wooden ones in the kitchenware sections of most supermarkets; soak them in water for about 30 minutes to keep them from scorching on the grill.

grilling and broiling p. 28

preparing bell peppers and chiles p. 183

Grilled Lamb with Mango Chutney

2 mangoes, peeled and diced

1 Tbsp fresh lime juice

2 tsp minced fresh cilantro

1 tsp plus 2 Tbsp minced gingerroot

½ tsp minced jalapeño

Salt and freshly ground pepper

1 tsp *each* ground cardamom and cumin

1 small yellow onion, grated

4 cloves garlic, minced

½ tsp freshly grated nutmeg

½ cup plain yogurt

2 lb boneless leg of lamb

Makes 6–8 appetizer servings

Toss the mangoes, lime juice, cilantro, the 1 tsp ginger, the jalapeño, ½ tsp salt, and ¼ tsp pepper in a bowl to make a chutney. Set aside.

Toast the cardamom and cumin lightly in a small, dry pan over low heat. Add the onion, the 2 Tbsp ginger, garlic, 1 tsp pepper, and nutmeg; sauté until aromatic, about 1 minute. Immediately transfer to a mixing bowl and let cool. Stir in the yogurt and set aside.

Trim the lamb of excess fat and cut into 3-inch-long strips. Put the lamb and the yogurt mixture in a resealable plastic bag, close, and squeeze to coat evenly. Refrigerate for 1–4 hours.

Remove the lamb from the marinade and thread onto 14–16 skewers.

Prepare a grill for a hot fire. Grill the lamb skewers on the first side until browned, about 2 minutes. Turn over and continue cooking until the meat registers 145°F for medium-rare, about 2 minutes more. Serve at once with the chutney.

Marinating meat in yogurt and spices is a traditional Indian technique that tenderizes the meat, thanks to yogurt's natural acids. When cooked in a beehive-shaped clay oven called a *tandoor*, the meat is called *tandoori*. Here, grilling adds a similar smoky flavor. The marinade may be blended up to 12 hours in advance; keep covered and refrigerated.

grilling and broiling p. 28

marinating p. 68

Roast Leg of Lamb Boulangère

1 bone-in leg of lamb (9–10 lb)

Salt and freshly ground pepper

6 cloves garlic, slivered

5 russet potatoes, peeled and sliced ⅛ inch thick

4 yellow onions, thinly sliced

3 cups beef broth, heated, or as needed

Makes 10–12 servings

Preheat the oven to 400°F. Trim the lamb of excess fat and season with salt and pepper. Make small slits all over the lamb and insert one piece of slivered garlic in each.

Place the lamb on a rack in a roasting pan. Roast for 1 hour, basting occasionally. Remove the pan from the oven and remove the lamb on its rack. Pour off the grease. Layer the sliced potatoes and onions in the roasting pan, seasoning with salt and pepper. Pour in the broth, adding just enough to moisten the potatoes well.

Place the lamb directly on the potatoes. Continue to roast until the potatoes and onions are tender and a thermometer inserted in the center of the meat registers 135° for medium-rare, 45–60 minutes more.

Let the leg rest for 15–20 minutes before carving it. Serve with the potatoes and onions.

The French term *boulangère* means "in the style of the baker's wife"; typically, it refers to meat or fish roasted or baked (in the baker's oven) in combination with onions and potatoes.

roasting and baking p. 30

resting p. 70

carving leg of lamb p. 100

Beef Tenderloin with Wild Mushrooms

½ oz dried porcino mushrooms

¼ tsp *each* onion powder, garlic powder, dried thyme, ground cumin, paprika

Salt and freshly ground pepper

1½ lb beef tenderloin, trimmed of silverskin and excess fat

4 Tbsp olive oil (divided use)

1 Tbsp minced shallot

3 cloves garlic, minced

1 lb assorted wild mushrooms, roughly chopped

1 Tbsp unsalted butter

2 Tbsp chopped fresh flat-leaf parsley

Makes 4 servings

Using an electric spice mill, grind the dried mushrooms to a fine powder. Transfer to a large bowl and combine with the onion powder, garlic powder, thyme, cumin, paprika, ½ tsp salt, and ¼ tsp pepper. Rub the tenderloin evenly with 1 Tbsp of the oil and place in the bowl with the mushroom mixture. Turn to coat evenly. Cover and refrigerate for 3 hours.

Preheat the oven to 350°F. Transfer the tenderloin to a small roasting pan and roast until an instant-read thermometer registers 140°F for medium-rare, about 45 minutes. Remove from the oven and let rest.

While the meat is resting, heat the remaining 3 Tbsp oil in a large skillet over medium-high heat. Add the shallot and garlic and sauté for 30 seconds. Add the chopped mushrooms and turn to coat. Raise the heat to high and sauté until the mushrooms are cooked and the liquid is starting to evaporate. Stir in the butter and parsley. Taste and season with salt and pepper.

Carve the meat into ¼-inch-thick slices and serve with the mushrooms.

This dish combines fresh and dried mushrooms for depth of flavor. Fresh mushrooms that may be used include oyster, cremini, chanterelle, shiitake, and white. While fresh porcini are often hard to find, dried ones are widely available and add an intense woodsy aroma and flavor to any dish they're used in. Only a small amount is needed in most recipes. When selecting dried mushrooms, look for large, creamy-tan pieces; very dark and crumbly pieces may be rather old and dried out.

cleaning mushrooms p. 186

trimming meat p. 97

Pork Roast with Jus Lié

1 boneless pork loin roast
(about 3½ lb)

Salt and freshly ground pepper

3 cloves garlic, mashed to a
paste

½ tsp fresh rosemary leaves

1 tsp fresh thyme leaves

4 Tbsp vegetable oil (divided
use)

½ cup coarsely chopped yellow
onion

¼ cup sliced carrot

¼ cup sliced celery

2 cups chicken broth

1 bay leaf

½ cup dry white wine

Cornstarch slurry: 2 Tbsp
cornstarch blended with 2 Tbsp
cold water or chicken broth
(optional)

Makes 8–10 servings

Preheat the oven to 325°F. Trim the pork loin of silverskin and excess fat. Season with salt and pepper, and rub the garlic, rosemary, and thyme into the meat.

Heat 2 Tbsp of the oil in a flameproof Dutch oven over high heat. Sear the pork until browned on every surface, including the ends, about 12 minutes total. Transfer the loin to a rack set in a roasting pan. Place in the oven and roast, basting occasionally, until the meat registers 150°F on an instant-read thermometer, 1½–1¾ hours.

While the pork is roasting, heat the remaining 2 Tbsp oil in the pan used to sear the pork loin. Add the onion and sauté until golden brown, 5–6 minutes. Add the carrot and celery and cook until the celery becomes translucent, 3–4 minutes more. Add the chicken broth and bay leaf and simmer slowly over low heat until the broth is very flavorful and slightly reduced, 10–12 minutes.

Transfer the roast to a platter, tent it loosely with aluminum foil, and keep warm while finishing the sauce. Add the wine to the roasting pan and stir to deglaze the pan, scraping up any browned bits from the pan bottom. Add this to the simmering broth, return the broth to a simmer, and skim to remove excess fat and other impurities. If needed, add just enough of the cornstarch slurry while stirring to thicken the sauce slightly. Strain the sauce into a sauceboat.

Carve the pork roast into slices and serve with the sauce.

One of a family of classic French sauces, *jus lié* is made by simmering broth with meat or poultry pan drippings and thickening it with a slurry of starch and water. Such a sauce is made quickly and capitalizes on savory pan drippings to add flavor to the finished dish.

roasting and baking p. 30

trimming meat p. 97

making a pan sauce
p. 98

VARIATION

Pork Roast Stuffed with Apples and Apricots

Cut 3 Granny Smith apples into small dice and 12 dried apricots into large dice. Toss together the apples and apricots with 2 tsp peeled, minced gingerroot and salt and freshly ground pepper to taste. With a long, thin knife, cut a pocket lengthwise through the center of the pork from a short end, without puncturing the sides of roast. Using the handle of a wooden spoon, push the apple and apricot stuffing into the pork, packing it tightly. Tie the loin to keep it compact during searing and roasting. Substitute red wine for the white wine and beef broth for the chicken broth, and proceed as directed.

tying a roast p. 97

Rack of Lamb Persillé

Persillade

1 cup fresh white bread crumbs

2 Tbsp unsalted butter, melted

1 Tbsp chopped fresh flat-leaf parsley

2 cloves garlic, mashed to a paste

Salt and freshly ground pepper

1 rack of lamb (2 lb, about 8 chops), frenched

1 tsp chopped fresh rosemary

1 tsp chopped fresh thyme

Vegetable oil for rubbing

1 small yellow onion, diced

1 stalk celery, diced

1 small carrot, diced

1 cup beef broth

Cornstarch slurry: 1 Tbsp cornstarch blended with 1 Tbsp cold water or beef broth (optional)

Makes 4 servings

Preheat the oven to 400°F.

For the persillade, mix together the bread crumbs, butter, parsley, garlic, and salt and pepper to taste to make an evenly moistened mixture. Set aside.

Season the lamb with salt and pepper and rub with the rosemary, thyme, and oil.

Place the lamb on a rack in a flameproof roasting pan.

Roast for 15 minutes, basting occasionally. Scatter the onion, celery, and carrot around the lamb, reduce the oven temperature to 325°F, and continue to roast until an instant-read thermometer inserted in the center of the meat registers 140°F for medium-rare, 15–20 minutes more. Set the meat aside and tent loosely with aluminum foil to keep warm.

To make a pan sauce, place the roasting pan over medium-high heat and cook until the vegetables are browned and the fat is clear, about 5 minutes. Pour off any fat. Add the broth and stir to deglaze, scraping up any browned bits from the pan bottom. Simmer for about 20 minutes. If needed, add just enough of the cornstarch slurry while stirring to thicken the sauce slightly. Strain through a fine-mesh sieve, if desired.

Transfer the lamb to a baking sheet. Carefully pack the persillade on the top of the lamb rack.

Return the lamb to the oven and roast until the crumbs are lightly browned, about 10 minutes.

Let rest for 8–10 minutes, then cut the lamb rack into chops. Return the sauce to a simmer and taste and season with salt and pepper. Serve with the chops.

This dish gets its name from the addition of persillade, a mixture of butter-moistened bread crumbs, parsley, and garlic. Patted onto the meat during the last 10 minutes of roasting, the crumbs create a crumbly, golden brown crust along the edge of each chop.

making a pan sauce
p. 98

frenching rack of lamb
p. 100

making bread crumbs
p. 26

Veal Shoulder Poêlé

1 boneless veal shoulder roast (about 3 lb)

Salt and freshly ground pepper

2 cloves garlic, minced

½ tsp finely chopped fresh rosemary

1 tsp finely chopped fresh basil

1 tsp finely chopped fresh thyme

½ tsp finely chopped fresh marjoram

6 Tbsp clarified butter (divided use), or as needed

2 slices thick-cut bacon or 2 oz smoked ham, diced

1 yellow onion, finely diced

2 stalks celery, finely diced

2 small carrots, finely diced

2 Tbsp tomato paste

1 cup dry white wine

1 cup beef or chicken broth

2 bay leaves

Cornstarch slurry: 2 Tbsp cornstarch blended with 2 Tbsp cold water or broth (optional)

Makes 6–8 servings

Preheat the oven to 300°F.

Spread open the veal and season with salt and pepper. Mix the garlic and herbs together and spread this mixture evenly over the inside of the veal. Roll and tie the roast with kitchen string.

Heat 4 Tbsp of the clarified butter in a Dutch oven over medium heat. Add the bacon and cook for 1–2 minutes. Add the onion, celery, and carrots; cook until a light golden brown, about 8 minutes. Add the tomato paste and cook, stirring frequently, until the tomato paste darkens, about 1 minute.

Place the veal on top of the vegetables and baste with 2 Tbsp more of the clarified butter.

Cover the pot and *poêlé* in the oven, basting with pan drippings (or additional clarified butter, if needed) every 20 minutes for 1 hour. Remove the lid to allow veal to brown, and roast until an instant-read thermometer inserted in the center of the meat registers 150°F for medium, about 30 minutes more. Transfer the veal to a warmed platter and cover to keep warm.

To make a pan sauce, place the Dutch oven over medium heat. Add the wine, broth, and bay leaves and stir to deglaze the pan, scraping up any browned bits from the pan bottom. Simmer for 20 minutes. Skim the sauce to remove any excess fat from the surface. If needed, add just enough of the cornstarch slurry while stirring to thicken the sauce slightly. Taste and season with salt and pepper. Remove the bay leaves.

Remove the strings from the veal. Slice thinly across the grain and serve with the sauce.

Veal shoulder is a cut that responds beautifully to gentle cooking such as *poêléing*, also known as butter-roasting (see page 79). Mild veal makes an excellent backdrop for more intense flavors, so experiment with other aromatic fillings such as finely chopped spinach sautéed with anchovies and garlic, an herb paste made from basil or cilantro, or a mixture of roasted bell peppers, capers, and currants.

tying a roast p. 97

making clarified butter p. 26

Pork Chops Forestière

4 bone-in center-cut pork chops
(about 8 oz each)

Salt and freshly ground pepper

All-purpose flour for dredging

Vegetable oil for pan-frying

1 small shallot, minced

1 cup sliced assorted
mushrooms such as oyster,
cremini, stemmed shiitake,
chanterelle, and white

1 tsp fresh thyme leaves

¼ cup dry white wine

¼ cup beef or chicken broth

2 Tbsp unsalted butter

Makes 4 servings

Season the pork chops with salt and pepper. Dredge in the flour.

Pour oil into a large sauté pan to a depth of ¼ inch and heat over high heat. Add the pork chops and pan-fry on the first side until deep golden brown, 3–4 minutes. Turn the pork chops and continue cooking on the second side until the pork is cooked through and the exterior is golden brown, 3–4 minutes more. Transfer to a warmed platter and cover to keep warm while completing the sauce.

Pour off all but 2 Tbsp oil and add the shallot to the pan and sauté over medium heat until limp, about 1 minute. Increase the heat to high, add the mushrooms and thyme, and sauté until the mushrooms are lightly browned, about 2 minutes.

Add the wine and stir to deglaze the pan, scraping up any browned bits from the pan bottom. Add the broth and any juices released by the pork chops. Simmer over high heat until the liquid has reduced by about half, 6–7 minutes. Swirl in the butter to thicken the sauce slightly.

Serve the pork chops at once with the sauce.

Forestière, or "of the forest," refers to the use of wild mushrooms in a dish. Nowadays, many of the wild mushrooms sold in supermarkets are in fact cultivated and as a result are available year-round instead of only in their natural season. Wavy-capped, apricot-colored chanterelle mushrooms are an exception, since they are still usually foraged rather than cultivated; look for them at farmers' markets in the autumn and spring.

pan-frying p. 34

making a pan sauce p. 98

Veal Scaloppine Marsala

8 veal top round cutlets
(about 3 oz each)

Salt and freshly ground pepper

All-purpose flour for dredging

2 Tbsp vegetable oil

¼ cup minced shallot

¼ cup dry red wine

1 sprig fresh thyme

1 bay leaf

½ cup chicken broth

½ cup Marsala wine

2 Tbsp unsalted butter

Makes 4 servings

Place each cutlet between sheets of parchment and pound to a ¼-inch thickness. Season with salt and pepper and dredge in the flour.

Heat the oil in a sauté pan over medium-high heat. Add the veal and sauté until golden brown and cooked through, about 2 minutes on each side. Transfer to a warmed plate and cover to keep warm.

Add the shallot to the pan and sauté over medium heat, stirring often, until translucent, about 1 minute. Add the red wine, thyme, bay leaf, and 1 tsp pepper and stir to deglaze the pan, scraping up any browned bits from the pan bottom. Simmer the wine until nearly cooked away, about 3 minutes. Add the broth and simmer for 5–6 minutes more. Add the Marsala and any juices released by the veal. Simmer until the liquid has reduced by half, 2–3 minutes. Discard the bay leaf, or strain the sauce, if desired. Turn the heat to low and whisk in the butter. Taste and season with salt and pepper. Serve the veal at once, and spoon the sauce over the scaloppine.

Scaloppine is the Italian term for boneless cutlets of meat such as veal. Dredging the veal in flour helps seal in juices beneath a delicate crust. The flour also helps thicken the sauce that is created at the end. Use a regular pan rather than a nonstick one for this recipe, as you want lots of sticky brown bits clinging to the pan after frying the cutlets. This helps create a sauce with deeper color and flavor.

sautéing and stir-frying p. 32

dredging and breading p. 68

Beef Tenderloin with Pizzaiola Sauce

Pizzaiola Sauce

1 cup dry white wine

4 tsp minced fresh flat-leaf parsley

2 tsp chopped fresh basil

2 tsp chopped fresh oregano

1 bay leaf

1 pepperoncini pepper, chopped

2 Tbsp olive oil or vegetable oil

1 yellow onion, minced

2 cloves garlic, minced

1½ cups canned crushed tomatoes

4 beef tenderloin steaks (5–6 oz each)

Salt and freshly ground pepper

2 Tbsp olive oil or vegetable oil, plus more as needed

1½ cups sliced white, oyster, and/or porcini mushrooms

Makes 4 servings

For the sauce, simmer the wine in a small saucepan over medium-high heat until reduced by half, 4–5 minutes. Remove from the heat and add the herbs and pepperoncini. Set aside to steep for 30 minutes before preparing the rest of the sauce.

Heat the oil in a saucepan over medium-high heat. Add the onion and garlic and sauté, stirring often, until light golden, about 5 minutes. Add the crushed tomatoes and simmer for 5 minutes more.

Remove the bay leaf from the wine mixture and discard it. Add the wine mixture to the pan with the tomatoes and continue to simmer for 5 minutes. Remove from the heat and set aside.

Blot the beef dry and season with salt and pepper.

Heat the oil in a heavy sauté pan over high heat. Add the beef and sauté to the desired doneness, 3–4 minutes per side for medium-rare. Transfer the steaks to a warmed platter and cover to keep warm while completing the sauce.

Return the sauté pan to medium-high heat and add enough oil to coat the bottom of the pan. Add the mushrooms and sauté until browned and any juices they have released cook away, about 4 minutes. Add the pizzaiola sauce and any juices released by the steaks. Reduce the heat to medium and simmer until the sauce develops a good flavor and consistency, about 5 minutes.

Taste and season with salt and pepper. Serve the steaks at once with the sauce.

Pepperoncini are small, hot, yellow-green peppers, pickled in vinegar and sold in glass jars in supermarkets and Italian delicatessens. Often used as a garnish on Greek salads and Italian submarine sandwiches, they add a welcome burst of heat to this spicy "pizza-maker's" sauce.

sautéing and stir-frying p. 32

preparing bell peppers and chiles p. 183

Pork and Green Onion Stir-Fry

1½ lb boneless pork loin

12 green onions

1 Tbsp cornstarch

1 Tbsp oyster sauce

2 tsp sugar

2 tsp soy sauce (divided use)

1 Tbsp peanut oil or vegetable oil

2 cloves garlic, minced

1 Tbsp Chinese rice wine or dry
sherry wine

¾ cup chicken broth

Salt and freshly ground pepper

4 cups steamed white rice

Makes 4 servings

Cut the pork into thin shreds, about ¼ inch wide by 2 inches long.

Trim the root ends of the green onions, split lengthwise, and cut into 1-inch pieces on the diagonal. Set aside

Mix together the cornstarch, oyster sauce, sugar, 1 tsp of the soy sauce, and 1 tsp water in a small bowl.

Heat the oil in a wok over medium-high heat. Add the garlic and stir-fry until aromatic, about 30 seconds. Add the pork and stir-fry until it stiffens and is cooked through, about 3 minutes.

Add the remaining 1 tsp soy sauce and the wine and stir-fry for 1 minute. Add the broth and bring to a boil.

Stir the cornstarch mixture to recombine and add to the meat. Bring to a boil, stirring frequently, and add the green onions. Taste and season with salt and pepper. Stir to combine and serve over the rice.

Oyster sauce adds a distinctive and authentic flavor to Chinese stir-fried dishes. Made from cooked oysters, soy sauce, salt, and seasonings, it is dark brown and slightly syrupy, with a rich, savory flavor that's not at all fishy.

stir-frying p. 32

preparing garlic p. 181

cooking rice and pilaf p. 206

VARIATIONS

Beef with Red Onions and Peanuts

Substitute boneless beef (sirloin, top round, or tenderloin) for the pork. Replace the green onions with 1 red onion, cut into julienne. Add 1 cup trimmed snow peas along with the red onion. Just before serving, scatter the stir-fry with 3 Tbsp roasted peanuts.

Spicy Hunan Lamb

Substitute boneless lamb leg for the pork. Add the following ingredients to the stir-fry sauce: 2 tsp *each* minced gingerroot, minced garlic, and hot bean paste. Replace the green onions with 1 cup finely julienned red bell pepper, 1 cup sliced mushrooms (white or wild varieties), and 1 dried black Chinese mushroom, rehydrated and cut into strips.

rehydrating and plumping p. 182

Apple-Sautéed Venison with Gin and Juniper

Marinade

1 cup apple cider

¾ cup chicken broth

½ cup gin

3 Tbsp Dijon mustard

3 cloves garlic, chopped

2 whole cloves

1 tsp juniper berries

4 venison chops or steaks
(about 8 oz each)

8 Tbsp unsalted butter, softened
(divided use)

18 pearl onions, peeled

3 Tbsp dry vermouth

2 Tbsp olive oil

Salt and freshly ground pepper

1 sprig fresh rosemary

Makes 6 servings

For the marinade, whisk together the apple cider, broth, gin, mustard, garlic, cloves, and juniper berries in a nonreactive bowl. Add the venison, turning to make sure that it is well coated with marinade. Cover and refrigerate for at least 2 hours or up to overnight.

Remove the venison from the marinade, then strain and reserve the marinade.

Melt 2 Tbsp of the butter in a saucepan over medium heat. Add the pearl onions and sauté until golden brown, about 5 minutes. Remove from the pan and cover to keep warm. Add the dry vermouth and reserved marinade to the pan. Bring to a gentle simmer and continue cooking until reduced by one-third, about 5 minutes.

While the liquid is reducing, heat the olive oil in a large sauté pan over medium heat. Pat the venison dry, season with salt and pepper, and sauté on the first side until browned, about 6 minutes. Turn and continue to sauté until an instant-read thermometer registers 160°F for medium, 6 minutes more.

When the marinade and vermouth mixture has reduced to a sauce-like consistency, blend in the remaining 6 Tbsp softened butter a little at a time. Add the onions and reheat the sauce gently until it is warmed through.

Serve the venison on a platter and spoon the sauce over the meat. Top with the onions and rosemary.

Commercially available venison comes from farm-raised deer and can usually be special-ordered from your butcher. It is a lean, deep red meat with a rich, woodsy flavor. Juniper berries (which give gin its distinctive aroma) are a popular seasoning for game, especially in Eastern European and Scandinavian countries.

sautéing and stir-frying
p. 32

marinating p. 68

Braised Rabbit with Tomatoes and Pine Nuts

1 rabbit (about 3 lb), cut into 6 pieces

Salt and freshly ground pepper

2 Tbsp all-purpose flour, plus more for dredging

3 Tbsp vegetable oil (divided use)

1 yellow onion, chopped

2 cloves garlic, minced

¼ tsp fresh rosemary

1 bay leaf

1 sprig fresh thyme

1 cup dry white wine

1 cup chicken or beef broth

3 plum (Roma) tomatoes, peeled, seeded, and chopped

2 Tbsp toasted pine nuts

Makes 3–4 servings

Preheat the oven to 350°F.

Season the rabbit with salt and pepper. Dredge in the flour.

Heat 2 Tbsp of the oil in a Dutch oven or other flameproof casserole over high heat. Sear the rabbit in the hot oil to brown, 1–2 minutes on each side; transfer to a plate and set aside.

Reduce the heat to medium-high and add the remaining 1 Tbsp oil. Add the onion and sauté until golden brown, 4–5 minutes. Add the garlic, rosemary, bay leaf, and thyme. Continue to sauté until the garlic is aromatic, about 1 minute. Add the 2 Tbsp flour and cook, stirring frequently with a wooden spoon, to make a blond roux, about 5 minutes.

Add the wine, whisking well to work out any lumps. Add the broth and stir to combine. Return the rabbit to the pan and add the tomatoes. Bring to a simmer.

Cover the casserole tightly and braise in the oven until the rabbit is tender, about 45 minutes, turning the rabbit pieces every 15 minutes to cook evenly. With a slotted spoon, transfer the rabbit to a warmed platter or plates and cover to keep warm while completing the sauce.

Place the Dutch oven over high heat and simmer the cooking liquid until it has a good flavor and saucelike consistency, about 10 minutes. Skim to remove any excess fat from the surface, taste, and season with salt and pepper. Remove and discard the bay leaf. Strain if desired. Spoon the sauce over the rabbit, garnish with the pine nuts, and serve.

Fresh herbs, tomatoes, and pine nuts add a rustic Italian backdrop to rabbit in this country-style dish. With its lean white meat, rabbit responds best to braising and other moist-heat cooking methods, which bring out its silky texture. Check with your butcher in advance before planning this dish; you may need to place a special order. Ask the butcher to disjoint the rabbit for you into 6 serving pieces.

braising and stewing p. 40

toasting nuts p. 26

Braised Short Ribs

3 lb beef short ribs
(6–7 oz each)

Salt and freshly ground pepper

3 Tbsp vegetable oil

1 yellow onion, diced

1 stalk celery, diced

1 carrot, diced

2 Tbsp tomato paste

3 Tbsp all-purpose flour

1 cup beef broth, or as needed

1 cup dry red wine

1 bay leaf

¼ tsp dried thyme

Makes 4 servings

Preheat the oven to 350°F. Trim the short ribs of excess fat and gristle, and season with salt and pepper.

Heat the oil in a large Dutch oven over high heat. Sear the short ribs until browned on all sides, about 5 minutes total. Transfer the ribs to a pan and set aside.

Add the onion, celery, and carrot to the Dutch oven and cook, stirring occasionally, until the onion is golden brown, 7–8 minutes. Add the tomato paste and cook until it darkens, about 1 minute. Add the flour and cook, stirring frequently, to make a blond roux, about 5 minutes.

Add the broth and wine to the Dutch oven, whisking well to work out any lumps. Return the short ribs to the pot with any juices released by the ribs. Add more broth if needed to cover the ribs by about one-third. Add the bay leaf and thyme.

Bring to a gentle simmer over medium heat. Cover the pot and transfer it to the oven. Braise the short ribs until fork-tender, about 1½ hours, turning every 20 minutes to keep them evenly moistened.

Transfer the ribs to a deep platter and moisten with some of the cooking liquid. Cover and keep warm while completing the sauce.

Place the Dutch oven over high heat and simmer the cooking liquid until it has a good flavor and saucelike consistency, about 10 minutes. Remove and discard the bay leaf. Taste and adjust the seasoning with salt and pepper.

Serve the ribs with the sauce.

Most braises and stews improve with age; if possible, let this one rest at least overnight in the refrigerator before serving. To reheat, use the large Dutch oven it was cooked in. Keep the heat very low until the braise or stew has "melted," then raise the heat and simmer until the liquid comes to a full boil. Stir frequently to prevent scorching, and adjust the seasonings again carefully just before you serve the braise.

braising and stewing
p. 40

trimming meat p. 97

Osso Buco

4–8 veal shank crosscuts (about 4 lb total), 1½–2 inches thick

Salt and freshly ground pepper

All-purpose flour for dredging

2 Tbsp olive oil

1 large yellow onion, diced

1 carrot, diced

1 leek, white and light green parts, sliced

2 cloves garlic, minced

3 Tbsp tomato paste

¾ cup dry white wine

1¾ cups beef broth, or as needed

1 tsp minced fresh thyme

½ tsp minced fresh rosemary

Gremolata

3 Tbsp chopped fresh flat-leaf parsley

2 anchovy fillets, minced

1 tsp grated lemon zest

Makes 4 servings

Preheat the oven to 350°F. Trim the veal shanks of excess fat and season with salt and pepper. Dredge them in the flour.

Heat the oil in a Dutch oven or other flameproof casserole over medium-high heat. Sear the veal until browned on all sides, about 8 minutes total. Remove the veal to a pan and set aside.

Pour off all but 2 Tbsp of the fat from the Dutch oven. Add the onion to the pan and cook, stirring occasionally, until golden brown, 5–6 minutes. Add the carrot and cook, stirring occasionally, until the carrot starts to brown, 3 minutes. Add the leek and garlic and cook, stirring frequently, until aromatic, 2 minutes more. Add the tomato paste and cook, stirring frequently, until the tomato paste darkens, about 1 minute.

Add the wine to the pan, stirring to incorporate the tomato paste. Simmer until the wine is reduced by half, about 4 minutes. Return the veal to the Dutch oven with any juices released by the veal. Add enough broth to cover the veal by two-thirds.

Bring to a gentle simmer over medium to low heat. Cover the pot and transfer it to the oven. Braise the veal shanks for 2 hours, turning the meat occasionally. Add the thyme and rosemary and braise, partially covered, until fork-tender, about 1 hour more.

Transfer the veal shanks to a warmed platter or plates and moisten with some of the cooking liquid. Cover and keep warm while completing the sauce.

Place the Dutch oven over high heat and simmer the cooking liquid until it has a good flavor and saucelike consistency, about 10 minutes. Taste and adjust the seasoning with salt and pepper.

Meanwhile, make the gremolata. Mix together the parsley, anchovies, and lemon zest.

Spoon the sauce over the osso buco, sprinkle with gremolata, and serve.

Gremolata is a finely minced seasoning garnish typically made of lemon zest, minced parsley, and garlic. Here, it includes an interesting addition of anchovies. Sprinkled over rich, heavy meat dishes like this osso buco just before serving, it adds a welcome burst of bright aroma and flavor.

braising and stewing
p. 40

dredging and breading
p. 68

Lamb and Chicken Stew with Couscous

2 lb boneless leg of lamb

8 skinless bone-in chicken thighs (4–5 oz each)

Salt and freshly ground pepper

3 Tbsp olive oil

1 yellow onion, diced

4 cloves garlic, minced

1 Tbsp minced gingerroot

2 tsp ground cumin

2 tsp ground turmeric

1 tsp ground coriander

½ tsp freshly grated nutmeg

2 bay leaves

Pinch of saffron threads, crushed

⅛ tsp ground cloves (optional)

3 cups chicken broth

6 fresh or frozen artichoke hearts, halved

2 cups coarsely diced carrot

2 cups coarsely diced turnip

3 cups finely diced zucchini

1 cup finely diced green bell pepper

One 15-oz can garbanzo beans (chickpeas), rinsed and drained

4 plum (Roma) tomatoes, peeled and cut into wedges

1 cup fresh lima beans, boiled until tender and drained, or thawed frozen lima beans

3 cups couscous, cooked according to package directions

Makes 10–12 servings

Open out the lamb leg and trim away excess fat and gristle. Cut into 2-inch cubes. Season the lamb and chicken with salt and pepper.

Heat the oil in a large, heavy Dutch oven over high heat. Sauté the lamb until lightly browned on all sides, about 3 minutes total. Remove and set aside.

Reduce the heat to medium-high. Add the onion, garlic, ginger, cumin, turmeric, coriander, nutmeg, bay leaves, saffron, and cloves (if using) and sauté until evenly blended, about 2 minutes. Add the lamb and any juices released by the lamb, the chicken, and the broth. If using fresh artichoke hearts, add them now. Simmer, covered, until the lamb and chicken are just cooked through, about 40 minutes. Add the carrots and turnips and simmer, covered, until tender, another 15 minutes. If using frozen artichoke hearts, add them now.

Uncover, add the zucchini and bell pepper, and simmer for 4–5 minutes. Add the garbanzos, tomatoes, and lima beans and simmer until all of the ingredients are tender and very hot, another 4 minutes. Taste and adjust the seasoning with salt and pepper.

Mound the couscous and ladle the stew over the mound. Serve at once.

Harissa, the traditional condiment for couscous, is a fiery hot red pepper sauce from North Africa, available in the special foods section of many larger supermarkets or in shops specializing in Middle Eastern and Moroccan products. Dilute *harissa* sauce with a little water to use it as a condiment for this dish. Other delicious accompaniments are toasted almond slices, raisins or currants, and parsley sprigs.

braising and stewing
p. 40

trimming artichokes
p. 185

boiling, parboiling, or blanching p. 37

Beef Stew

3 lb boneless beef shank, chuck, or brisket

Salt and freshly ground pepper

4 Tbsp vegetable oil (divided use)

1 small yellow onion, diced

2 Tbsp tomato paste

3 Tbsp all-purpose flour

2 cups beef broth

1 spice sachet (p. 46), including 1 crushed garlic clove

1 large yellow or white waxy potato, peeled and cut into large dice

12 pearl onions, peeled

1 stalk celery, coarsely diced

1 carrot, coarsely diced

½ cup fresh or thawed frozen peas

1 Tbsp chopped fresh flat-leaf parsley or chives (optional)

Makes 4–6 servings

Trim the beef of excess fat and gristle. Cut into 2-inch cubes and season with salt and pepper.

Heat 2 Tbsp of the oil in a Dutch oven over high heat. Working in batches without crowding, sear the beef to a deep brown on all sides, about 8 minutes. Transfer the beef to a pan and set aside.

Add the remaining 2 Tbsp oil to the Dutch oven and heat over medium-high heat. Add the onion and cook, stirring occasionally, until golden, about 5 minutes. Add the tomato paste and cook until it darkens, about 1 minute. Add the flour and cook, stirring frequently, to make a blond roux, about 5 minutes.

Add the broth to the pot, whisking well to work out any lumps. Return the beef to the pot along with any juices released by the beef.

Bring to a gentle simmer over low to medium heat and add the sachet. Cover the pot and continue to stew over very low heat or transfer to a 350°F oven. Stew the beef for 45 minutes, stirring occasionally. Add the potato, pearl onions, celery, and carrot and stew until the beef is tender to the bite and the vegetables are fully cooked, 30–35 minutes more.

Remove and discard the sachet. Add the peas and simmer 2–3 minutes more, or until all of the ingredients are very hot. Taste and season with salt and pepper. If using, stir in the parsley or use to garnish individual portions, and serve.

Tougher cuts of meat, like beef shank, round, or chuck, make the best stews. Long cooking tenderizes the meat while releasing flavor into the surrounding sauce. Although supermarkets often sell precut packages of "beef for stewing," you'll get higher-quality meat (with less gristle and odd ends) if you buy a single cut and cube it yourself.

braising and stewing
p. 40

preparing potatoes
p. 205

VARIATION

Lamb Navarin

Replace the beef with lamb shoulder and half of the beef broth with dry white wine. Double the amount of carrot, and replace the potato and peas with 2 cups diced turnips or rutabagas. Include some fresh or dried rosemary in the sachet. Proceed as directed.

Pork Goulash

2½ lb boneless pork shoulder
or butt

2 Tbsp sweet paprika

Salt and freshly ground pepper

⅓ cup vegetable oil

6 yellow onions, diced

2 cloves garlic, minced

¼ cup all-purpose flour

3 cups chicken broth

¾ cup dry white wine

2 bay leaves

2 tsp caraway seeds

2 tsp minced fresh marjoram

1 tsp minced fresh thyme

1 tsp grated lemon zest

Sour cream for serving

Makes 8 servings

Trim the pork of excess fat and cut into 2-inch cubes. Combine the paprika, 1 tsp salt, and 1 tsp pepper in a large bowl and toss with the cubed pork to coat evenly.

Heat the oil in a large, heavy Dutch oven or soup pot over high heat. Sear the pork, stirring occasionally, until browned on all sides, about 5 minutes. Remove the pork with a slotted spoon to another pan and cover to keep warm.

Reduce the heat to medium-high. Add the onion and cook, stirring often, until softened, 6–8 minutes. Add the garlic and continue to sauté until aromatic, 1 minute more.

Add the flour and cook, stirring frequently with a wooden spoon, to make a blond roux, about 5 minutes.

Add the broth and wine to the pan and whisk well to remove any lumps. Bring to a full boil. Return the pork to the pan along with any juices released by the pork.

Bring to a gentle simmer over low heat. Add the bay leaves and caraway seeds. Cover and simmer the goulash, stirring occasionally, for 45 minutes. Uncover and add the marjoram, thyme, and lemon zest and simmer until the pork is fork-tender, 15 minutes more.

Remove and discard the bay leaves. Taste and season with salt and pepper. Serve, passing sour cream at the table.

Goulash, which comes from the Hungarian word *gulyas,* or shepherd, is a rich meat stew flavored with paprika. Because paprika is a key ingredient, buy a good-quality imported Hungarian paprika in a tin and store tightly closed in a cool, dark place. Paprika quickly loses its color and flavor when exposed to light. Egg noodles tossed with butter and toasted bread crumbs make a delicious accompaniment for this savory stew. The pork may be replaced with an equal amount of boneless beef round or chuck.

braising and stewing
p. 40

zesting and juicing citrus
p. 182

Fish and
Shellfish

If you were to name the best loved dishes from the world's great cuisines, you'd find many seafood dishes high on the list. Their recipes are often deceptively simple, relying as they do upon the seafood's absolute freshness. Re-creating these dishes requires a trip to the local fish market, stocked with salmon, trout, or other fish that are pan-dressed, filleted, or cut into steaks; live lobsters; shrimp in a range of sizes, cooked and peeled or in the shell; a variety of clams and oysters in the shell; and squid or octopus. Preparing these different types of seafood gives you the opportunity to experience how cooking techniques may be adapted for different textures, depending on whether a fish is naturally lean or oily, meaty or delicate.

Types of fish and shellfish

The way fish swim, the water they swim in, and their diets all influence the flavor and texture of their flesh. Being familiar with these distinctions is useful when you want to substitute one type of fish for another in a recipe or want to find a recipe for a type of fish that is new to you. A fish can have a firm, meaty texture or be delicate and tend toward flakiness. Its flavor can be mild or robust; often, the fattier the fish, the more pronounced its flavor.

Finfish have gills and fins. They live in oceans, ponds, rivers, and streams. Some species live in salt water, others in fresh water. Round fish varieties include trout, bass, snapper, tuna, and salmon. The most popular flatfish varieties include flounder, sole, halibut, cod, haddock, and turbot. Sharks, skate, and ray are cartilagenous fish, meaning they have cartilage instead of bones.

Clams, mussels, oysters, and scallops are all bivalve mollusks, shellfish with two shells joined by a hinge. Clam and oyster varieties often carry the name of the area where they were harvested. Mussel types include standard (or horse) mussels, pen shell, and New Zealand green lipped. The two main types of scallop are sea scallops and bay scallops.

Lobsters, crabs, crayfish, shrimp, and prawns are all crustaceans. They have jointed exterior skeletons or shells. There are both salt- and freshwater crustaceans. The texture of their flesh is affected by the temperature of the water where they are harvested. Squid, octopus, and cuttlefish belong to a group of shellfish known as cephalopods. Instead of an exterior shell or skeleton, they have an interior shell called a quill.

Today, many varieties of seafood, including catfish, trout, salmon, mussels, and oysters, are farm raised. Fish raised on farms are usually of consistent size and quality, although their flavor may be less pronounced than that of "wild" varieties.

Selecting seafood

To enjoy great fish on a consistent basis, you need a great fish market. Your market may be a shop specializing in fish or a department in a larger store, but any high-quality fish market has certain hallmarks. The fish looks fresh, with moist flesh and skin. All the fish and shellfish are iced or cooled, and the entire display is clean and orderly. The staff handle the fish carefully and keep all work surfaces and scales clean and sanitized. You can select both familiar and unfamiliar types of fish with confidence because someone in the shop can describe the fish to you in terms of its culinary characteristics. You enjoy coming to the shop or counter because it smells pleasantly of the sea.

Stop at the fish counter last, right before heading home, in order to keep your purchase as cold as possible. Once home, keep fresh fish in the coldest part of your refrigerator, and remember to put a plate or dish underneath any packages that might drip or leak. Keep frozen seafood in the freezer until you are ready to thaw it.

Many fish are now frozen right on the fishing ships using blast freezers. The fish freezes very quickly without forming the large ice crystals a home freezer would create. As long as the fish or seafood is slowly and carefully thawed—overnight in the refrigerator, not more quickly at room temperature—there is little difference between the flavor and texture of a flash-frozen fish and a fresh one.

The basic market forms for fish are whole, drawn, pan-dressed, fillets, and steaks. A whole fish remains exactly as it was when taken from the water. If the fish is gutted before it is sold, it is known as a drawn fish. Pan-dressed fish have been gutted and usually scaled. The head, tail, and fins have been removed, although they may remain on some smaller fish, such as trout.

Steaks can be cut from large fish such as tuna, salmon, or halibut. The steak is produced by cutting a drawn fish into crosswise pieces. The backbone is left intact; the skin may or may not be removed. Although the scales are generally removed before fish is cut into steaks, it's a good idea to check for any stray scales before cooking.

Fillets are boneless cuts. Flatfish, such as flounder and sole, can be cut into four fillets, two from the upper surface of the fish (the side with dark skin) and two from the lower (the side with white or light skin). Round fish such as trout, salmon, or snapper are cut into two fillets, one from each side of their bodies. Fillets from larger fish are often cut into pieces or individual portions. Fish with relatively tough skin such as catfish or perch are skinned before they are sold as fillets.

Oysters, clams, and mussels are sold live by the dozen or by weight. Lobsters and crab are sold live by the pound. Shrimp are sold by weight, the price varying according to its "count," the number of shrimp in a pound. The larger the shrimp, the higher the price.

Best cooking methods for fish and shellfish

FISH OR SHELLFISH	CHARACTERISTICS	BEST COOKING METHODS
Bass	Moderately fatty, fairly firm, smooth	Steaming, poaching, sautéing, roasting, grilling
Bluefish	Oily, flaky, soft, strong taste	Roasting, baking, grilling, broiling
Catfish	Moderately fatty, firm, sweet	Pan-frying, baking, grilling, broiling, shallow-poaching
Cod	Lean, firm, mild taste	Poaching, shallow-poaching, sautéing, steaming, roasting, baking, grilling, broiling
Flounder	Lean, flaky, mild taste	Sautéing, pan-frying, deep-frying, shallow-poaching, baking
Grouper	Lean, firm, mild taste	Sautéing, grilling, broiling, roasting, baking, steaming, shallow-poaching
Halibut	Lean, fine texture, flaky, mild taste	Poaching, sautéing, steaming, shallow-poaching, roasting, baking, grilling, broiling
Perch	Lean, delicate, sweet flavor	Sautéing, pan-frying, baking
Pompano	Moderately fatty, firm, full flavor	Sautéing, grilling, broiling, roasting, baking, steaming, shallow-poaching
Salmon	Moderately fatty, firm, rich flavor	Sautéing, grilling, broiling, roasting, baking, shallow-poaching, poaching
Shad	Lean, flaky, sweet	Poaching, steaming, shallow-poaching, roasting, baking
Snapper	Lean, firm	Sautéing, grilling, broiling, roasting, baking, steaming, shallow-poaching
Sole	Lean, flaky, delicate flavor	Sautéing, pan-frying, shallow-poaching, baking
Swordfish	Lean, very firm	Sautéing, grilling, broiling, roasting, baking, stewing
Trout	Moderately oily, flaky	Sautéing, pan-frying, baking, poaching
Tuna	Moderately oily, firm	Sautéing, grilling, broiling, roasting, baking, stewing
Clams		Steaming, poaching, simmering, stewing, sautéing, baking, grilling
Lobster		Steaming, boiling, poaching, simmering, stewing, sautéing, baking, grilling, broiling
Mussels		Steaming, poaching, simmering, stewing, sautéing, baking, grilling
Oysters		Steaming, poaching, simmering, stewing, sautéing, baking, grilling
Scallops		Sautéing, stir-frying, deep-frying, grilling, broiling, poaching, steaming
Shrimp		Sautéing, stir-frying, deep-frying, grilling, broiling, poaching, steaming

3 Removing the backbone

Without turning the fish over, insert the blade just underneath the backbone. Lay your guiding hand flat on top of the bone structure to keep the fish stable. Keeping the knife parallel to the work surface, run the blade down the entire length of the fish underneath the bones. The knife's cutting edge should be angled upward very slightly to cut as much flesh from bone as possible.

4 Trimming the fillets

Remove the belly bones by making smooth strokes against the bones to cut them away cleanly. Trim away excess fat only on the belly edge of the fillets. Cut away the remnants of the backbone by running the blade just underneath the line of the backbone, lifting it up and away from the fillet as you cut.

Filleting a flatfish

Flatfish, such as sole, can be cut into two wide or four narrow fillets. Place the fish pale-belly side down. To make two fillets, cut from the outer edge of the fish, beginning at the tail end just inside the fin. Hold the knife parallel to the work surface and work toward the head to divide the top fillet from the bottom one. Adjust the direction and length of your strokes to go over the ridge of bones in the center of the fillet. Hold the fillet up and away from the bones as you work, to expose the bone structure. Continue cutting to the other edge and remove the top fillet in a single piece. Repeat on the other side. To make four fillets, make cuts along each side of the center bone ridge and then fillet from the center toward the fins.

Filleting a round fish

A boning knife with a flexible blade is ideal for the delicate work of filleting fish.

1 Cutting in behind the head

To fillet a fish, use a filleting or boning knife. Place the fish on a work surface with its back toward you. Make a cut behind the head and gills down to the bone, angling the knife away from the body, but do not cut the head away from the body.

2 Cutting the first fillet

Without lifting the knife, angle it so that the blade is parallel to the work surface and the cutting edge is pointing toward the fish's tail. Hold the knife handle lower than the blade, to remove as much flesh from the bone as possible. Run the knife down the length of the fish, under the flesh, to cut a fillet. Press the knife against the bones as you slice and do not saw back and forth. Remove the fillet from the bones and place skin side down.

Preparing salmon fillets

By freshly skinning and cutting a large fillet of salmon or other fish, you can create attractive slices that cook quickly.

1 Removing the skin

To remove the skin from a fillet or an entire side of fresh salmon before you cook it, use a flexible filleting knife or a chef's knife. Lay the fillet skin side down and nearly parallel to the edge of the cutting surface. Make a small cut at the tail end between the skin and flesh to make a small flap of skin that you can grip firmly. Hold the blade of the knife nearly parallel to the work surface, angling the blade toward the skin to avoid cutting into the flesh. Hold the flap at the tail end taut, using a cloth if needed for a surer grip. Use short, back-and-forth sawing motions as you simultaneously push the knife down the length of the fillet to cut the skin from the fillet. Moving the skin back and forth sideways while pressing the knife gently forward will help ease the knife along between the skin and flesh. Carefully flip the fillet over onto a platter or dish and remove any scales or debris sticking to it.

2 Removing the pin bones

Salmon have a row of narrow pin bones running the length of their fillets. Most fishmongers will remove the pin bones, either before selling the salmon or on request, but it is always good to check for any stray ones before cooking the fillet. Run your finger down the middle of the fillet against the grain (from the thicker head end to the thinner tail end) to locate the pin bones.

Grasp a pin bone firmly with clean tweezers or needle-nose pliers and pull it out with the grain toward the direction of the fish's head. Repeat, removing the bones methodically from one end to the other to make sure none are passed over.

3 Slicing the fillets

Once the skin and pin bones are removed, a fillet of salmon or other fish may be sliced into serving portions. Diagonal cuts of fish have a greater surface area, so they cook more quickly. These cuts, sometimes referred to on menus as *tranches,* are excellent for sautéed or pan-fried dishes and for grilling or broiling. To prepare tranches, hold a very sharp knife at an angle as you slice.

Other preparations

Depending on the size of the fillet, you can also prepare fingers, or *goujonettes,* and strips of salmon to sauté, stir-fry, or grill on skewers. Cut pieces across the grain about 2 inches long and up to ½ inch thick.

You can also wrap fillets around a filling or butterfly them in order to stuff them. To butterfly a fillet, hold the knife blade parallel to the work surface and place your guiding hand flat on top of the fillet. Make a horizontal cut through the fillet, leaving about 1 inch of fillet uncut, to act as a hinge.

Bring the water to a rolling boil, then plunge each lobster into the pot head first. Once the water returns to a boil, lower the heat to maintain a simmer. Allow about 8 minutes for a 1½-pound lobster and add 2 minutes for every additional pound. Do not crack the lobster before you cook it, or you will lose flavorful juices.

4 Cracking the shell

If you partially crack the shells of a whole lobster before serving it, diners will have an easier time. If desired, separate the legs and claws from the body. Roll the tail against the work surface to loosen the shell. Use a lobster cracker or a small mallet to crack the shells of the legs and claws gently and evenly. Avoid smashing the flesh. Reassemble the lobster on a platter.

If a recipe calls for only the meat of a cooked lobster, you will need to shell the lobster completely. Let cool completely for easier handling and to allow the meat to firm up enough to hold its shape. Twist the tail away from the body. Squeeze the tail shell to crack it partially and loosen it, then pull the tail meat away in one piece. Stand the claw on the work surface with its thumb edge down. Use the heel of the knife to cut into the outside edge of each claw, without cutting through to the meat, then swivel the knife sharply to the side to crack apart the claw shell. Remove the claw in one piece by wiggling the meat as you pull it out, taking care to slip the "thumb" out slowly. Use a large knife or kitchen shears to cut through the leg knuckles, then pull out the knuckle meat.

Preparing lobster

Purchasing live lobster for cooking guarantees the best flavor and texture. Lobster may be split for broiling, or boiled whole.

1 Splitting lobster for broiling

Lay a live lobster belly side down on a work surface, head pointing toward your cutting hand. Insert the tip of a chef's knife into the base of its head to kill the lobster quickly, and pull the knife all the way down through the shell, splitting the head in half.

2 Making the second cut

Turn the lobster 180 degrees. Place the tip of the knife at the same point as your first cut, and then cut completely through the shell of the body and tail.

3 Boiling whole lobster

To boil live lobster(s), choose a large pot to allow plenty of room. You will need 1 gallon of water for 1 lobster. For each additional lobster, add another quart of water to the pot.

Preparing shrimp

For shrimp presented whole and peeled, especially in sautéed or grilled dishes, remove the vein for a cleaner appearance.

1 Peeling shrimp

To peel shrimp, start from the belly side and peel away the legs along with the shell. Pull off the tail if desired.

2 Deveining shrimp

To devein shrimp, lay the peeled shrimp on a work surface, with the curved outer edge of the shrimp facing your cutting hand. Make a shallow cut into the shrimp's back with a paring knife. Use the tip of the knife to scrape out the gray or black vein, which is actually the shrimp's intestinal tract. To remove the vein without cutting into the shrimp (a nice touch for boiled or steamed shrimp), use the tip of your paring knife, a skewer, or a toothpick to pierce the shrimp just below the center point of the vein and slowly pull the vein out.

3 Butterflying shrimp

If you would like to butterfly shrimp for grilling or broiling, cut more deeply into the curve of the back as you are deveining the shrimp.

Cleaning mussels

Mussels need careful cleaning before cooking.

1 Scrubbing and debearding

Hold the mussel under cold running water. Use a brush with stiff bristles to thoroughly scrub the mussel, removing grit, sand, and mud from the shell's exterior. Mussels attach themselves to rocks and other surfaces by means of a fibrous, shaggy beard (which is sometimes absent in farmed mussels). Since removing the beard kills the mussel, plan on debearding them just before cooking. Pull the beard away from the shell until taut, and yank it sharply down toward the pointed hinge until it snaps away.

Shucking oysters

Whether you plan to enjoy oysters raw or simply want them as fresh as possible for cooking, purchase live oysters and shuck them yourself.

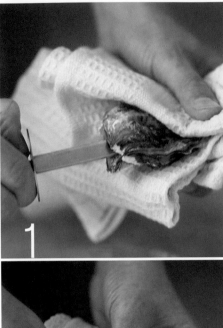

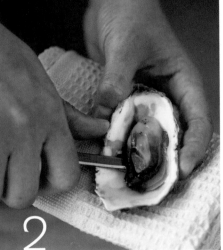

1 Opening the shell

To open an oyster shell, you will need to pry apart the hinge holding its two shells together. Be sure to work over a bowl in order to catch the juices, known as oyster liquor, and reserve for seafood soups, stews, sauces, and broths. Wear a thick glove or place a folded cloth in your noncutting hand for protection against cuts, and use an oyster knife or other flat, dull knife. To serve oysters on the half shell or to prepare them for broiling, open oysters with their deeper, more curved shell halves on the bottom. Hold the oyster so its hinged side is facing your cutting hand. Work the tip of the knife into the hinge that holds the upper and lower shells together and twist, turning the knife like a key in a lock, to break open the hinge.

2 Loosening the oyster

Once the shell is open, carefully slide the knife along the inside surface of the top shell to detach the oyster from its shell. Continue to work over a bowl, as the oyster may release more juice. Remove and discard the top shell. Slide the knife carefully underneath the oyster to release it from its bottom shell.

Testing fish and shellfish for doneness

Use a thermometer and your senses to check the doneness of fish and shellfish.

Testing temperature and other cues

In general, cook seafood until it registers 145°F on an instant-read thermometer, or until the flesh is opaque. Well-cooked fish will separate easily into flakes when prodded with a fork but should still be moist. Meaty fish such as salmon, tuna, or swordfish is sometimes cooked to medium-rare, or still translucent in the center. As with red meat, seafood will become more firm and less springy as it cooks. Press fish gently with a finger to help determine doneness, as well as checking the internal temperature.

The shells of shrimp, lobster, and crab will turn vivid pink or bright red and their flesh will become opaque when cooked through. Scallops will turn milky white and feel firm to the touch. The shells of bivalves such as clams, mussels, and oysters will open once properly cooked. Discard any shellfish whose shells remain closed after cooking, because they were likely dead before cooking.

Broiled Mahi-mahi with Pineapple Chutney

Pineapple Chutney

1 cup diced fresh pineapple

2 Tbsp minced green onion

2 Tbsp minced fresh cilantro

2 Tbsp minced red bell pepper

2 tsp fresh lime juice

Salt and freshly ground black pepper

Ground cayenne pepper

Vegetable oil for brushing

4 mahi-mahi fillets (about 8 oz each)

Juice of ½ lemon

1 cup fresh bread crumbs

½ cup ground blanched almonds

Makes 4 servings

For the chutney, toss together the pineapple, green onion, cilantro, and bell pepper in a bowl. Taste and season with the lime juice and salt, black pepper, and cayenne to taste. Set aside.

Preheat the broiler. Position the rack at least 4 inches from the heat source. Line a baking sheet with aluminum foil and brush lightly with oil.

Season the mahi-mahi with salt and pepper and drizzle with the lemon juice. Brush evenly with oil.

Combine the bread crumbs and almonds in a wide, shallow pan. Dip the mahi-mahi in the mixture and gently press over all sides. Transfer to the prepared baking sheet.

Broil the mahi-mahi until a light golden crust forms, 3–4 minutes. Turn once and broil until the mahi-mahi is cooked through, about 2 minutes more.

Serve at once on warmed plates with the chutney.

Nuts are a an excellent complement to fish. Here, almonds add crunch and flavor to these simple salmon fillets. Try using other ground nuts for variety.

grilling and broiling p. 28

preparing salmon fillets p. 127

making bread crumbs p. 26

VARIATION

Tuna with Lime Marinade

Replace the mahi-mahi with four 6-ounce tuna steaks. Combine ½ cup peanut oil with ¼ cup fresh lime juice, ¼ tsp salt, and a few grinds of black pepper. Brush the tuna with this marinade just before broiling or combine the tuna with the marinade in a resealable plastic bag for up to 2 hours. Coat the tuna in panko (Japanese-style bread crumbs) before broiling as directed.

Tamarind Mixed Seafood Grill

4 green onions, minced

½ cup tamarind concentrate

½ cup olive oil

¼ cup white vinegar

¼ cup fresh lime juice

2 Tbsp honey

2 Tbsp minced fresh basil

1 Tbsp Dijon mustard

3 cloves garlic, minced

1 Tbsp toasted cumin seeds

½ tsp red pepper flakes

1 lb sea bass or yellowtail fillets, cut into 2-inch cubes

1 lb jumbo shrimp, peeled and deveined, tails on

1 lb sea scallops

12 clams

Makes 4 servings

Whisk together the green onions, tamarind, oil, vinegar, lime juice, honey, basil, mustard, garlic, cumin, and red pepper flakes in a baking dish to make a marinade. Reserve 1 cup to use as a dipping sauce.

Add the sea bass, shrimp, and scallops to the dish, turn to coat, cover, and refrigerate for at least 30 minutes or up to 2 hours.

Meanwhile, prepare a grill for a hot fire. Soak 8 bamboo skewers in water for 30 minutes to prevent them from scorching.

Thread the shrimp and scallops alternately onto the bamboo skewers. Place the skewers, sea bass, and clams on the grill, discarding clams that do not close to the touch. Grill the skewers until the scallops are barely opaque and shrimp is pink, turning once or as needed to mark them evenly on all sides, 2–3 minutes total. Grill the clams until they open, 5–6 minutes, being careful to reserve their juices when removing them from the grill. Discard any that do not open. Grill the sea bass on the first side until marked. Gently turn the fish over and continue cooking until barely opaque, 5–6 minutes.

Serve the grilled seafood with the reserved dipping sauce.

The tropical tamarind tree is valued for its plump, dark brown pods, which are filled with a sticky, stringy pulp peppered with large seeds. Tart and refreshing, with a more complex astringency than that of citrus, tamarind pulp is used extensively in Indian and Southeast Asian cooking. Look for jars of tamarind concentrate in Indian or Asian groceries.

grilling and broiling p. 28

preparing shrimp p. 129

Broiled Salmon with Orange-Thyme Butter

4 Tbsp unsalted butter, softened

¾ cup blanched almonds, ground, plus 2 Tbsp

1 Tbsp fresh orange juice

1 tsp fresh thyme leaves

½ tsp orange zest

Salt and freshly ground pepper

Vegetable oil for brushing

4 salmon fillets (about 6 oz each), skin removed

1 Tbsp fresh lemon juice

1 cup fresh bread crumbs

Makes 4 servings

Blend the butter with the 2 Tbsp ground almonds, orange juice, thyme, orange zest, ¼ tsp salt, and ¼ tsp pepper. Place on a piece of plastic wrap. Roll into a 1-inch-diameter cylinder and secure the ends by twisting. Chill until firm, about 2 hours.

Preheat the broiler. Position the rack at least 4 inches from the heat source. Line a baking sheet with foil and brush lightly with oil. Season the fish with salt, pepper, and the lemon juice. Brush evenly with oil.

Combine the bread crumbs and remaining ground almonds in a wide, shallow pan. Dip the salmon in the mixture and gently press over all sides. Transfer to the prepared baking sheet and broil until a light golden crust forms, 3–4 minutes. Turn once and broil until the salmon is cooked through, about 2 minutes more. Top each fillet with a slice of the orange-thyme butter and pass under the broiler just long enough to begin melting the butter. Serve at once on warmed plates.

You can find packaged ground almonds in the baking aisle of most supermarkets, or you can grind whole almonds yourself. Pulse the nuts in short bursts in a mini food processor or clean coffee grinder. Stop when the nuts look like coarse sand; grinding for too long can make the nuts pasty with their own oils.

preparing salmon fillets p. 127

Oysters Diamond Jim Brady

12 oysters

1½ cups dry white wine

1 Tbsp minced shallot

2 tsp fresh lemon juice

2–3 fresh tarragon leaves

½ tsp cracked peppercorns

2 large egg yolks, lightly beaten

6 Tbsp crème fraîche
(divided use)

½ cup peeled, seeded, and
diced tomato

1–2 tsp Pernod, or to taste

Salt and freshly ground pepper

4 cups baby spinach leaves

Rock salt for baking

Makes 4 appetizer servings

Preheat the broiler, positioning the rack about 4 inches from the heat source. Rinse and shuck the oysters, reserving the oyster liquor and shells.

Combine the wine, shallot, lemon juice, tarragon, and peppercorns in a shallow pan over medium-low heat. Bring to a gentle simmer (the liquid should be barely bubbling around the edges of the pan and giving off some steam). Add the oysters and their liquor and poach until the edges just begin to curl, 2–3 minutes. Remove from the liquid with a slotted spoon and transfer to a warmed plate. Cover to keep warm.

Raise the heat to high and simmer the poaching liquid until reduced by two-thirds, about 5 minutes. Strain the poaching liquid through a fine-mesh sieve, cheesecloth, or paper coffee filter. (The liquid should cool slightly, but can still be warm when combined with the eggs in the next step.)

Combine the poaching liquid and egg yolks in the top of a double boiler or a stainless-steel bowl set over simmering water. Whisk constantly until the mixture falls in ribbons when the whisk is lifted, 3–4 minutes, to make a sabayon. Whisk in 2 Tbsp of the crème fraîche.

Season the tomatoes with the Pernod and salt and pepper to taste. Set aside.

Heat a sauté pan over high heat and add the spinach by the handful, sautéing just until the leaves wilt before adding more. Once all the spinach is added to the pan, sauté until the spinach is deep green, tender, and softened, about 3 minutes.

Preheat the broiler again. Place 2 tsp of the tomato mixture in the deep half of each oyster shell. Top each with 1 tsp of the remaining crème fraîche, 1 tsp of the wilted spinach, and an oyster, and coat it with the sabayon. Place the oysters in a baking dish on a bed of rock salt ½–¾ inch deep to keep them from tipping over as they broil.

Broil the oysters until the sabayon is browned, about 1 minute. You can serve the oysters directly from the bed of salt or transfer them to individual plates.

This rich, succulent oyster dish well deserves the name of the famously lavish and high-living Diamond Jim, millionaire of the Gilded Age. A light coating of creamy sabayon sauce (made from egg yolks whisked with the wine used to poach the oysters and thickened with crème fraîche) before broiling helps keep the oysters from drying out under the heat.

poaching p. 39

grilling and broiling p. 28

shucking oysters p. 130

Broiled Lobster with Bread Crumb Stuffing

2 live lobsters (1½–2 lb each)

2 Tbsp unsalted butter, plus
8 Tbsp clarified

1 small yellow onion, minced

1 stalk celery, minced

¼ cup minced red bell pepper

¼ cup minced green bell pepper

1 clove garlic, minced

2 cups fresh bread crumbs

¼ cup minced sun-dried
tomatoes

2 Tbsp minced fresh basil

2 Tbsp dry sherry wine

Salt and freshly ground pepper

Lemon wedges, as needed

Makes 4 servings

Preheat the broiler, positioning the rack about 3 inches from the heat source. Split the lobsters in half lengthwise. If the coral and tomalley are present, remove and reserve to add to the stuffing.

Place the lobster halves on a baking sheet, shell side up. Broil until the meat is opaque around the edges, 5–6 minutes. Set aside. Preheat the oven to 400°F.

Meanwhile, heat the 2 Tbsp butter in a sauté pan over low heat. Sauté the onion, celery, red and green bell peppers, and garlic, stirring frequently, until softened but not colored, 5–6 minutes. Remove from the heat. Add the tomalley and coral (if desired), bread crumbs, tomatoes, and basil. Stir in the sherry and season with salt and pepper.

Turn the lobsters cut side up. Spoon the bread crumb mixture into the body cavity of each lobster. (Do not place it over the tail meat.) Put them in the oven and roast until the lobster meat is opaque in the center, about 10 minutes. Crack the lobster's claws and serve the lobsters with the lemon wedges and hot clarified butter.

For extra flavor in the stuffing, mix in the lobster coral (eggs), if present, and tomalley (liver). After splitting the lobster, use a small spoon to scoop the pinkish orange coral and pale green tomalley from the area near the head.

preparing lobster p. 128

making clarified butter p. 26

making bread crumbs p. 26

Smoke-Roasted Salmon with Leek Compote

4 Tbsp unsalted butter

4 leeks, white and light green
parts, sliced

1 clove garlic, minced

½ cup chicken broth

¼ cup dry white wine

1 tomato, peeled, seeded,
and diced

1 Tbsp chopped fresh flat-leaf
parsley

Salt and freshly ground pepper

4 salmon fillets (6–8 oz each)

Fresh lemon juice, as needed

Makes 4 servings

Heat the butter in a sauté pan over low heat. Add the leeks and garlic and cook until the leeks are wilted, about 10 minutes. Add the broth and wine and simmer until the leeks are tender and the liquid has almost evaporated, 20 minutes. Add the tomato and parsley and season with salt and pepper. Set the leek compote aside and cover to keep warm.

Prepare a grill for a medium-hot fire. Season the fish with salt, pepper, and lemon juice.

Spread ¼ inch of hickory smoking chips in the bottom of a large disposable foil pan and place on the grill. When the chips begin to smolder, place the fish on a rack and set atop the chips. Don't allow the fish to touch the chips. Cover the pan and rack with aluminum foil and cook for 5–6 minutes (6–8 minutes for larger fillets). Remove from the heat and allow to sit for 2 minutes before opening. Serve the salmon over a bed of the leek compote.

Follow the timing given in this recipe for smoke-roasting exactly. More time in the smoke would give the fish an acrid flavor and discolor it. Look for hickory smoking chips in gourmet shops or well-stocked hardware stores.

grilling and broiling p. 28

preparing salmon fillets p. 127

cleaning leeks p. 186

Roast Monkfish with Pernod Sauce

1½ lb monkfish fillet

Marinade

1 Tbsp fresh lime juice

1 Tbsp cracked green peppercorns

1 Tbsp chopped fresh tarragon, plus sprigs for garnish

1 Tbsp minced shallot

Vegetable oil, as needed

1 Tbsp tomato paste

2 Tbsp Pernod or another anise-flavored liqueur

½ cup dry white wine

¼ cup heavy cream

8 Tbsp unsalted butter, cut into pieces

12–16 Niçoise olives, pitted and sliced

Salt and freshly ground pepper

Makes 4 servings

Trim the monkfish by pulling away the slippery membrane, using a small, sharp knife if needed, and trim away any connective tissue.

Preheat the oven to 350°F. For the marinade, combine the lime juice, peppercorns, chopped tarragon, and shallot in a resealable plastic bag and add the fish. Close the bag, squeeze several times to distribute the marinade evenly, and marinate the fish for 15–30 minutes.

Coat an ovenproof sauté pan with oil. Heat over high heat until very hot. Remove the monkfish from the marinade and sear in the hot oil, browning it on all sides, 3–4 minutes total.

Transfer the pan with the fish to the oven and roast until the monkfish is opaque throughout, 12–15 minutes. Transfer the monkfish to a cutting board and cover to keep warm while completing the sauce.

Using the same pan, sauté the tomato paste over medium heat, stirring occasionally, until it is a deep brown, about 5 minutes. Pour in the Pernod and stir to deglaze the pan. Add the wine and reduce until slightly thickened, 3 minutes. Add the cream and whisk in the butter. Add the olives. Taste and season with salt and pepper.

Slice the monkfish and fan it on a heated platter. Pour the sauce over, garnish with the tarragon sprigs, and serve.

Don't leave the monkfish in the marinade for longer than 30 minutes. If left too long, the acid in the lime juice will begin to "cook" the delicate flesh, resulting in a mushy texture in the finished dish. Pernod is the most well-known brand of *pastis,* a French liqueur with a distinctive anise flavor, usually drunk as an aperitif. You can find it in most well-stocked liquor stores.

roasting and baking p. 30

marinating p. 68

Baked Lemon-Stuffed Trout

4 trout (8–10 oz each), pan-dressed

Salt and freshly ground pepper

2 tsp fresh lemon juice

2 lemons, one cut into 8 rounds and one cut into wedges

16 sprigs fresh flat-leaf parsley

4 sprigs fresh thyme

1 Tbsp unsalted butter, softened, plus more for greasing

Makes 4 servings

Preheat the oven to 400°F.

Open each fish, season with salt and pepper, sprinkle with the lemon juice, and layer each with 2 lemon slices, 4 sprigs parsley, and 1 sprig thyme. Fold the fish closed.

Place the fish in a buttered 8 x 13–inch baking pan. Dot the fish with the butter.

Bake until the flesh along the backbone, where it is thickest, is opaque when cut into, and just starting to slide apart, 10–12 minutes.

Serve the trout with the lemon wedges.

A pan-dressed fish is one that's ready for the pan— meaning it's been gutted and (usually) scaled, with its head, tail, and fins removed. Because of its small size, trout is often sold with its head still on; you can cook it that way or ask your fishmonger to remove the head for you.

roasting and baking p. 30

filleting a round fish p. 126

Pancetta-Wrapped Halibut with Summer Vegetables

1 small zucchini or yellow squash, sliced into thin rounds

1 large tomato, peeled, seeded, and diced

½ yellow onion, sliced

2 cloves garlic, minced

1 Tbsp minced fresh basil

½ tsp minced fresh oregano

3 Tbsp olive oil (divided use)

Salt and freshly ground pepper

4 halibut fillets (about 6 oz each)

½ lemon

4 slices pancetta

Makes 4 servings

Preheat the oven to 375°F. Toss together the zucchini, tomato, onion, garlic, basil, oregano, 2 Tbsp of the olive oil, ½ tsp salt, and ½ tsp pepper in a bowl. Spread in a thin, even layer in a 9 x 13–inch baking dish. Place in the oven while preparing the fish.

Season the fish with salt and pepper and squeeze the lemon half over it. Wrap a piece of pancetta around each fillet and use a toothpick or skewer to secure it if needed. Heat the remaining 1 Tbsp oil in a large sauté pan over high heat. Add the fillets and sear on the first side just until the pancetta is starting to brown, about 1 minute. Carefully turn and continue cooking until the pancetta is lightly browned on the second side, about 2 minutes more.

Remove the vegetables from the oven. Transfer the fillets and their juices to the vegetable bed. Return to the oven and roast until the fish is cooked through and opaque, about 10 minutes. Serve each fillet over a bed of vegetables.

Pancetta is an unsmoked, cured Italian bacon, available in Italian delicatessens and specialty food shops. It is folded into a roll and can be sliced to order or sold in a single piece. Since it's not smoked, it has a milder flavor than American bacon. If substituting strip bacon, parcook it until limp so that it crisps well on the fish.

peeling and seeding tomatoes p. 184

dicing p. 17

Roasted Stuffed Swordfish

5 swordfish steaks (about ¾ inch thick and 6 oz each)

¼ cup plus 1 Tbsp olive oil

2 Tbsp fresh lemon juice

2 Tbsp chopped fresh basil

2 Tbsp chopped fresh thyme (divided use)

3 cloves garlic, minced (divided use)

Salt and freshly ground pepper

½ cup minced yellow onion

⅓ cup brandy

1 cup fresh bread crumbs

2 Tbsp minced fresh flat-leaf parsley

1 tsp lemon zest

Makes 4 servings

Finely dice 1 swordfish steak. Butterfly the remaining 4 steaks.

Blend the ¼ cup oil, lemon juice, basil, 1 Tbsp of the thyme, 2 cloves of the garlic, and salt and pepper to taste in a small bowl. Brush over the fish 15–45 minutes before grilling. Reserve the excess marinade.

Preheat the oven to 400°F. Heat the 1 Tbsp oil in a sauté pan over high heat. Add the diced swordfish, onion, and remaining garlic and sauté until lightly browned, 4–5 minutes. Add the brandy and simmer until reduced by half, 2 minutes. Meanwhile, combine the bread crumbs, parsley, remaining thyme, and lemon zest in a bowl and mix gently. Add the swordfish mixture and season with salt and pepper.

Divide the stuffing mixture among the swordfish steaks, fold the steaks over the stuffing, and use a toothpick or skewer to secure the opening. Place in a small baking dish. Bake the swordfish, brushing with some of the marinade every 2–3 minutes, until the stuffing is hot and the fish is cooked to the desired doneness, about 12 minutes for medium-rare. Serve at once.

This unusual preparation uses diced swordfish as part of a stuffing for swordfish steaks. Make sure to check that the fish in the stuffing is cooked as well as the steaks.

roasting and baking p. 30

butterflying p. 67

making bread crumbs p. 26

Fillet of Snapper en Papillote

6 Tbsp unsalted butter, softened (divided use), plus more for greasing pan

2 Tbsp minced shallot

2 cups asparagus tips

1 cup sliced white mushrooms

1 cup thinly sliced green onions, white and green parts

¾ cup heavy cream

½ cup dry white wine

Salt and freshly ground pepper

4 skinless red snapper fillets (about 6 oz each)

Makes 4 servings

Preheat the oven to 375°F.

Cut 4 pieces of parchment paper into heart shapes large enough to fit a fillet comfortably on one side with at least 2 inches of margin around the edge. Fold the hearts in half lengthwise to crease the paper. Use 1 Tbsp butter to coat both sides of each parchment paper heart.

Melt the remaining 2 Tbsp butter in a sauté pan over high heat. Sauté the shallot until translucent, about 2 minutes. Add the asparagus, mushrooms, and green onions. Continue to sauté until the asparagus turns bright green, about 1 minute more. Add the cream and wine, and simmer until the asparagus is barely tender, about 8 minutes. With a slotted spoon, remove the vegetables and allow the cream to continue to reduce until fairly thick, about 3 minutes. Taste and season with salt and pepper.

Season the fish with salt and pepper.

Place ½ cup of the vegetable mixture on one side of each buttered parchment paper heart. Top each mound of vegetable mixture with a snapper fillet, and spoon 2–3 Tbsp of the reduced cream over each fish fillet.

Fold each paper heart in half over the food and align the edges. Starting at the top of the heart, make small, tight folds all along the edge of the paper; when you come to the bottom of the heart, give it a good twist to seal the packet. This will prevent steam from escaping.

Preheat a buttered baking sheet in the oven for 5 minutes. Place the packets on the hot sheet. Bake for 10 minutes. It is impossible to visually gauge the doneness of food cooked *en papillote,* but the parchment paper will puff up high and become brown. Serve immediately. For a dramatic presentation, carefully cut the packages open with scissors or a sharp paring knife at the table.

A form of steaming, cooking *en papillote*—in a paper packet—is suited to naturally tender foods like fish. The food is wrapped in a packet of parchment paper (or sometimes aluminum foil) and placed in the oven to steam. Finely cut vegetables are usually included to add moisture for steam, and they also add flavor, color, and texture to the finished dish.

cleaning mushrooms
p. 186

Pan-fried Trout with Bacon

Vegetable oil for deep-frying

8 sprigs fresh flat-leaf parsley

4 slices thick-sliced bacon, minced

4 brook trout (8–10 oz each), pan-dressed

Salt and freshly ground pepper

Cornmeal for dredging

2 lemons, cut into wedges

Makes 4 servings

Pour the oil into a small, heavy saucepan to a depth of ½ inch. Heat over medium heat until it registers 350°F on a deep-frying thermometer. Pat the parsley sprigs dry if needed and fry, stirring gently to submerge the sprigs, until crisp, about 1 minute. Drain on absorbent towels, then reserve, uncovered, at room temperature.

Heat a large sauté pan over medium heat. Add the bacon and cook, stirring, until crisp, 2–3 minutes. With a slotted spoon, scoop out the crisp bacon, reserving the fat in the pan, and set aside.

Season the trouts with salt and pepper. Dredge in the cornmeal. Return the sauté pan with the bacon fat to medium-high heat and add enough oil to come to a depth of ¼ inch. When the oil is shimmering, add the cornmeal-dredged trout. (If the pan is not large enough to hold all 4 trout at once, cook 2 at a time; very slightly undercook the first 2 trout and place them in a 200°F oven while cooking the remaining trout.) Pan-fry until golden brown on both sides, 3–4 minutes per side. Adjust the heat as needed to prevent scorching.

Serve the trout at once, garnished with the reserved bacon pieces, deep-fried parsley, and lemon wedges.

The deep-fried parsley garnish adds a professional-looking touch to this hearty dish. Make sure you dry the sprigs well to prevent splattering while frying. Once fried, the parsley will be brilliant, almost translucent, green with a brittle crunch.

pan-frying p. 34

deep-frying p. 35

Sautéed Sole Meunière

4 sole fillets (about 6 oz each)

Salt and freshly ground pepper

All-purpose flour for dredging

2 Tbsp vegetable oil

4 Tbsp unsalted butter

1 Tbsp fresh lemon juice

2 Tbsp chopped fresh flat-leaf parsley

Makes 4 servings

Season the fish with salt and pepper and dredge in the flour. Heat a sauté pan over high heat, add the oil, and sauté the sole, turning once, until the flesh is opaque and firm, 2–3 minutes per side. Transfer the sole to warmed plates and cover to keep warm while completing the sauce.

Pour off the excess fat from the pan and add the butter. Cook over medium heat until the butter begins to brown and has a nutty aroma, 1 minute.

Add the lemon juice and swirl the pan until the lemon is blended into the butter and the sauce thickens. Add the parsley and immediately pour or spoon the pan sauce over the sole. Serve at once.

Meunière means in the style of a miller's wife—that is, dredged in flour, sautéed in butter, and served with brown butter sauce and parsley. Browning the butter gives it a rich, nutty flavor and aroma that pair well with mild sole. Serve with small boiled potatoes and lightly steamed green beans.

sautéing and stir-frying p. 32

dredging and breading p. 68

Hot and Sour Fish

deep-frying p. 35

Batter

2 cups all-purpose flour

2 Tbsp dark sesame oil

1½ Tbsp baking powder

Hot and Sour Sauce

1 Tbsp peanut oil

1 red bell pepper, diced

1 green bell pepper, diced

1 cup sliced white mushrooms

8 green onions, white and light green parts, sliced on the bias

2 cloves garlic, minced

2 Tbsp tomato paste

2 Tbsp Thai fish sauce (nam pla)

1 Tbsp sugar

2 Tbsp minced fresh cilantro

1 Tbsp Worcestershire sauce

1 Tbsp red wine vinegar

1 Tbsp soy sauce

½ tsp red pepper flakes

Salt and freshly ground pepper

Vegetable oil for deep-frying

4 grouper fillets (5–6 oz each)

Makes 4 servings

For the batter, combine the flour, 1½ cups cold water, sesame oil, and baking powder in a shallow pan and mix until smooth. Set aside.

For the hot and sour sauce, heat the oil in a large sauté pan over medium heat. Add the red and green bell peppers, mushrooms, green onions, and garlic and sauté until the garlic is aromatic and the vegetables softened, about 5 minutes. Add ¾ cup water, the tomato paste, fish sauce, and sugar and mix together. Add the cilantro, Worcestershire sauce, vinegar, soy sauce, and red pepper flakes and simmer until flavorful with a saucelike consistency, 15–20 minutes. If needed, adjust the consistency with water, then taste and adjust the seasoning with salt and pepper. Cover to keep warm.

Pour the vegetable oil into a tall pot to a depth of 2 inches and heat over medium heat until it registers 350°F on a deep-frying thermometer. Season the fish with salt and pepper, dip in the reserved batter, then deep-fry in batches without crowding until golden brown, 4–5 minutes. Drain on absorbent towels, then serve with the hot and sour sauce.

Use a wide, flat slotted spoon or spatula to let excess batter drip off the fillets before transferring them into the hot oil for frying. Thai fish sauce, or *nam pla,* is a thin, clear, brown sauce with a pungent, savory flavor. It is very common in Southeast Asian cooking, used as both an ingredient and a condiment. Look for it in Asian grocery stores.

Flounder à l'Orly

Beer Batter

1¼ cups all-purpose flour

1½ tsp baking powder

1 cup lager beer

1 large egg

Salt and freshly ground pepper

Vegetable oil for deep-frying

4 flounder fillets (about 6 oz each)

½ tsp fresh lemon juice

All-purpose flour for dredging

Fresh parsley sprigs for garnish

Lemon wedges for serving

1½ cups tomato sauce (p. 160), warmed

Makes 4 servings

For the beer batter, whisk together the flour and baking powder. Add the beer and egg all at once and whisk until combined, about the thickness of pancake batter, and very smooth. Pour into a wide, shallow dish or pan. Stir in ¼ tsp salt and ¼ tsp pepper.

Pour oil into a tall pot to a depth of 3 inches. Heat over medium-high heat until it registers 350°F on a deep-frying thermometer. Blot the fish dry and season with the lemon juice, salt, and pepper. Dredge in the flour, then dip in the beer batter. Deep-fry each fillet until golden brown and cooked through, 3–4 minutes. Drain very briefly on absorbent towels.

Garnish with the parsley sprigs and lemon wedges and serve immediately with the tomato sauce.

Fish cooked *à l'Orly* means that it is breaded, fried, and served with a tomato sauce. A white flaky fish such as sole would work well here in place of the flounder.

deep-frying p. 35

dredging and breading p. 68

Deep-fried Breaded Calamari

2 tsp fresh lemon juice

½ tsp Worcestershire sauce

Salt and freshly ground pepper

2½ lb squid tentacles and rings

All-purpose flour for dredging

Egg wash: 1 large egg whisked with 2 Tbsp cold milk or water

1 cup fresh white bread crumbs

Vegetable oil for deep-frying

2 cups tomato sauce (p. 160), warmed

Makes 4–6 appetizer servings

Combine the lemon juice, Worcestershire sauce, and salt and pepper to taste. Add the squid and toss to coat.

To bread the squid, put the flour, egg wash, and bread crumbs in 3 separate large bowls. Dredge the squid pieces in the flour, dip in the egg wash, and roll in the bread crumbs.

Pour the oil into a tall pot to a depth of 5 inches. Heat the oil over medium-high heat until it registers 375°F on a deep-frying thermometer. Deep-fry the squid in batches without crowding until they are evenly browned and cooked through, 3–4 minutes. Drain very briefly on absorbent towels, and season to taste with salt.

Serve the squid with the warm tomato sauce for dipping.

The secret to tender calamari is to cook it quickly at a high temperature—or else to braise it slowly for a long time. Overfrying calamari will result in a tough, rubbery texture. To save time, make sure you ask your fishmonger for cleaned and ready-to-cook calamari, as removing the heads and viscera from whole calamari is a messy and time-consuming job.

deep-frying p. 35

dredging and breading p. 68

Shrimp in Chili Sauce

Chili Sauce

4 green onions, white and green parts, minced

¾ cup ketchup

¼ cup chicken broth

2 Tbsp minced gingerroot

2 Tbsp rice vinegar

2 Tbsp soy sauce

2 Tbsp Chinese rice wine or dry sherry wine

1 Tbsp cornstarch

4 cloves garlic, minced

2 tsp sugar

1 tsp chili paste

Batter

1 large egg white

2 Tbsp peanut oil or vegetable oil

1 Tbsp cornstarch

3 cups peanut oil or vegetable oil

2 lb medium shrimp, peeled and deveined

One 15-oz can baby corn, drained

One 15-oz can straw mushrooms, drained

1 lb snow peas

Dark sesame oil for drizzling

4 cups steamed white rice

Makes 4 servings

For the chili sauce, combine the green onions, ketchup, chicken broth, ginger, vinegar, soy sauce, wine, cornstarch, garlic, sugar, and hot chili paste in a bowl. Set aside.

For the batter, whisk together the egg white, 2 Tbsp peanut oil, and cornstarch in a bowl. Set aside; whisk to recombine just before coating the shrimp, if necessary.

Heat the 3 cups peanut oil in a wok over high heat until it registers 375°F on a deep-frying thermometer. Toss the shrimp in the batter to coat. With a skimmer or slotted spoon, lower the shrimp into the hot oil and deep-fry until pink, with a crispy and translucent coating, about 3 minutes. Remove the shrimp from the wok with the slotted spoon and drain on absorbent towels.

Pour off all but 2 Tbsp of the oil from the wok. Add the corn, straw mushrooms, and snow peas and stir-fry until the peas are bright green and hot, 2–3 minutes.

Return the shrimp to the pan, add the reserved chili sauce, and continue to stir-fry until the sauce thickens and the shrimp is evenly coated, about 2 minutes. Drizzle with sesame oil. Serve over a bed of hot white rice.

Hot chili paste can be found in the Asian foods section of most supermarkets or in Asian specialty markets. Bright red-orange in color, this fiery sauce is made of puréed red bell peppers, vinegar, garlic, and salt, and is often used in dipping sauces.

deep-frying p. 35

sautéing and stir-frying p. 32

preparing shrimp p. 129

Steamed Cod with Gingered Hoisin Sauce

4 cod steaks or fillets
(about 6 oz each)

Salt and freshly ground pepper

½ cup hoisin sauce

3 Tbsp honey

2 Tbsp minced gingerroot

3 cloves garlic, minced

1 tsp fermented black beans

8 large outer leaves savoy
cabbage

4 green onions

4 tsp toasted sesame seeds

Makes 4 servings

Place the cod in a shallow dish and season with salt and pepper.

Combine the hoisin sauce, honey, ginger, garlic, and fermented black beans in a small bowl. Pour half of the sauce over the fish and turn to coat. Cover and refrigerate for 2–8 hours. Reserve the remaining sauce.

Bring a large pot of salted water to a boil. Cook the cabbage leaves until they are limp, 2–3 minutes. Drain leaves and rinse under cold water. Blot dry on absorbent towels.

Trim the root ends of the green onions and split each in half lengthwise. Cut each piece into 3-inch lengths.

Remove the cod from the marinade and blot dry. Overlap 2 cabbage leaves and place 1 piece of cod in the center. Top with one-fourth of the green onions and 1 teaspoon of the hoisin mixture. Fold the leaves up and around the fish so that it is completely enclosed and secure with toothpicks or skewers. Repeat with the remaining fish pieces.

Place the packets, seam side up, in a bamboo or metal steamer over a pot containing 1 inch of boiling water. Make sure the water does not touch the steamer. Cover, reduce the heat to low, and steam until the fish is opaque throughout, about 15 minutes.

Place each packet on a plate, still seam side up. Remove the toothpicks and open the leaves. Drizzle the remaining hoisin mixture over the fish and cabbage or serve it on the side. Sprinkle each serving with 1 teaspoon sesame seeds. Serve at once.

Fermented black beans add a distinctive salty pungency to this Chinese dish. You can find them in jars or plastic bags in Asian markets; they keep well and make a savory addition to stir-frys of vegetables, seafood, or chicken.

steaming p. 36

marinating p. 68

VARIATION

Whole Steamed Bass

Use a whole bass, about 3 lb, with a large steamer: Rinse and season the fish inside and out with salt and pepper. Make a bed of the green onions on a round or oblong heatproof plate that fits inside your steamer. Set the fish on the green onions. Pour half of the hoisin mixture over the fish, cover, and steam until the fish is cooked through, 25–30 minutes. Scatter with the sesame seeds and serve with the green onions and the remaining hoisin mixture.

Moules Marinière

¾ cup dry white wine

2 Tbsp minced shallot

3 cloves garlic, minced

1 bay leaf

¼ tsp cracked peppercorns

1 sprig fresh thyme

5 doz mussels, scrubbed and debearded

4 Tbsp unsalted butter, softened

3 Tbsp chopped fresh flat-leaf parsley

1 Tbsp chopped fresh chives

Salt and freshly ground pepper

Makes 4 servings

Combine the wine, shallot, garlic, bay leaf, peppercorns, and thyme in a soup pot over high heat. Bring to a simmer. Add the mussels, discarding any that remain open when touched. Cover and steam until the shells open, 5–6 minutes. Using a slotted spoon, transfer the mussels to a heated serving bowl and cover to keep warm while completing the sauce. Discard any that did not open.

Strain the steaming liquid through a double thickness of moistened cheesecloth or a coffee filter into a sauté pan. Bring to a simmer over high heat, then whisk in the butter over low heat. Add the parsley and chives, taste, and season with salt and pepper.

Serve the sauce ladled over the mussels.

Marinière, or "sailor style," is a typical French way of preparing mussels. As the mussels cook, they release their own aromatic juices into the simmering white wine, creating a flavorful broth. Finished with a quick swirl of butter and a sprinkle of parsley and chives, it's perfect for sopping up with crusty French bread.

steaming p. 36

cleaning mussels p. 129

Poached Turbot with Lemon Beurre Blanc

4 sprigs fresh tarragon

4 turbot fillets (about 6 oz each)

Salt and freshly ground pepper

12 Tbsp unsalted butter, softened (divided use)

1 Tbsp minced shallot

¼ cup bottled clam juice

¼ cup chicken broth

¼ cup dry white wine

1 Tbsp fresh lemon juice

½ cup heavy cream

Zest of 1 lemon

Makes 4 servings

Pull the tarragon leaves from the stems and reserve the leaves and stems.

Preheat the oven to 300°F. Season the turbot with salt and pepper. Coat an ovenproof sauté pan with 4 Tbsp of the butter and sprinkle with the shallot. Cut a round of parchment paper the same diameter as the sauté pan.

Place the turbot in the pan and add the clam juice, chicken broth, white wine, and lemon juice. Bring to a simmer over medium heat and cover with the parchment round. Poach in the oven until the fish is firm and opaque throughout, about 8 minutes.

Transfer the turbot from the pan to warmed plates, reserve the poaching liquid, and cover to keep warm while completing the sauce.

To make a beurre blanc sauce, add the tarragon stems to the poaching liquid. Bring to a boil and reduce by half, about 3 minutes. Stir in the cream and continue to reduce to a saucelike consistency, 2 minutes more. Whisk in the remaining 8 Tbsp butter, a little at a time, until melted. Taste and season with salt and pepper.

Pour the sauce over the fish and garnish with zest and tarragon leaves.

Adding an acidic ingredient to a fish-poaching liquid helps firm the fish's texture as well as contributing flavor. Experiment with different citrus juices (try blood orange, Meyer lemon, or pink grapefruit) and white wines for variety. Beurre blanc, or "white butter" sauce, is a classic accompaniment for poached fish. Since it is thickened only with butter, it is more fragile than a flour-based white sauce. Carefully whisk in the butter, a little at a time, over low heat; serve at once to prevent the sauce from breaking down.

poaching p. 39

zesting and juicing citrus p. 182

Sole Vin Blanc

9 Tbsp unsalted butter, softened (divided use)

1 Tbsp minced shallot

4 sole fillets (about 6 oz each)

Salt and freshly ground pepper

½ cup dry white wine

¼ cup fish or chicken broth

1 Tbsp fresh lemon juice

½ cup heavy cream

Fresh tarragon sprigs for garnish (optional)

Makes 4 servings

Preheat the oven to 300°F. Grease an ovenproof sauté pan with 1 Tbsp of the butter and sprinkle with the shallot. Cut a round of parchment paper with the same diameter as the sauté pan.

Season the sole with salt and pepper. Roll the sole into a corkscrew shape (known as a *paupiette*). Place the sole in the prepared pan, seam side down, and pour the wine, broth, and lemon juice over it. Bring to a simmer over medium heat and cover with the parchment paper round. Transfer to the oven and poach until the fish is firm and opaque, 15–16 minutes.

Transfer the sole from the pan to warmed plates and cover to keep warm while completing the sauce.

To prepare the vin blanc sauce, bring the poaching liquid to a boil over high heat and reduce by half, 3 minutes. Add the cream and continue to reduce to a saucelike consistency. Whisk in the remaining 8 Tbsp butter until melted. Season to taste with salt and pepper.

Serve the sauce over the sole. If desired, garnish with tarragon sprigs.

Look for a good-quality, crisp, dry white wine such as Chablis, Pinot Gris, or Sancerre to use in this dish, since the better the *vin blanc* (white wine), the better the final result.

poaching p. 39

VARIATIONS

Poached Sea Bass with Clams, Bacon, and Peppers

Substitute sea bass for the sole. Add 2 doz littleneck clams, scrubbed, to the pan along with the fish before covering and placing in the oven. Cook just until the clams open, 10–12 minutes. Discard any that do not open. Meanwhile, sauté 5 strips bacon, minced, over medium heat until crisp, 3–4 minutes. Add 1 bell pepper, cut into julienne, and sauté until tender, 2–3 minutes more. Omit the heavy cream from the sauce. Scatter the bacon and bell pepper over the sea bass and clams just before serving. Scatter with minced fresh chives.

julienne p. 17

Tilapia with Capers and Tomatoes

Substitute tilapia for the sole. Add 1 cup peeled, seeded, and diced tomato (or drained canned diced tomatoes) and 1–2 Tbsp capers to the fish as it cooks. Omit the heavy cream from the sauce. Garnish with minced fresh chives.

peeling and seeding tomatoes p. 184

Prawn Curry

1 coconut

¼ cup clarified butter or vegetable oil

1 yellow onion, chopped

3 Tbsp grated gingerroot

2 small jalapeños, seeded and minced

1 tsp ground turmeric

½ tsp ground cardamom

½ tsp ground cumin

½ tsp ground cayenne pepper

¼ tsp ground cloves

3 bay leaves

2 lb large shrimp, peeled and deveined

1 cup chicken broth

1 cup plain whole-milk yogurt

3 cloves garlic

2 Tbsp fresh lemon juice

2 tsp sugar

1 tsp salt

Cornstarch slurry: 2 tsp cornstarch blended with 2 tsp cold water or chicken broth (optional)

4 cups steamed white rice

Makes 4 servings

Place the coconut on a flat, level surface. Using a hammer and nail, pierce the "eyes" and pour the coconut "water" into a bowl through a sieve lined with a coffee filter. Wrap the coconut in a towel and a plastic bag, then pound with the hammer until the coconut splits in several pieces. Unwrap, insert a sturdy knife between the hairy brown shell and coconut meat, and carefully twist to release the meat from the shell. Peel off the thin brown skin with a vegetable peeler. Chop or grate ½ cup of the snowy white nut meat. Reserve the remaining coconut meat and the coconut "water" for another use.

Heat the clarified butter in a sauté pan over medium heat. Add the onion and sauté until golden brown, 6–8 minutes. Remove with a slotted spoon and set aside.

Add the coconut, ginger, jalapeños, turmeric, cardamom, cumin, cayenne, cloves, and bay leaves to the pan and sauté until very hot, about 3 minutes. Add the shrimp, broth, yogurt, garlic, lemon juice, sugar, and salt and simmer until the shrimp turn pink and are opaque throughout and the dish is very aromatic, about 5 minutes.

If needed, add just enough of the cornstarch slurry while stirring to thicken the sauce slightly. Remove and discard the bay leaves.

Serve the curry with steamed rice.

Grated fresh coconut keeps almost indefinitely in the freezer. To make your own coconut milk, heat ½ cup coconut water and pour it over 1 cup grated fresh or thawed frozen coconut. Let rest for 30 minutes, then pour through a doubled cheesecloth into a second bowl. Gather the cloth and twist firmly to extract the liquid.

braising and stewing
p. 40

making clarified butter
p. 26

preparing shrimp p. 129

Cioppino

Garlic Crostini

2 Tbsp olive oil

1 clove garlic, minced

Salt and freshly ground pepper

Ten ½-inch-thick slices crusty French or Italian bread

2 Tbsp olive oil

1 yellow onion, diced

10 green onions, white and green parts, diced

1 green bell pepper, diced

1 bulb fennel, sliced

8 cloves garlic, minced

1 cup dry white wine

One 32-oz can diced tomatoes

2 cups bottled clam juice

2 cups chicken broth

½ cup tomato purée

3 bay leaves

12 littleneck clams, scrubbed

3 blue crabs, disjointed

1½ lb swordfish fillet, coarsely diced

1 lb large shrimp, peeled and deveined

½ lb scallops

¼ cup fresh basil, chopped

Makes 10 servings

Preheat the broiler.

For the crostini, whisk together the olive oil, garlic, ¼ tsp salt, and a grinding of pepper in a small bowl and brush evenly over the bread slices. Place on a baking sheet and broil on both sides until browned, about 2 minutes per side. (Watch carefully to prevent the garlic from burning.) Set aside.

Heat the oil in a soup pot over medium-high heat. Add the yellow onion, green onions, bell pepper, fennel, and garlic. Sauté until the onions are translucent, 6–8 minutes. Add the white wine and reduce by half, about 5 minutes.

Add the tomatoes, clam juice, broth, tomato purée, and bay leaves. Cover the pot, adjust the heat to a slow simmer, and cook until very flavorful but still brothy, about 45 minutes. Add a small amount of water if necessary to adjust the consistency. (Cioppino should be more of a broth than a stew.)

Remove and discard the bay leaves. Add the clams and crabs. Simmer until the crab shells are bright red and the clams have just started to open, about 10 minutes. Add the swordfish, shrimp, and scallops and simmer just until the fish is cooked through, 8–10 minutes more. The clams should be completely open. Discard any that are not.

Add the basil and taste and season with salt and pepper. Ladle the cioppino into bowls and garnish with the garlic crostini.

Cioppino is a fish stew whose origin is attributed to Italian immigrants—mostly fishermen from Genoa—who settled in San Francisco and brought their taste for boldly flavored, easily made fish stews with them. In San Francisco, you'll find cioppino made from large, sweet-fleshed Dungeness crabs and a mixture of local Pacific rockfish, but the more readily available blue crabs and swordfish are suggested here.

braising and stewing p. 40

preparing shrimp p. 129

5 Pasta

When Italians visit the United States, they are sometimes amazed at the size of the pasta portions they find here. In Italy, pasta is typically served in small amounts as a first course before a meat or fish dish; it is seldom offered as the main course itself. But we Americans welcomed this versatile food to our tables with typical national gusto. Rather than restricting pasta to the first course or a side dish, we often serve up steaming bowls of spaghetti and meatballs, platters of fettuccine alfredo or penne puttanesca, or ravioli stuffed with cheeses or meat as a main dish. We like it hot or cold, unadorned or gilded, plain or flavored, flat or filled. Inventive American cooks marry pasta with flavors and ingredients from around the globe to make it one of this country's most versatile and best-loved foods.

Types of pasta

Dried pasta is made from hard-wheat flours, such as semolina, which produces a stiff dough that is difficult to knead or roll by hand. Dried pastas of excellent quality and in a variety of shapes, sizes, colors, and flavors are widely available. Since they keep almost indefinitely in a cool, dry, dark cupboard, you can always have some on hand.

Look for prepared fresh pasta in the refrigerated cases stocked with prepared foods, cheeses, and olives in most supermarkets, or try the freezer case. You can keep purchased fresh pasta in the refrigerator for up to 5 days or the freezer for up to 2 months with virtually no loss of quality.

All-purpose or bread flour works well for making fresh pasta at home. Eggs provide moisture, flavor, and structure. (Dried pasta sometimes includes eggs, but water is typically the only liquid used.) Some fresh pasta recipes also call for a small amount of water or oil to make the dough tender and pliable. Salt develops flavor in the dough. You can substitute a quantity of whole-wheat, semolina, cornmeal, buckwheat, rye, or chickpea flour for all-purpose to give your pasta a unique flavor and texture. Ingredients such as spinach or saffron may be added for flavor and color.

Preparing and serving pasta

Sauces are customarily paired with pasta shapes that complement both their texture and flavor. Hearty sauces require sturdier shapes, such as bucatoni, to stand up to their weight, while smooth sauces, such as pesto, benefit from thinner strands that are easily coated. The delicate flavor of fresh pasta is best matched with a simple sauce based on oil, cream, or butter. Stuffed pastas also call for light sauces, as their fillings provide flavor and moisture of their own. See the chart below for guidancc in matching sauces to pasta shapes.

Pasta doesn't always demand a traditional simmered sauce. Keep a chunk of fresh Parmesan cheese, some olive oil, and garlic on hand and you can whip up dinner in less time than it takes to run out for a pizza. With some key pantry staples in your inventory—sun-dried tomatoes, canned tomatoes, olives, capers, dried mushrooms, anchovies, and artichoke hearts, to name a few—you can prepare or devise countless delicious pasta sauces. Stock your refrigerator and freezer with ingredients like eggs, prosciutto, pancetta, chorizo or other cured sausage, heavy cream, butter, pesto, and fresh herbs and vegetables for great impromptu pasta meals.

Pairing shapes and sauces

TYPE	EXAMPLES	BEST SAUCES
Long, thin strands	Capellini, spaghetti, linguine, vermicelli, bucatini bavette, macheroni alla chitarra	Olive oil or tomato sauces
Long, wide ribbons	Fettuccine, tagliatelle, pappardelle, trenette, lasagnette	Smooth, light butter- or cream-based sauces
Tubes	Penne, rigatoni, macaroni, bucatoni, mostaccioli, tortiglioni, ziti	Chunky sauces with meat and vegetables
Pockets	Shells, orecchiette	Chunky sauces with meat and vegetables
Twists	Fusilli, rotini, gemelli	Slightly chunky meat or vegetable sauces
Frilled	Radiatore, farfalle, farfallini, fusilli, gigli, campanelle, cresti di gallo	Smooth sauces with vegetables
Small	Orzo, ditali, ditalini, stelline	Soups, butter, herbs
Stuffed	Ravioli, tortellini, cappelletti, manicotti, agnolotti, rotolo, cannelloni	Butter, broth, pesto, grated cheese

Cooking pasta

Boiling pasta in a large amount of salted water ensures the best flavor and consistent texture.

Determining portions

Deciding on the amount of pasta to cook for each diner depends on how the dish will be served. A light first course in a meal with several courses, for example, will require less pasta than a hearty main-dish pasta served with only a salad. A general guideline for a main course calls for about 4 ounces of fresh pasta or 2 ounces dried pasta per person.

Choosing a pot

A large pot that is taller than it is wide is best for boiling most pastas. Stuffed pastas such as raviolis, however, are best cooked in wide, shallow pans that allow for easier removal. Fill the pot with plenty of water and bring the water to a rolling boil. For every pound of pasta, allow about 1 gallon of water. Add 2 tablespoons of salt per gallon of water for the best-tasting finished dish. The water should taste noticeably salty, like seawater.

Boiling pasta

Once the water comes to a full boil, add the pasta all at once. Long strands should be submerged gently as they soften. Stir the pasta a few times to separate the strands or shapes, then cook until al dente—that is, tender but still offering resistance to the bite. Fresh pasta cooks rapidly, often taking less than 1 minute. Dried pasta requires 5–12 minutes, or even longer, depending on the size and shape. When it is ready, pour the pasta into a colander and toss well to drain away as much water as possible.

Cooking stuffed pasta

Gently lower filled pastas into boiling water and reduce the heat to maintain a simmer, to prevent the stuffed shapes from breaking open. When done, stuffed pastas will rise to the surface. Be sure to allow time for thoroughly cooking the filling, but don't let the pasta overcook. Lift stuffed pastas from the cooking water with a slotted spoon to avoid breaking them. Transfer to a colander to drain, or blot the spoon gently with absorbent towels to remove excess water.

Holding and reheating pasta

Cooked pasta is best served immediately, but it can be held for a little while if needed. After draining, plunge the pasta into a bowl of cold water and stir gently until the pasta is cold. Drain a second time. Toss the cooled pasta with a small amount of oil to keep it from sticking and clumping together. To reheat pasta, lower it into simmering salted water for a few minutes, then drain and serve at once.

Saucing pasta

Combine pasta and sauce as close to serving time as possible.

There are 2 methods of saucing pasta. After draining the pasta, transfer it to a heated serving bowl. Pour or spoon the sauce over the pasta. With a large fork and spoon, gently but thoroughly toss the pasta until it is evenly coated with the sauce.

You can also add the pasta to the pan containing the simmering sauce, tossing the pasta and sauce together right in the pan. This method helps the hot pasta absorb the sauce and melds the flavors and textures of the dish. This method works best with slightly undercooked pasta, since the pasta continues to cook in the pan with the sauce.

Whichever saucing method you choose, be sure to distribute the sauce as evenly as possible over the pasta. Because pasta loses its heat rapidly, be sure to warm serving bowls or plates (see page 27) to help maintain the food's temperature as long as possible at the table. If you are serving the pasta in a buffet or passing it family-style at the table, use large bowls or deep serving platters so that the pasta can be mounded to conserve heat. For the best texture, especially with homemade noodles, serve the pasta at once.

Making fresh pasta

Egg pasta can be prepared quickly, whether you mix it traditionally by hand or conveniently by machine. The tender, silky dough is simple to knead and roll with the aid of a pasta machine.

1 Mixing ingredients by hand

For small batches, pasta dough can be efficiently mixed by hand. Combine the flour and salt in a bowl and make a well in the center. Place the eggs, flavoring ingredients, and oil in the well. Using a fork and working as rapidly as possible, incorporate the flour into the liquid ingredients little by little, until a shaggy mass forms. As the dough is mixed, adjust the consistency with additional flour or a few drops of water to compensate for the natural variations in ingredients, humidity, temperature, or the addition of either dry or moist flavoring ingredients.

2 Kneading the dough by hand

Once the dough is mixed, turn it out onto a floured surface and knead until its texture becomes smooth and elastic. Use the heels of your hands to push the dough away from you, then reverse the motion, folding the dough over on itself toward you. Give the dough a quarter turn periodically so that it is evenly kneaded. Kneading by hand generally takes 10–12 minutes. Do not rush the kneading process, or the texture of the finished pasta will suffer. Properly kneaded dough is uniform in texture and no longer tacky to the touch.

3 Mixing and kneading the dough by machine

Large batches of pasta dough are easier to make with a food processor or stand mixer. To mix in a food processor, fit the machine with the metal blade and combine all the ingredients in its work bowl. Process just until the dough is blended into a coarse meal that forms a ball when gathered. Do not overprocess. Remove the dough, transfer to a lightly floured work surface, and knead by hand as described above. To use a stand mixer, fit it with the dough hook attachment to combine all the ingredients, then mix at low speed for 3–4 minutes, until the dough is just moistened. Increase the speed to medium and knead the dough another 3 minutes, until the dough forms a smooth ball that pulls cleanly away from the sides of the bowl.

4 Rolling the dough in a pasta machine

Gather the dough into a ball, cover, and let relax at room temperature for at least 1 hour. Letting the dough relax allows it to be rolled into thin sheets more easily. Cut off a piece of dough and flatten it. The amount will vary according to the width of your pasta machine. Cover the remaining dough to keep it from drying. Set the rollers to the widest opening, fold the dough in thirds, and guide the flattened dough through the machine as you turn the handle. Roll the dough to form a long, wide strip. Pass the dough through the widest setting 2 or 3 times, folding the dough in thirds each time.

5 Rerolling the dough

Lightly flour the dough strip to prevent sticking. Set the rollers to the next thinnest opening and run the dough through the rollers again, without folding. Repeat, narrowing the setting, dusting the dough each time, and passing the dough through the rollers twice on each setting, until it reaches the desired thinness—the second-to-last setting for most pastas, or the thinnest setting for lasagna.

6 Cutting and drying the dough

Cut each rolled sheet of dough into shorter lengths, about 1 foot long, for easier handling. For best results—cleaner cuts and no sticking—let the pasta sheets dry slightly, until the surface is leathery to the touch. This is especially important for cutting shapes by hand, but machine cutting is also easier with slightly dried pasta. Feed the dough through the desired cutting attachment. If you are not cooking the pasta immediately, you can dry it for storage. Spread small shapes in a single layer on a clean, dry towel or baking sheet. Gather long pasta into loose nests, arrange them on a clean baking sheet with plenty of space between each one, and let the pasta dry completely in a cool, dry place before placing in an airtight container. Store in the refrigerator for up to 2 days.

Making stuffed pasta

Fill fresh pasta sheets with a succulent mixture of seafood, vegetables, meat, or cheese for tempting dishes such as ravioli and tortellini.

1 Preparing the pasta

When making stuffed pastas, you can add a small amount of vegetable oil to the dough to help it stick together better when sealed around a filling. Roll the pasta out to the thinnest setting on a pasta machine (see page 157). While rolling and filling one portion of the dough, keep the rest tightly wrapped in plastic wrap to make sure it stays moist and pliable. Cut and fill the sheets as soon as possible after they are rolled. As they dry, they become more difficult to seal properly.

2 Forming ravioli

Lightly flour a clean, dry work surface and lay down a thinly rolled pasta sheet. Use a round cookie cutter to cut out as many rounds as possible, or use a sharp knife to cut squares. Using a teaspoon or a pastry bag (see page 271), place or pipe a small amount of the filling in the center of each circle or square. The amount of filling will vary depending on the size of the pasta round or square. Lightly moisten the edges of the pasta round or square with a pastry brush dipped in cool water. Top each with another pasta round or square and press firmly with your fingertips to seal. Use the tines of a fork to crimp the edges together. Refrigerate the finished ravioli while you roll out, cut, and fill the remaining pasta dough.

3 Forming tortellini

Lightly flour a clean, dry work surface and lay down a thinly rolled pasta sheet. Use a round cookie cutter to cut out as many rounds as possible, or use a sharp knife to cut squares. Using a teaspoon or a pastry bag (see page 271), place or pipe a small amount of the filling in the center of each circle or square. The amount of filling will vary depending on the size of the pasta round or square. Lightly moisten the edges of the pasta round or square with a pastry brush dipped in cool water, fold in half to make a half-moon or triangle, and press firmly to seal with your fingertips. To shape the tortellini, wrap the half circle or triangle around the tip of your forefinger, pulling the 2 corners together to overlap and pinching them firmly to seal.

Fresh Pasta Dough

2 cups all-purpose flour, plus
more as needed

½ tsp salt

3 large eggs

1 tsp olive oil

Makes 1 lb; 4–6 servings

Combine the flour and salt in a large bowl and whisk to blend. Make a well in the center. Place the eggs, olive oil, and 1 Tbsp water in the well. Working as rapidly as possible, gradually pull the flour from the edges of the well into the liquid ingredients with a fork and stir until a shaggy mass forms. As the dough is mixed, adjust the consistency with additional flour or water so that it is pliable but not sticky. (The dough can also be mixed in a food processor. Add liquid until the dough just holds together when pressed; it should not form a ball on the blade.)

Turn the dough out onto a floured work surface and knead until the texture becomes smooth and elastic, about 10–12 minutes. Gather and smooth the kneaded dough into a ball, cover, and let the dough relax at room temperature for at least 1 hour.

In batches, roll the pasta dough into thin sheets, let dry for 15–20 minutes, and cut into the desired shapes by hand or machine. The pasta is ready to cook now, or it can be refrigerated, covered, for up to 2 days.

Letting the dough rest for at least 1 hour after kneading before rolling allows the elastic strands of gluten present in the dough to relax. This makes for a more pliable dough that can be rolled into thin sheets more easily.

making fresh pasta
p. 156

VARIATIONS

Black Pepper Pasta Dough

Add 2 tsp cracked peppercorns to the flour with the salt. Proceed as directed.

Herbed Pasta Dough

Add ½ cup chopped fresh herbs such as thyme, basil, or oregano along with the eggs. Proceed as directed.

Curried Pasta Dough

Add 2–4 tsp curry powder to the flour with the salt. Proceed as directed.

Tomato Sauce

3 Tbsp olive oil

2 yellow onions, finely diced

8 cloves garlic, minced

2½ lb plum (Roma) tomatoes, peeled, seeded, and chopped

1 Tbsp chopped fresh basil

Salt and freshly ground pepper

Makes 6 servings

Heat the olive oil in a large saucepan over medium-high heat. Add the onions and sauté until translucent, about 6 minutes. Add the garlic and sauté until fragrant, about 1 minute. Add the tomatoes, bring the sauce to a boil, reduce the heat, and simmer for 20–25 minutes. Add the basil and simmer for 5 minutes more. Taste and season with salt and pepper.

Tomatoes, originally native to South America, were not introduced to Italy until the sixteenth century. Now, of course, it's almost impossible to think of Italian cuisine without dozens of delicious tomato-based dishes coming to mind.

sautéing and stir-frying p. 32

peeling and seeding tomatoes p. 184

VARIATIONS

Canned Tomato Sauce

Replace the fresh tomatoes with whole canned tomatoes that have been seeded and coarsely chopped. (Reserve the juices to add to the pot as well.) Be sure to taste the tomatoes before starting the sauce. If the tomatoes need extra body or flavor, sauté ¼–⅓ cup tomato paste with the onions after the onions are translucent. Or replace half of the whole tomatoes with tomato purée.

Meat Sauce

After sautéing the onions, add up to 2 lb ground or finely diced beef (or a combination of beef and veal; or replace half the ground meat with an Italian-style sausage, removed from its casings). Season the meat with herbs, including 2 tsp *each* dried oregano and basil. Sauté until browned before adding the tomatoes, then proceed as directed. Add 3 Tbsp minced fresh oregano, parsley, and/or basil just before removing from the heat.

Fettuccine with Puttanesca Sauce

¾ lb dried fettuccine or 1 lb fresh (p. 159)

¼ cup olive oil

2 anchovy fillets, finely chopped

4 cloves garlic, finely minced

¼ tsp red pepper flakes, or to taste

5 plum (Roma) tomatoes, peeled, seeded, and chopped

¼ cup chopped fresh flat-leaf parsley

¼ cup pitted, chopped kalamata olives

2 Tbsp capers, rinsed and chopped

Salt and freshly ground black pepper

Makes 4 servings

Bring a large pot of salted water to a boil. Add the pasta and boil until al dente. Cooking time may vary by brand; follow package directions. If using fresh pasta, boil until tender, 1–2 minutes. Drain immediately.

Meanwhile, heat the olive oil in a sauté pan over medium heat. Add the anchovies, garlic, and red pepper flakes. Sauté, stirring frequently, until the anchovies are is lightly browned, 1–2 minutes.

Add the tomatoes, parsley, olives, and capers and simmer until thoroughly heated, 1–2 minutes. Taste and season with salt and black pepper.

Pour the sauce over the drained pasta and toss to coat evenly. Serve at once.

There is nothing demure about this robust pasta dish. In fact, its name (which translates as "in the style of a prostitute") borders on the ribald. It is based on a recipe that hails from the slums of Naples. The quickly prepared combination of olives, capers, and anchovies can be quite salty, so be sure to taste the sauce before adding additional salt.

cooking pasta p. 155

saucing pasta p. 155

Pasta Primavera with Basil Cream Sauce

¾ lb dried whole-wheat linguine or fettuccine

2 Tbsp olive oil

1 leek, white and light green parts, diced

½ lb asparagus, trimmed and cut into ½-inch pieces, including tips

1 cup fresh or thawed frozen peas

1 cup white mushrooms, sliced

1 cup heavy cream

⅓ cup grated Parmesan

Salt and freshly ground pepper

2 Tbsp basil chiffonade

Makes 4 servings

Bring a large pot of salted water to a boil. Add the pasta and boil until al dente. Cooking time may vary by brand; follow package directions. Drain immediately.

Meanwhile, heat the olive oil in a large sauté pan over medium-high heat. Add the leek and sauté until bright green and tender, 7–10 minutes. Add the asparagus, peas, and mushrooms and sauté until the vegetables are tender and the moisture has cooked away, 5–10 minutes.

Add the cream, Parmesan, and salt and pepper to taste. Gently bring to a simmer, cooking just until the sauce begins to thicken.

Add the pasta to the sauté pan with the vegetables and cream sauce and toss together. Finish by adding the basil chiffonade. Taste and season with salt and pepper. Serve at once.

Pasta primavera, whose name invokes the Italian for "springtime," was invented in the 1970s by Sirio Maccioni, the owner of New York's celebrated Le Cirque restaurant. Feel free to vary the vegetables at will, adding sugar snap peas, tender young green beans, sliced zucchini, or pinky-sized baby carrots.

trimming asparagus p. 185

shredding and chiffonade p. 17

Pasta alla Carbonara

¾ lb dried spaghetti or bucatoni

¼ lb pancetta, minced

2 Tbsp olive oil

1½ cups heavy cream

1 large egg

Salt and freshly ground pepper

Chopped fresh flat-leaf parsley
for garnish

Makes 4 servings

Bring a large pot of salted water to a boil. Add the pasta and boil until al dente. Cooking time may vary by brand; follow package directions.

Meanwhile, sauté the pancetta in the olive oil in a large skillet over medium heat until crisp, 2–3 minutes. Remove about half of the pancetta with a slotted spoon and set aside.

Drain the pasta and add to the pan. Toss to coat evenly with the oil.

Whisk the cream with the egg. Reduce the heat to low, add the egg mixture to the pan, and cook gently while stirring constantly just until heated through, about 1 minute. Taste and season with salt and pepper. Top with the reserved pancetta and the parsley, then serve.

This Roman specialty makes a great quick meal. Traditionally, the beaten eggs are added to the pasta off the heat; however, in light of current concerns about raw eggs, this recipe calls for briefly cooking the egg sauce before serving.

cooking pasta p. 155

Mushrooms and Artichokes over Black Pepper Pasta

6 fresh or thawed frozen
artichoke hearts

1 Tbsp fresh lemon juice
(optional)

Salt

1 Tbsp unsalted butter

1 shallot, minced

6 cups sliced mixed mushrooms
such as white, cremini, trumpet,
oak, and portobello

1 cup dry white wine

1 cup heavy cream

1 lb fresh black pepper pasta
(p. 159) cut into fettuccine,
linguine, or other long ribbon
shape

2 plum (Roma) tomatoes,
peeled, seeded, and chopped

¼ cup chopped fresh sage

Chopped fresh flat-leaf parsley
for garnish

Makes 4 servings

If using fresh artichoke hearts, bring a large pot of water seasoned with the lemon juice to a simmer. Add the artichoke hearts to the simmering water and cook until stems are tender enough to pierce easily with the tip of a knife, 12–15 minutes. Scoop out the artichoke hearts with a slotted spoon, reserving the water. When cool enough to handle, cut the artichokes into halves or quarters, depending on size. Add more water to the pot as needed to cook the pasta, salt the water, and bring to a boil.

Meanwhile, melt the butter in a large skillet over medium heat. Add the shallot and sauté until translucent, about 2 minutes. Add the mushrooms, raise the heat to high, and sauté until tender and very hot, about 4 minutes. Add the wine and cook until almost all the liquid is absorbed. Add the cream and reduce until slightly thickened. Remove the pan from the heat and cover to keep warm.

Add the pasta to the boiling water and boil until tender, 1–2 minutes. Drain immediately.

Add the cooked or thawed frozen artichoke hearts and the tomatoes to the cream mixture and heat over low heat until warmed through. Stir in the fresh sage. Add the pasta and toss until evenly coated and very hot. Taste and season with salt. Sprinkle with parsley and serve.

Adding black pepper to the pasta dough offers a pleasant hint of spice to this autumnal dish. If you don't have time to make your own pasta, you can often find flavored fresh pastas in gourmet supermarkets or Italian specialty shops.

trimming artichokes
p. 185

cleaning mushrooms
p. 186

Shrimp with Curried Pasta

Curry-Lime Butter

4 Tbsp unsalted butter, softened

Zest and juice of ½ lime

2 tsp curry powder

½ tsp ground ginger

Salt and freshly ground pepper

1 lb large shrimp, peeled and deveined

2 Tbsp vegetable oil

2 Tbsp unsalted butter

1 small shallot, minced

1 cup chicken or fish broth

1 cup dry white wine

1 lb fresh fettucine (p. 159)

⅔ cup plain whole-milk yogurt

Green onions, white and green parts, sliced on the bias, for garnish

Toasted cashew halves for garnish

Makes 4 servings

For the curry-lime butter, blend the 4 Tbsp butter with the lime juice and zest, curry powder, and ginger. Season with salt and pepper. Set aside.

Season the shrimp with salt and pepper. Heat the oil in a sauté pan over high heat. Add the shrimp and sauté until the shrimp are just cooked through, 4–5 minutes. Remove from the pan with a slotted spoon and set aside.

Add the 2 Tbsp unsalted butter to the pan and heat until the foaming subsides. Add the shallot and sauté, stirring frequently, until translucent, 2–3 minutes. Add the broth and wine and stir to deglaze the pan, scraping up any browned bits from the pan bottom. Let simmer until reduced by one-fourth, 4–5 minutes. Whisk in the curry-lime butter gradually until smooth (the mixture may appear broken at first but will come together as it cooks). Cover to keep warm while preparing the pasta.

Bring a large pot of salted water to a boil. Add the pasta and boil until tender, 1–2 minutes. Drain immediately.

While the pasta drains, bring the sauce back to a simmer and whisk in the yogurt. Add the hot pasta to the sauce and lift and toss to coat evenly and heat through. Taste and season with salt and pepper.

Transfer the pasta to a warmed bowl or plates. Top with the shrimp. Spoon the sauce remaining in the pan over the shrimp and garnish with the green onions and cashews. Serve at once.

Curry powders vary in flavor, heat, and aroma, but most are a pungent blend of ground coriander, cumin, turmeric, pepper, fenugreek, and cardamom. Experiment with different brands to find your favorite for this fusion dish, which blends tangy lime zest, curry powder, and yogurt with white wine, shrimp, and fettucine.

making fresh pasta p. 156

sautéing and stir-frying p. 32

toasting nuts p. 26

Roasted Eggplant Ravioli

1 medium globe eggplant
or 4 Japanese eggplants

1 head garlic

3 Tbsp olive oil (divided use)

1 yellow onion, minced

½ cup shredded mozzarella

½ cup grated Parmesan

2 Tbsp minced fresh chives

1 Tbsp minced fresh flat-leaf
parsley

Salt and freshly ground pepper

1 lb fresh pasta dough (p. 159)

1½ cups tomato sauce (p. 160),
warmed

Makes 4 servings

Preheat the oven to 350°F.

Cut the eggplant(s) in half and put them face down on an aluminum foil–lined baking sheet. Cut the top off of the garlic head to expose each of the cloves (so that they will come out easily after they are roasted). Place the garlic bulb, cut side down, next to the eggplant. Drizzle 2 Tbsp of the oil over the eggplant and the garlic.

Roast the eggplant halves and garlic until tender, about 30 minutes for Japanese eggplant, 45 minutes for globe eggplant. Set aside and let cool to room temperature.

Peel the eggplant and scoop out and discard any seed pockets. Squeeze the garlic cloves out of their skins. Purée the eggplant and garlic in a food processor until smooth. You should have about ⅔ cup. Transfer to a bowl.

Heat the remaining 1 Tbsp olive oil in a skillet over medium heat. Add the onion and sauté until translucent, 5–7 minutes. Add the onion to the eggplant purée, along with the mozzarella, Parmesan, chives, parsley, 1 tsp salt, and ½ tsp pepper. Mix well. Taste and season with salt and pepper.

Roll out the dough into thin sheets (see page 157). Cut the sheets into 24 three-inch circles. Keep the dough circles covered with plastic wrap until they are ready to be filled.

Brush the edge of a pasta circle lightly with a pastry brush dipped in cool water. Place 1 Tbsp eggplant filling in the center of the circle. Place another circle on top of the filling, keeping the edges of the dough lined up. Lightly press the edges of the dough together. Crimp the edges with the tines of a fork to seal them. Repeat with the remaining pasta circles.

Bring a large, wide pot of salted water to a boil. Reduce the heat, add the ravioli, and simmer until tender, about 5 minutes. Drain immediately.

Serve the ravioli over a pool of hot tomato sauce.

Most mature globe eggplants are ribboned with vertical seed pockets. Since the seeds can be bitter (and won't purée smoothly), remove them after roasting, when the eggplant flesh has softened.

making fresh pasta
p. 156

making stuffed pasta
p. 158

Lobster Tortellini in a Coconut-Curry Broth

Lobster Filling

1 live lobster (about 2 lb)

2 Tbsp minced fresh chives

1 Tbsp minced fresh basil

1 tsp minced gingerroot

Salt

½ tsp fresh lemon juice

1 lb fresh pasta dough (p. 159)

Coconut-Curry Broth

3 cups fish or shellfish broth

3 cups chicken broth

One 14-oz can coconut milk

2 Tbsp thinly sliced lemongrass

½ tsp prepared red curry paste

2 cups bite-sized torn kale

Freshly ground pepper

1 red or yellow bell pepper, peeled and julienned

½ cup thinly sliced radish

2 Tbsp minced fresh mint

Makes 4 servings

For the filling, bring a large pot of salted water to a boil and submerge the lobster. Cook until the shell is bright red, 10–12 minutes. Cool slightly, then crack; reserve the lobster claw meat intact for a garnish and coarsely chop the remaining lobster meat. Toss gently with the chives, basil, ginger, 1 tsp salt, and the lemon juice. Refrigerate until ready to use.

Roll out the dough into thin sheets (see page 157). Cut the sheets into 16 three-inch squares. Keep the dough squares covered with plastic wrap until they are ready to be filled.

Brush the edges of each square lightly with a pastry brush dipped in cool water. Place a scant 2 tsp filling in the center of each square. Fold the squares in half on the diagonal to make a triangle, pinch to seal, and overlap 2 corners to form tortellini. Set aside, covered.

For the coconut-curry broth, combine the fish and chicken broths, coconut milk, lemongrass, and red curry paste in a saucepan over medium heat. Bring to a simmer and cook for 5–10 minutes. Add the kale and cook just to heat through, 2–3 minutes. Taste and season with salt and pepper.

Meanwhile, bring a large, wide pot of salted water to a boil. Reduce the heat, add the tortellini, and simmer until tender, about 5 minutes. Drain immediately.

To serve, ladle the broth into serving bowls, and add 5 or 6 tortellini to each bowl. Garnish with the reserved claw meat, the bell pepper, radish, and a sprinkle of mint.

For this recipe, you will want to use only the pale, tender inner portion of the lemongrass stalk. Chop off the hard knob at the base of the stalk, peel off and discard the outer layers, and thinly slice the lower 3 to 4 inches of the stalk. The rest of the lemongrass can be saved for flavoring broths and soups.

making stuffed pasta p. 158

preparing lobster p. 128

Chorizo Ravioli with Tomato-Basil Coulis

2 tsp vegetable oil

6 cloves garlic, minced

1 tsp minced jalapeño

6 oz chorizo sausage, coarsely chopped

Salt

1 tsp chili powder

½ tsp coarsely chopped fresh oregano, plus more for garnish

¼ tsp ground cayenne pepper

1 lb fresh pasta dough (p. 159)

1½ cups tomato sauce (p. 160), warmed

Makes 4 servings

Heat the oil in a skillet over medium heat. Add the garlic and jalapeño and sauté until aromatic, 1 minute. Add the chorizo, 1 tsp salt, the chili powder, the ½ tsp oregano, and the cayenne and sauté until aromatic, about 2 minutes more. Transfer to a bowl to cool.

Roll out the dough into thin sheets. Cut the sheets into 32 two-inch circles and cover with plastic wrap until they are ready to be filled. Brush the edge of a pasta circle lightly with water. Place 2 tsp chorizo filling in the center of the circle. Place another circle on top of the filling, keeping the edges of the dough lined up. Lightly press the edges of the dough together. Crimp the edges with the tines of a fork to seal them. Repeat with the remaining pasta circles.

Bring a large, wide pot of salted water to a boil. Reduce the heat, add the ravioli, and simmer until tender, about 5 minutes. Drain. Serve the ravioli over hot tomato sauce, garnished with oregano.

Chorizo is a hard, cured Spanish sausage, made from pork that's been marinated with garlic and paprika, either the mild *dulce* (sweet) or more fiery *picante* (hot). It's usually rather spicy, with a rusty-red color and slightly chunky texture.

making stuffed pasta p. 158

cooking pasta p. 155

Orecchiette with Sausage Sauce

½ cup olive oil

1 lb mild or hot Italian sausage, casings removed

¼ cup finely chopped onion

2 cloves garlic, minced

1 pinch red pepper flakes

½ cup dry white wine

¼ cup brandy

2 cups canned crushed tomatoes

1 Tbsp chopped fresh rosemary

4 cups heavy cream

¼ cup fresh peas, blanched

1 cup white mushrooms, sliced

1 lb dried orecchiette or other shaped pasta

Salt

Grated Parmesan for serving

Makes 6 servings

Heat the olive oil in a large sauté pan over medium heat and cook the sausage until golden brown, stirring to break it up. Using a slotted spoon, set aside on a plate. Pour off the excess fat, leaving about ¼ inch in the pan. Add the onion and sauté until translucent. Add the garlic and red pepper flakes and sauté until golden. Add the wine and brandy and cook until most of the liquid is absorbed. Add the tomatoes and cook for 5 minutes.

Add the sausage, rosemary, and cream. Bring to a simmer and cook over low heat until the cream thickens slightly, 3–4 minutes. Add the peas and mushrooms. Set aside and cover to keep warm.

Meanwhile, cook the pasta in a large pot of salted boiling water until al dente. Cooking time may vary by brand; follow package directions. Drain immediately. Add the pasta to the warm sauce and toss until well coated with sauce. Serve with Parmesan alongside.

The sausage alone will likely provide enough salt for this dish. Add salt only after tasting the sauce to see whether it is needed. Use high-quality sausage from a good butcher.

boiling, parboiling, or blanching p. 37

Spinach and Escarole Lasagna

½ recipe fresh pasta dough (p. 159), rolled out to thinnest setting or ¹⁄₁₆ inch thick and cut into 3 x 10–inch strips, or about 10 dried lasagna noodles

Cheese Filling

15 oz ricotta

1 cup grated Parmesan

⅓ cup minced fresh flat-leaf parsley

Salt and freshly ground pepper

¼ tsp freshly grated nutmeg, or to taste

2 large eggs, lightly beaten

4 Tbsp olive oil (divided use)

2 cloves garlic, minced (divided use)

1 head escarole, trimmed and chopped

1 bunch spinach, trimmed and chopped

4 cups tomato sauce (p. 160)

2½ cups shredded mozzarella (divided use)

½ cup grated Parmesan (divided use)

Makes 8 servings

If using dried pasta, bring a large, wide pot of salted water to a boil. Add the lasagna and stir to separate. Cook until al dente, about 8 minutes. Drain the noodles and rinse with very cold water. Drain again and lay flat on clean kitchen towels. (If using fresh pasta, omit this first step.)

Preheat the oven to 375°F.

For the filling, combine the ricotta, Parmesan, parsley, ½ tsp salt, ¼ tsp pepper, and nutmeg. Add the eggs and mix well. Set aside.

Heat 2 Tbsp of the oil in a large skillet over medium-high heat. Add 1 tsp of the minced garlic and sauté for 15 seconds. Add the escarole and sauté, turning frequently, until the greens have wilted and cooked through, about 4 minutes. Season well with salt and pepper, transfer to a bowl, and set aside.

Add the remaining 2 Tbsp oil to the skillet and return to medium-high heat. Add the remaining minced garlic and sauté for 15 seconds. Add the spinach and sauté, turning frequently, until the greens have wilted and cooked through, about 2 minutes. Season well with salt and pepper, transfer to a bowl, and set aside.

To assemble the lasagna, spread 1 cup of tomato sauce in a 9 x 13–inch baking dish. Add a layer of cooked dried pasta or fresh pasta. Spread half of the ricotta filling evenly over the pasta, followed by the escarole and its juices. Top with 1½ cups of tomato sauce. Spread half of the mozzarella over the sauce and sprinkle with half of the Parmesan. Place another layer of pasta on top and spread with the remaining ricotta filling, then the spinach and its juices. Top with 1½ cups of tomato sauce. Tuck any long noodles into the pan to prevent them from curling and drying, scatter the remaining mozzarella on top, and sprinkle with the remaining Parmesan.

Bake the lasagna for 15 minutes. Reduce the oven temperature to 325°F and bake for 30 minutes more. If the top browns too fast, cover it lightly with oiled aluminum foil. The cheese should be melted and bubbly and the top should be a light golden brown when done.

Remove the lasagna from the oven and let it stand for about 15 minutes before cutting into portions and serving.

For best results, use a "classic" or "natural" brand of ricotta, made only of whey, milk, cream, and salt. These traditional ricottas yield a sweeter, creamier result than brands made with stabilizers, thickeners, and preservatives.

sautéing and stir-frying
p. 32

roasting and baking
p. 30

Forest Mushroom Individual Lasagnas

½ recipe fresh pasta dough (p. 159), rolled out to thinnest setting or ¹⁄₁₆ inch thick and cut into eight 3 x 10–inch strips, or 8 dried lasagna noodles

3 Tbsp butter, plus more for greasing pan

1 cup sliced shallots plus 3 Tbsp minced

5 Tbsp all-purpose flour

2 cups whole milk

1 cup heavy cream

Salt and freshly ground pepper

2 Tbsp olive oil

5 cloves garlic, minced

2 lb assorted mushrooms such as oyster, cremini, chanterelle, white, and stemmed shiitake, coarsely chopped

6 Tbsp dry white wine or Marsala

½ cup sour cream

2 Tbsp minced fresh flat-leaf parsley

1 tsp minced fresh thyme

½ cup grated Parmesan

Makes 8 servings

If using dried pasta, bring a large, wide pot of salted water to a boil. Add the lasagna and stir to separate. Cook until al dente, about 8 minutes. Drain the noodles and rinse with very cold water. Drain again and lay flat on clean kitchen towels. (If using fresh pasta, omit this first step.)

Preheat the oven to 375°F.

Heat the butter in a saucepan over medium-low heat. Add the sliced shallots and cook, stirring occasionally, until light brown, 8–10 minutes. Add the flour and cook, stirring constantly, to make a blond roux, about 5 minutes. Slowly add the milk and cream, whisking constantly to prevent lumps from forming. Raise the heat and bring the mixture to a boil. Reduce the heat to low and simmer for 20 minutes, stirring occasionally. Remove from the heat, taste, and season with salt and pepper. Set aside.

Heat 1 Tbsp of the olive oil in a sauté pan over high heat until it shimmers. Add the minced shallots and garlic and sauté for 30 seconds. Add half of the mushrooms and sauté until the mushrooms are golden and the liquid they release starts to evaporate, about 3 minutes. Transfer the mushrooms to a bowl. Return the pan to the heat and add the remaining 1 Tbsp oil. Add the remaining mushrooms and sauté until golden and the liquid starts to evaporate, about 3 minutes. Add the wine and simmer until most of the liquid is absorbed, about 3 minutes. Transfer to the bowl with the other mushrooms. Stir to combine and let cool completely.

Add the sour cream, parsley, and thyme to the cool mushroom mixture. Taste and season with salt and pepper.

Working with one noodle at a time, spread about ⅓ cup of mushroom filling over the length of each noodle. Gently roll the noodles up, pushing in the filling at the sides as you go. Place each roll, seam side down, in a buttered 11½ x 8–inch baking pan. Pour the shallot cream sauce evenly over the rolls and sprinkle with the Parmesan.

Bake the lasagnas until the filling is hot and the top is lightly browned, about 15 minutes. Serve at once.

Instead of the usual layered pasta dish, this elegant variation wraps individual lasagna noodles around a creamy mushroom filling. The neat rolls are glazed with a shallot cream sauce and dusted with Parmesan. Serve one roll as an appetizer or more to make an entrée.

roasting and baking
p. 30

cleaning mushrooms
p. 186

Gnocchi with Herbs and Butter

3 russet potatoes, peeled

Salt

3 Tbsp unsalted butter
(divided use)

1 large egg

1 large egg yolk

½ tsp freshly ground pepper

1 pinch freshly grated nutmeg

¾ cup all-purpose flour, or
as needed

3 Tbsp grated Parmesan

¼ cup minced fresh flat-leaf
parsley

Makes 4 servings

Cut the potatoes into equal-sized pieces (about 6 pieces per potato, 3 cups chopped). Place them in a pot with enough cold water to cover by 2 inches. Salt the water. Gradually bring the water to a simmer over medium heat. Cover and simmer until the potatoes are easily pierced with a fork, 10–12 minutes.

Drain the potatoes. Return them to the pot and let them dry briefly over very low heat until no more steam rises from them, or spread them out on a baking sheet and dry them in a 150°F oven. While the potatoes are still very hot, push them through a ricer or food mill into a bowl.

Bring another large pot of salted water to a boil.

Meanwhile, make the gnocchi dough. Add 1 Tbsp of the butter, the egg and egg yolk, 1 tsp salt, the pepper, and the nutmeg to the riced potatoes. Mix well. Incorporate enough of the flour to make a stiff dough.

Divide the dough into egg-sized pieces. On a lightly floured board, use the flat of your hand to roll out each piece into a cylinder about 1 inch in diameter. Cut the cylinders into pieces about 1 inch long. Gently roll the gnocchi against the tines of a fork or wires of a whisk to create ridges.

Add the gnocchi to the boiling water and boil until they rise to the surface, 2–3 minutes. Lift the gnocchi from the water with a slotted spoon or drain in a colander.

Melt the remaining 2 Tbsp butter over medium-high heat in a large skillet. Add the gnocchi and toss until very hot and coated with butter. Add the Parmesan and parsley. Serve at once.

A food mill or potato ricer gives the best texture to the puréed potatoes called for in this gnocchi dough. Both tools push the cooked potatoes through a metal strainer, producing fine, light strands of potato easily blended into a smooth paste. Blenders and food processors break down the potato starch too fast, producing a loose, gluey mass that won't hold its shape.

boiling and simmering
p. 37

preparing potatoes
p. 205

Cannelloni with Swiss Chard and Walnuts

Cream Sauce

2½ Tbsp unsalted butter

7 Tbsp all-purpose flour

2 cups whole milk

1 cup heavy cream

Salt and freshly ground pepper

⅛ tsp freshly grated nutmeg (optional)

2 Tbsp unsalted butter, plus more for greasing pan

1 Tbsp minced shallot

1 bunch Swiss chard, trimmed and chopped (about 5½ cups)

¾ cup grated Gruyère cheese

¼ cup coarsely chopped toasted walnuts

2 Tbsp brandy

1 large egg, well beaten

8 savory crêpes (p. 262)

½ cup grated Parmesan

Makes 4 servings

Preheat the oven to 375°F.

For the cream sauce, melt the butter in a saucepan over medium heat. Add the flour and cook, stirring frequently, to make a blond roux, about 5 minutes. Whisk the milk and cream into the roux. Bring the cream sauce back to a boil. Add ½ tsp salt, ¼ tsp pepper, and the nutmeg, if using. Reduce the heat and allow the sauce to simmer, stirring frequently, until it is thickened and no longer tastes floury, about 20 minutes. Remove from the heat and cover to keep warm.

Melt the butter in a skillet over medium heat. Cook the shallot, stirring occasionally, until limp and translucent, 5–7 minutes. Add the chard by the handful, sautéing just until wilted before adding more. Once all of the chard is added to the pan, sauté until it is deep green, tender, and softened, 3–4 minutes more. Drain the mixture, if necessary, and season generously with salt and pepper.

Blend 1 cup of the cream sauce with the Gruyère, walnuts, brandy, and egg in a bowl. Fold in the sautéed chard to make a filling for the cannelloni.

To prepare the cannelloni, spread 2 Tbsp filling over the center of each crêpe and roll into a cylinder. Place the cannelloni, seam side down, in a buttered 9 x 13–inch flameproof baking dish.

Ladle the remaining cream sauce over the cannelloni. Sprinkle the Parmesan evenly over the top.

Bake the cannelloni until heated through, 25–30 minutes. If desired, brown the Parmesan lightly under the broiler just before serving.

There are two types of cannelloni. One is a dried pasta tube shape that is cooked, then filled. However, this version is a specialty of the Piedmontese region, made with crêpes rather than dried pasta. Use escarole, spinach, or other cooking greens to replace the Swiss chard, if you prefer. You can prepare the filling ahead of time and hold it, covered, in the refrigerator. This dish makes a great centerpiece for a meatless menu.

roasting and baking p. 30

toasting nuts p. 26

Brown Butter Spätzle

1¼ cups all-purpose flour, sifted

⅔ cup whole milk

2 large eggs

Salt and freshly ground pepper

1 pinch freshly grated nutmeg, or to taste (optional)

2 Tbsp unsalted butter

2 Tbsp minced fresh chives, parsley, or dill (optional)

Makes 4 servings

Bring a large pot of salted water to boil.

Meanwhile, combine the flour, milk, eggs, ½ tsp salt, ¼ tsp pepper, and the nutmeg (if using) in a large bowl and whisk well to make a smooth but thick batter. Let the batter rest for 10 minutes to relax, for tender spätzle.

Push the batter through a spätzle maker or colander into the boiling water. Simmer until cooked throughout, 5–6 minutes. Drain the spätzle well.

Melt the butter in a sauté pan. Add the spätzle and sauté until very hot and lightly browned, 3–4 minutes. Sprinkle with the herbs (if using) and serve at once.

These chewy little dumplings are traditionally made in a spätzle maker, which looks like a flat cheese shredder with very wide holes. With the spätzle maker suspended horizontally over the cooking pot, the dough is pressed through the holes and drops into the simmering water below. A metal colander with large holes can be substituted.

boiling and simmering p. 37

sautéing and stir-frying p. 32

Pasta Salad with Pesto Vinaigrette

Pesto

½ cup lightly packed fresh basil leaves, coarsely chopped

¼ cup grated Parmesan

¼ cup toasted pine nuts

1 clove garlic, minced

3 Tbsp extra-virgin olive oil

Salt and freshly ground pepper

½ lb dried penne

¼ cup extra-virgin olive oil

2 Tbsp red wine vinegar

1 cup cherry tomatoes, halved

1 cup diced lean ham

½ red onion, diced

½ cup green olives, pitted and chopped

¼ cup toasted pine nuts

Makes 4–6 servings

For the pesto, put the basil in a food processor or mortar and pestle. Add the Parmesan, pine nuts, and garlic and grind together. While grinding, gradually add the 3 Tbsp olive oil to form a thick paste. Taste and season with salt and pepper.

Bring a large pot of salted water to a boil. Add the pasta and boil until al dente. Cooking time may vary by brand; follow package directions. Drain and rinse in cold water until the pasta is cool.

Combine the ¼ cup olive oil, vinegar, and the pesto in a large bowl. Add the cooked penne, tomatoes, ham, onion, olives, and pine nuts. Toss until evenly coated. Season with salt and pepper.

Cover, refrigerate, and marinate for at least 1 hour or up to 4 hours before serving.

This pesto recipe doubles or triples easily. If you are making a big batch, leave the Parmesan out of the portion you want to store, transfer to a clean jar, and cover with a thin layer of olive oil to prevent the sauce from darkening and drying out. Cover tightly and keep refrigerated for up to 2 weeks.

toasting nuts p. 26

making vinaigrette p. 250

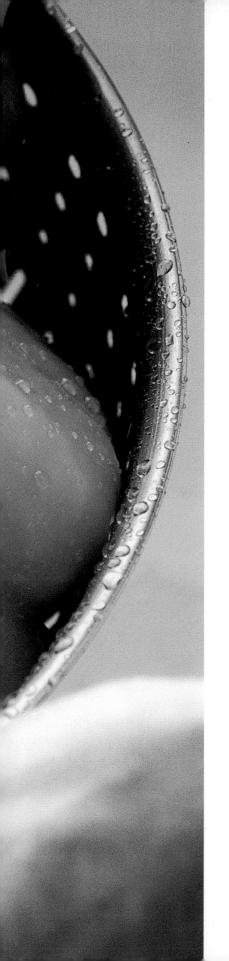

6 Vegetables

From the first tender pea shoots of spring to the last brilliant orange pumpkins in autumn, vegetables are the cook's harbinger of the changing seasons. When the local crop of asparagus or sweet corn first starts to trickle into the market in early spring or midsummer, we can't wait to get it home. We admire such vegetables for their many culinary virtues: bright colors, distinctive flavors, valuable nutrients, and remarkable versatility. Vegetables can be savored just as they come from the farm, or they can be prepared using virtually any cooking method. Enjoy them on their own or incorporated into soups, salads, side dishes, and main courses.

Steamed and boiled vegetables have vivid colors and good texture. You can let the vegetable stand alone or choose from myriad seasonings and garnishes. Simple steamed broccoli, for example, is tender and sweet. Drizzling it with olive oil and a scattering of toasted pine nuts, and you have a completely different dish. Sautéed, pan-fried, and deep-fried vegetables have intensified flavors.

Selecting vegetables

The essential point to remember when choosing vegetables is that they are, in general, highly perishable. The more fresh and appealing a vegetable looks when you buy it (or pick it, if you have a garden), the greater its level of nutrients.

As soon as any vegetable is harvested, it begins to undergo significant changes. The more delicate the vegetable, the more dramatic the change. Sweet corn and peas, for instance, begin converting sugars into starch, giving over-the-hill corn and peas a telltale sticky texture and pasty taste. When you consider the time that it takes to get foods from the field to the market, you can see why it is best to shop frequently for vegetables, keep them refrigerated, and cook them within a few days. At some times of the year, you may find that frozen vegetables, which are typically processed right in the field upon harvesting, are a good alternative to less-than-ripe fresh produce. Peas, spinach, corn, and green beans are good examples of vegetables that might be best frozen.

Root vegetables (sometimes called winter vegetables) are significantly less perishable and can generally be stored without any marked loss of quality for several weeks or, if carefully handled, even months. Hard-skinned squashes, turnips, carrots, parsnips, and cabbages fall into this category of vegetables. The traditional way to store these vegetables is in a root cellar under a good covering of straw or hay, where they benefit from a constant cool temperature and relatively high humidity. Since most of us don't have root cellars, however, it is best to use them within a week or two of purchase.

If vegetables are sold as organic, they must meet specific guidelines regarding the land they are grown on and the types of fertilizers and other cultivating aids that can be used. Look for the "Organic" symbol on the label or posted near the display.

Some markets offer precut vegetables. These can be a great boon, saving on preparation time. When you inspect the package, look for fresh, moist surfaces. Even if the produce is labeled "prewashed," you should rinse it in cool water to refresh it.

Preparing and serving vegetables

Each vegetable has distinct properties when it is properly cooked. Fully cooked green beans, for example, have a very different texture from fully cooked carrots. Different cooking methods also result in different textures in the finished dish. Stir-fried vegetables may be fairly crisp, while stewed and braised vegetables are often cooked until they nearly fall apart. Personal preference and the cuisine your recipe draws from also influence how you judge doneness.

The most reliable doneness tests for vegetables are taste and touch. Bite into a piece of the vegetable when it is raw, and then again at various points as it cooks. Notice the flavor and texture. If tasting the vegetable isn't practical, pierce it with a knife, fork, or skewer and gauge the resistance it gives. Consider the way you will be using the vegetable to determine the right degree of doneness. Will it be served alone or as part of a complex dish?

Most stand-alone vegetable dishes, whether steamed, boiled, sautéed, or grilled, turn out best when the vegetables are cooked just until tender. You should be able to bite into the vegetable easily, but it should still offer a slight resistance.

Stewed and braised vegetables should be fully cooked. Aim to cook vegetables for these dishes until they are completely tender but retain their shape and color. When you boil or steam vegetables for a purée, cook them until they almost fall apart on their own. At this point, they should be easy to push through a sieve or purée in a blender.

In some recipes, vegetables are blanched, not to cook them through but to set their colors, make them easier to peel, or to improve their flavor. Blanched vegetables are boiled very briefly, just long enough to cook the outermost layer, then submerged in cold water to stop the cooking process. The vegetable retains, for the most part, the texture it had when raw. Similarly, vegetables are sometimes boiled, steamed, or roasted to near doneness, then finished in a second step, sometimes using a different technique such as grilling or sautéing. Boiling or cooking to near doneness is known as parboiling or parcooking.

Vegetables can be the centerpiece of a meal or can be used to add flavor, eye appeal, and texture to meals featuring meat, fish, or poultry. The recipes in this chapter offer a wide range of choices for those who want to expand their repertoire of vegetable dishes.

Selecting and preparing vegetables

VEGETABLE OR FAMILY	REPRESENTATIVE MEMBERS	WHAT TO LOOK FOR	BEST COOKING METHODS
Cabbage family	Bok choy, broccoli, broccoli rabe, brussels sprouts, cauliflower, green/red/savoy/napa cabbage, kohlrabi	Firm, heavy heads; good color; florets tightly closed	Boiling, steaming, stir-frying, grilling, braising, stewing
Corn		Husk firmly attached, kernels plump	Boiling, steaming, roasting, grilling, stewing
Eggplant	Globe, Japanese	Skin firm and glossy, leaves unwilted	Grilling, broiling, roasting, stewing, pan-frying, deep-frying
Greens, leafy	Arugula, chard, collards, dandelion, kale, mustard, spinach	No wilting or yellowing in leaves, heads heavy for size	Sautéing, stir-frying, steaming, boiling, stewing, braising
Legume family	Green beans, haricots verts, fava beans, garden peas, snow peas, sugar snap peas	Beans and pea pods plump, crisp, evenly colored	Steaming, boiling, sautéing, stir-frying, stewing, braising
Mushroom family	Chanterelle, porcino, enoki, morel, portobello, oyster, shiitake, white; truffles	Caps plump; stems, if any, firmly attached; earthy smell; gills, if any, intact	Sautéing, stir-frying, stewing, braising, grilling, roasting, baking, pan-frying, deep-frying
Onion family	Fresh: leeks, green onions	Green portions intact and unwilted; bulb firm	Sautéing, grilling, broiling, stewing, braising
	Dried: cipolline, red onions, shallots, sweet onions, white onions, yellow onions	Firm and heavy for size, outer layers tight with good color	Sautéing, grilling, broiling, stewing, braising, roasting, baking, pan-frying, deep-frying
Pepper family	Bell, chile	Fruit plump, skin glossy and taut	Roasting, grilling, broiling, sautéing, stir-frying, stewing, deep-frying
Roots and tubers	Beets, carrots, parsnips, potatoes, rutabagas, salsify, turnips	Firm and heavy for size, no withering; greens, if attached, unwilted	Boiling, steaming, roasting, baking, sautéing, stir-frying, grilling, broiling, stewing, braising
Squash family	Summer: chayote, crookneck, pattypan, yellow, zucchini	Good color, firm, with no bruises or soft spots	Sautéing, stir-frying, pan-frying, deep-frying, grilling, broiling, roasting, stewing, braising
	Winter: acorn, butternut, hubbard, spaghetti; pumpkin	Firm; heavy for size; stem, if any, firmly attached	Boiling, steaming, roasting, baking, sautéing, stewing, braising
Tomatoes	Beefsteak, cherry, currant, pear, plum (Roma)	Good color, skin glossy and intact, heavy for size, slightly yielding when ripe	Sautéing, stir-frying, roasting, grilling, broiling, stewing, braising, simmering

Dicing onions

Onions grow in layers, so you need a special approach to cut them into neat, relatively even dice.

1 Halving and peeling

Cut onions just before you plan to cook them, since once they are cut their flavor starts to escape. First trim away the roots, leaving the root end of the onion intact, then cut the onion in half from stem end to root end. Peel away the outer layers, discarding both the papery skin and the thin, tough layer just beneath it.

2 Slicing horizontally

Place an onion half cut side down on the cutting board. Holding your knife with its blade parallel to the work surface, carefully make 2 or 3 horizontal cuts in the onion, spacing them from ½ inch apart (for coarse dice) to ¼ inch apart (for fine dice). Do not cut all the way through the root end. This will hold together the onion layers for easier and neater dicing.

3 Slicing vertically

Next, make parallel cuts lengthwise with the tip of the knife. Again, do not cut through the root end. For coarse dice, allow about ½ inch between each cut. For fine dice, space the cuts ¼ inch apart.

4 Cutting crosswise to dice

To complete the dice, make even cuts crosswise through all the layers of the onion, perpendicular to the horizontal and vertical cuts. Work from the loose layers of the stem end to the intact root end of the onion half. Check that all pieces are the same size and shape, cutting any pieces smaller, if needed.

Alternative method

An alternative method for slicing or dicing an onion calls for a series of parallel cuts to be made from the root to the stem end, following the natural curve of the onion. After peeling and halving the onion, you can remove the core by cutting a V-shape notch in the root end. Lay the onion on a surface, cut side down. Hold the knife so that the edge of the blade is at a 90-degree angle to the onion's surface. As you make successive cuts of the required thickness, reposition the blade to maintain a perpendicular angle with the surface of the onion to produce even strips. Cut the strips crosswise to make dice.

Preparing garlic

Depending on how it is prepared, garlic contributes distinctly different flavors.

1 Separating and peeling cloves
To separate the cloves from an entire head of garlic, wrap it in a clean towel and press down on it firmly with the heel of your hand. To loosen the skin from each clove, place the clove on a cutting board, lay your knife blade flat against it and the heel of your palm on the flat side, and press down on the blade to crush the garlic clove lightly, breaking the paper. Peel away the skin.

2 Chopping or mincing
For the best flavor, prepare garlic as close to the time of cooking as possible and cut away any green sprouts in the cloves. Lay the cloves on a cutting board and smash them well, pressing down firmly with the side of your knife blade. Smashing the cloves will ease mincing as well as develop the garlic's flavor to the fullest. Use a rocking motion to chop or mince the garlic to the desired fineness.

3 Mashing garlic
Sprinkle roughly chopped garlic with a little salt. Hold your knife so that its blade is nearly flat against the cutting board. Press the flat side of the cutting edge firmly and repeatedly against the garlic and drag it across the board to make a smooth paste.

Preparing ginger

Proper peeling and chopping releases the maximum amount of flavor from the fresh root.

1 Peeling, then grating or slicing
Use a vegetable peeler to remove the tan skin of fresh gingerroot, peeling only as much as you will need at a time. Peel off as thin a layer as possible, since much of the flavor of ginger lies just beneath its skin. You will notice, particularly in older ginger, a distinct "grain" that makes it easier to slice cleanly in one direction, producing shreds in the other. For a moist, fine purée, use a ginger grater, a small ceramic dish lined with tiny points or pyramids, or a flat, file-like metal grater to reduce the fibers of gingerroot into a softer texture. You can also mince ginger. Cut it into thin slices against the grain, then chop it finely as you would garlic. Ginger is often used in slices to infuse stock soups, broths, and poaching liquids. Thicker pieces hold up well for long simmering, while thin slices will release flavor quickly in shorter cooking times.

Zesting and juicing citrus

The peels of lemons, limes, and oranges are rich in aromatic oils, while their juices add bright flavor to savory and sweet dishes.

1 Zesting citrus

When selecting citrus fruits for their zest, choose those with firm skins rather than very soft or withered peels, as the firm skins are easier to shave or grate. If possible, choose organic fruit for zesting, since pesticides accumulate in the peel. Depending on how the zest will be used in a recipe, remove it in wide pieces, thin strips, or fine gratings. Take care not to cut into the bitter white pith. Use a vegetable peeler for thick strips that can infuse a liquid with flavor and be easily removed later. You can also cut these pieces crosswise for thin strips. Specially designed zesters create thin, delicate strips of zest for sauces or garnish. For finely grated zest, use a grater with very small holes and rotate the fruit frequently as you grate to avoid scraping off too much pith.

If you need both citrus zest and juice for a dish, note that it is easier to zest before juicing.

2 Juicing citrus

A citrus fruit at room temperature gives more juice than chilled fruit. Before cutting and juicing it, roll the fruit firmly against a hard surface to crush its pulp—this will help release even more juice. Slice in half crosswise, then use a fluted reamer or mechanical juicer to extract as much juice as possible.

Rehydrating and plumping

Drying concentrates the flavors and changes the texture of fruits and vegetables.

1 Soaking in hot liquid

Dried chiles, mushrooms, tomatoes, and fruits such as apples, cherries, apricots, and raisins add intense flavor to many dishes. These ingredients must often be "plumped," or rehydrated by soaking them in a liquid, before use. Rinse dried foods first to remove any debris, and check for mold or blemishes. Place the dried fruit or vegetable in a bowl and add enough boiling or very hot liquid to cover. Water is always a safe choice, but soaking food in wine, fruit juice, or broth adds even more flavor to the finished dish. If needed, weigh down the ingredients with a saucer or small pot lid to submerge all the pieces. Let the food steep until soft and plump, usually about 10 minutes. Pour off the liquid, reserving if desired. To remove grit, strain the liquid through cheesecloth.

Preparing bell peppers and chiles

Peppers may be prepared in several ways for the dishes of Latin America, Southeast Asia, the Mediterranean, and the American Southwest.

1 Cutting and seeding peppers

Cut a bell pepper or chile in half or quarters lengthwise, from the stem end to the root end. Using the tip of a paring knife, cut away the stem, pale membranes (also called ribs), and seeds. Since the heat of chiles comes from a substance called capsaicin that is found in their seeds and membranes, you can lower a dish's heat level by removing all or most of the seeds and membranes. When working with very hot chiles, you might choose to wear plastic gloves to protect your skin from the irritating oils they contain. Be careful not to touch your eyes, nose, and mouth after touching cut chiles. Wash your hands after working with hot chiles.

2 Peeling raw peppers

The skins of peppers and chiles are thin, tough, and firmly attached to the flesh. Peppers and chiles are often peeled before they are used in a dish, to improve the dish's flavor and texture. The thin but relatively tough skin can be removed using a swivel-blade peeler or paring knife. This approach is ideal for dishes that highlight the peppers' sweet flavor or that include raw peppers, such as a salad or salsa. Cut the pepper into sections first to create edges of skin that make peeling easier.

3 Roasting and peeling peppers

When peppers and chiles are charred over a flame, grilled, roasted, or broiled, not only are the flavors brought out, but the skins are loosened as well. If you have gas burners, hold the peppers over the flame with tongs or a large kitchen fork, turning to char them evenly. If your grill is hot, char the peppers over hot coals or high heat. To roast or broil peppers and chiles in a hot oven or under a broiler, halve them; remove their stems, seeds, and membranes; and place them cut side down on an oiled sheet pan. Broil or roast until their skin is black and blistered. Once the entire pepper is evenly charred, transfer to a paper bag or bowl and close or cover tightly. By the time they are cool enough to handle, about 10 minutes, steam will have loosened the skin enough that it peels away easily. Peel and rub it away with your fingertips, using a paring knife if the skin clings in some places.

Peeling and seeding tomatoes

This common recipe step ensures smoother sauces and more attractive dishes.

1 Scoring and blanching

Bring a large pot of water to a rolling boil. Cut a shallow X into the blossom (bottom) end of the tomato with the tip of a paring knife. The cut should be just deep enough to slice through the skin. Scoring the tomato will make it easier to remove the peel after blanching. Lower the tomatoes into the water with a slotted spoon, blanching no more than 3 or 4 at a time if they are small, or only 2 if large. After 10–15 seconds, depending on the tomatoes' size and ripeness, remove them from the water with a slotted spoon.

2 Peeling tomatoes

Immediately plunge the tomatoes into ice water to stop the cooking. Peel away the tomato skins starting at the X, using a paring knife if necessary.

3 Seeding tomatoes

Halve round tomatoes crosswise at their widest points. Cut plum (Roma) tomatoes lengthwise to seed them more easily. Gently squeeze each tomato half to extract the seeds, using your finger to help loosen and remove them.

Preparing spinach and leafy greens

Wash fresh spinach thoroughly to remove grit from its crinkly leaves, and remove the tough stems for salads and fillings.

1 Washing and trimming spinach

Spinach and other leafy greens can be very sandy and need careful washing. Fill a large bowl or a sink with cold water. Submerge the leaves in the water, turn them gently, then lift them out and transfer them to a colander. Change the water and repeat the washing as needed until the water remains clear. If the stems are thick and tough, trim them away. Fold a leaf in half lengthwise along its rib, veined side facing outward. With your other hand, grasp the stem firmly and strip it away from the leaf; the rib should also tear away cleanly.

Trimming artichokes

Before you serve artichokes or just their hearts, trim away the thorns and scoop out the choke.

1 Trimming whole artichokes

Once artichokes are cut and exposed to air, they start to turn brown. An acid such as lemon juice slows this discoloration. Whenever you are cutting artichokes, cut a lemon in half to rub on cut surfaces, or fill a bowl with water and add a squeeze of lemon juice and salt to hold the artichokes after trimming. Cut the stem flush with the base of the artichoke, or leave it intact but peel the stem and trim off the rough bottom. For artichokes served whole, use a chef's knife to cut off the top inch of the artichoke, then use kitchen scissors to remove any remaining barbed leaf tips and create a neat appearance. For artichoke hearts, pull away the outer leaves, leaving only the tender inner leaves at the center. To remove the choke before cooking, spread open the leaves of the artichoke. Use a grapefruit spoon, tablespoon, or melon baller to scoop out and discard the pale, purple-tinged leaves.

2 Preparing artichoke bottoms

To prepare artichoke bottoms, cut away the outer leaves with a paring knife. Trim and peel the stem or cut it flush with the artichoke base. Make a cut crosswise through the artichoke at its widest point. Scoop out the choke at the center with a grapefruit spoon or teaspoon. The bottom should look like a bowl. Hold the trimmed artichoke bottoms in lemon water to prevent browning.

Trimming asparagus

Removing the tough ends and skin of mature asparagus highlights its tenderness and fresh flavor.

1 Trimming asparagus

Bend the asparagus spear until the woody end snaps off, then trim the end of the spear neatly.

2 Peeling asparagus

Lay the trimmed asparagus spear on a flat surface. With a vegetable peeler, very lightly scrape the length of the stalk, from just beneath the tip's leaf buds down to the trimmed end. Remove only the outer, dark green layer of the stalk. A pale hint of light green should be left on the asparagus.

Cleaning mushrooms

Clean mushrooms just before preparing them, and don't let them soak up too much water.

1 Rinsing or wiping

Clean mushrooms with as little water as possible; they absorb water like sponges, which can interfere with cooking. If the mushrooms were relatively clean when you bought them, you may need only to rub them gently with a cloth or soft brush. If you have a number to clean or they are very dirty, put them in a colander and rinse in cool water just long enough to remove any dirt. Let the mushrooms drain well on layers of absorbent towels before you cut them. Some mushrooms, such as shiitake, must have their tough, woody stems removed. Even mushrooms with tender stems generally left intact should have the dried, discolored ends of their stems trimmed away.

Cleaning leeks

A leek's layered leaves trap grit and sand that must be rinsed away carefully.

1 Trimming the leeks

Rinse whole leeks, paying special attention to the roots, where dirt can cling. Lay the leek on a cutting board and trim away the root end and the tough, dark green portion of the leaves. Cut the leaves away at an angle to avoid losing the tender light green leaves at the center of the stalk.

2 Washing the layers

Cut the leek lengthwise in halves or quarters, depending on the recipe. Rinse the leek under running water, gently separating its leaves to flush out grit and sand.

Preparing corn kernels

Some recipes call for corn kernels to be cut away from the cob.

1 Cutting away the kernels

Husk the corn and slice off one end. Firmly hold the ear upright on its cut end and slice away the kernels down the length of the cob, pressing the knife blade as close to the cob as possible. A traditional recipe for creamed corn or corn chowder may call for "milking" the corn. For this technique, lay the ear down on a flat surface and lightly score each row of kernels with the tip of a knife, cutting through the center of each kernel. Then, using the back of the knife or a large spoon, scrape out the flesh and milk of the kernels into a shallow bowl or pan.

Grilled Vegetables Provençale

4 cloves garlic

½ cup olive oil

2 tsp minced fresh rosemary

2 zucchini, cut lengthwise into
½-inch-thick slices

1 small globe eggplant, peeled
and cut lengthwise into
½-inch-thick slices

1 green bell pepper, cut into
6 wedges

1 red bell pepper, cut into
6 wedges

1 sweet onion, cut horizontally
into ½-Inch-thick slices

Salt and freshly ground pepper

1 tomato, peeled, seeded,
and diced

2 Tbsp balsamic vinegar, or
to taste

2 Tbsp fresh basil chiffonade

Makes 4–6 servings

Lightly smash the garlic cloves. Put the garlic in a small, heavy saucepan and add the oil and rosemary. Place over very low heat and heat slowly until the garlic is tender, about 8 minutes. Remove the flavored oil from the heat, remove and discard the garlic, and set the oil aside to cool to room temperature.

Prepare a grill for a medium fire.

Brush the zucchini, eggplant, bell peppers, and onion slices with the flavored oil and season with salt and pepper. Grill the vegetables until marked, 2–4 minutes. Turn once and complete cooking on the second side until the vegetables are marked and fully cooked, 3–6 minutes more. As each vegetable finishes cooking, remove from the grill and dice. Transfer to a serving bowl.

Add the tomatoes and any remaining flavored oil to the the grilled vegetables and toss well. Taste and season with salt, pepper, and balsamic vinegar. Fold in the basil chiffonade or use it to garnish individual portions.

Cutting the vegetables as directed here will ensure that they all cook in the same amount of time. To keep the onion's rings together while grilling, push a toothpick through the rings horizontally on either side.

grilling and broiling p. 28

**preparing bell peppers
and chiles** p. 183

shredding and chiffonade
p. 17

Citrus-Roasted Beets

1 lb beets (about 6 small beets)

Zest of 1 orange

Salt and freshly ground pepper

2 Tbsp olive oil

2 Tbsp fresh orange juice

3 Tbsp chopped fresh cilantro,
flat-leaf parsley, or mint

Makes 4 servings

Preheat the oven to 350°F. Trim the stem ends of the beets, leaving about 1 inch intact; leave the root ends untouched. Place the beets in a small baking dish with water to a depth of ¼ inch. Scatter half of the orange zest, 1 tsp salt, and ½ tsp pepper over the top. Cover the pan tightly with aluminum foil and bake until the beets are tender enough to pierce easily with the tip of a paring knife, about 1 hour.

When the beets are cool enough to handle, trim the ends and slip off the skins. Quarter each beet lengthwise and cut each quarter into ½-inch-thick slices.

Whisk together the olive oil, remaining orange zest, orange juice, and cilantro in a serving bowl. Add the roasted beets and toss well. Season with salt and pepper. Serve warm.

For a truly eye-catching dish, try combining several different colors of beets, such as red, golden, or the candy-striped Chioggia beets, which when cut reveal a pattern of pink and white concentric rings.

roasting and baking
p. 30

zesting and juicing citrus
p. 182

Roasted Eggplant Stuffed with Curried Lentils

½ cup brown lentils

2 cups vegetable broth or water

2 small globe eggplants

1 Tbsp olive oil, plus more for greasing pan

¼ cup minced yellow onion

1 clove garlic, minced

½ tsp grated gingerroot

½ cup minced white mushrooms

½ tsp salt

½ tsp lemon zest

½ tsp curry powder

¼ tsp ground cinnamon

¼ tsp ground turmeric

Freshly ground pepper

Makes 4 servings

Bring the lentils and broth to a boil in a small pot. Cover and reduce the heat to low. Simmer until the lentils are tender to the bite, 25–30 minutes. Remove from the heat and set the lentils aside in their cooking liquid.

Preheat the oven to 350°F. Grease an 8 x 11–inch baking pan.

Halve the eggplants lengthwise and scoop out some of the flesh, leaving a ½- to ¾-inch "wall." Mince the scooped flesh and set aside. Transfer the eggplant halves to the prepared baking pan, skin side down.

Heat a large nonstick skillet over medium heat. Swirl in the oil, then add the onion, garlic, and ginger. Sauté, stirring occasionally, until the onion is golden brown, 6–8 minutes. Add the minced eggplant, mushrooms, salt, lemon zest, curry, cinnamon, turmeric, and pepper to taste. Sauté over medium heat, stirring occasionally, until the mushrooms begin to release some moisture, about 5 minutes.

Drain the lentils, reserving the cooking liquid, and add the lentils to the eggplant and mushroom mixture. Add enough of the cooking liquid (about ¼ cup) to moisten the vegetables well, then simmer until the liquid is reduced, 6–8 minutes.

Fill the hollowed eggplant halves with the lentil mixture. Cover with aluminum foil and bake until the eggplants are tender and cooked through, 35–40 minutes. Serve at once.

Small globe eggplants are the perfect size for this dish and can sometimes be found in the supermarket produce section or at farm stands. If you cannot find them, however, use a larger eggplant, leaving the same size "wall" but cooking for up to 10 minutes longer, and cut it into serving portions after baking.

roasting and baking
p. 30

mincing p. 17

Italian-Style Spinach

1 Tbsp olive oil

2 Tbsp diced pancetta or 1 slice bacon, diced

¼ cup minced yellow onion

1 clove garlic, minced

8 cups spinach leaves

Salt and freshly ground pepper

¼ cup grated Parmesan

¼ tsp freshly grated nutmeg

Makes 4–6 servings

Heat the olive oil in a large sauté pan over medium heat. Add the pancetta and sauté until the fat renders and the pancetta is translucent, about 1 minute. Raise the heat to high and add the onion and garlic. Sauté until the garlic is aromatic, about 1 minute more. Add the spinach by the handful, sautéing just until the leaves wilt before adding more. Once all the leaves are added to the pan, sauté until they are deep green, tender, and softened, 3–4 minutes more. Drain the mixture if necessary and season generously with salt and pepper. Remove from the heat and stir in the Parmesan and nutmeg. Serve at once.

Dark, leafy greens abound in vitamins and robust flavor. Try a mixture of other greens, such as beet or turnip tops (which cook quickly like spinach), Swiss chard, kale, or escarole (which need a few minutes longer), or broccoli rabe, which has a pleasant bitterness.

sautéing and stir-frying p. 32

preparing spinach and leafy greens p. 184

VARIATIONS

Creamed Swiss Chard with Air-Dried Beef

Replace the spinach with 8 cups trimmed Swiss chard leaves, and replace the pancetta with ¼ cup finely diced air-dried beef or ham. Gently sauté the beef in 2 Tbsp olive oil before adding the onion. Once all the chard is in the pan, add ⅓ cup heavy cream and return to a simmer; cook until the Swiss chard is tender, about 5 minutes.

preparing spinach and leafy greens p. 184

Broccoli Rabe and Cannellini Beans

Replace the spinach with 6 cups trimmed broccoli rabe (1½ lb). Add 1 cup cooked and drained or rinsed canned cannellini beans and ½ cup broth or water. Bring to a simmer and cook until the broccoli rabe is bright green and tender, 4–5 minutes. To make this dish a main dish, fold in very hot, well-drained, cooked bow tie pasta or elbow macaroni.

Escarole with Sun-Dried Tomatoes

Replace the spinach with 8 cups chopped escarole (about 1 head), and replace the pancetta with ¼ cup sun-dried tomatoes cut into thin strips. Gently sauté the tomatoes in 2 Tbsp olive oil before adding the onion. For a vegan dish, omit the Parmesan cheese.

rehydrating and plumping p. 182

Belgian Endive à la Meunière

4 heads Belgian endive

2 tsp sugar

Salt and freshly ground pepper

2 Tbsp fresh lemon juice
(divided use)

1 cup whole milk, or as needed

All-purpose flour for dredging

¼ cup vegetable oil

3 Tbsp unsalted butter

2 Tbsp minced fresh flat-leaf
parsley

Makes 4 servings

Split each endive in half lengthwise and remove any bruised or damaged outer leaves. Bring a large pot of water to a boil and season with the sugar, 1 tsp salt, and 1 tsp of the lemon juice. Add the endives and boil, covered, until tender, 3–4 minutes. Transfer to a colander and drain, cut side down. When just cool enough to handle, press and drain on absorbent towels.

Transfer the endives to a cutting board and flatten each piece slightly by pressing down on it with the palm of your hand. Season the endives with salt and pepper. Put the milk and flour in separate bowls. Dip each endive half in the milk and then dredge in the flour.

Heat the oil in a large skillet over medium-high heat. Add the endives, in batches if necessary, and fry on the first side until golden brown, 2–3 minutes. Turn and fry on the second side until crisp and brown, 2 minutes more. Transfer the endives to a serving dish and cover to keep warm.

Pour off any excess oil from the pan and wipe out the browned flour with a paper towel. Add the butter and cook over medium heat until the butter begins to brown and take on a nutty aroma, about 30 seconds. Add the remaining lemon juice and the parsley and swirl it until the mixture thickens slightly. Pour the pan sauce over the endives and serve immediately.

Belgian endives are deliberately protected from light as they grow to produce pale, satiny heads. Choose tight heads that show no scars or other blemishes. The leaves should be closed into a tight point and should have a pale ivory color, shading to a light yellowish green (or sometimes violet) at the tips.

pan-frying p. 34

boiling, parboiling, or blanching p. 37

Green Beans with Toasted Walnuts

¾ lb green beans

1 Tbsp olive oil

1 Tbsp minced shallot

1 clove garlic, minced

¼ cup chicken broth or water

Salt and freshly ground pepper

1 Tbsp walnut oil

1 Tbsp chopped toasted walnuts

2 tsp minced fresh chives

Makes 4 servings

Trim the ends from the green beans and cut them on the diagonal into 2-inch pieces.

Heat the olive oil in a large sauté pan over medium heat. Add the shallot and garlic and sauté until translucent, about 1 minute. Add the green beans and the broth and bring to a simmer.

Cover and pan-steam over low heat, stirring occasionally, until the beans are tender, 10–12 minutes. Remove from the heat and add 1 tsp salt, ¼ tsp pepper, the walnut oil, walnuts, and chives. Toss until well combined. Taste and season with salt and pepper. Serve at once.

Pressed walnut oil, available in specialty and gourmet shops, has a rich, nutty aroma and flavor. Too delicate for cooking, it is best put to use as a condiment or combined with milder olive or vegetable oils in salad dressings.

steaming p. 36

toasting nuts p. 26

Broccoli in Garlic Sauce

6 cups broccoli florets

3 Tbsp soy sauce

2 Tbsp Chinese rice wine or dry sherry wine

2 Tbsp rice vinegar

2 Tbsp chicken broth

1 Tbsp cornstarch

2 tsp chili paste

1 tsp sugar

2 Tbsp peanut oil

1 green onion, white and green parts, thinly sliced on the bias

1 Tbsp minced gingerroot

3 cloves garlic, minced

½ red bell pepper, julienned

Salt

4 cups steamed rice

Makes 4 servings

Bring a pot of water to a boil and blanch the broccoli for 2 minutes, until a vivid green but still firm. Drain. (If the broccoli is being cooked in advance, refresh it in ice water and drain again. Refrigerate until ready to stir-fry.)

Combine the soy sauce, wine, rice vinegar, broth, cornstarch, chili paste, and sugar in a small bowl. Set aside.

Heat the oil in a wok over medium-high heat. Add the green onion, ginger, and garlic and stir-fry until aromatic, about 1 minute. Raise the heat to high, add the bell pepper, and stir-fry for 1 minute more. Add the broccoli and stir-fry until all of the broccoli is hot, about 1 minute. Whisk the soy sauce mixture to recombine and add to the broccoli. Bring to a boil without stirring, about 30 seconds. Then stir just until the sauce coats the vegetables. Taste and season with salt, if necessary. Serve at once over the rice.

Blanching, or cooking briefly in boiling salted water, helps the broccoli hold its bright color. The precooking also ensures that it will cook through in the rapid final stir-fry.

boiling, parboiling, or blanching p. 37

julienne p. 17

Cheddar Corn Fritters

¾ cup all-purpose flour

2 tsp sugar

1–2 tsp chili powder (optional)

Salt and freshly ground pepper

3 ears corn or 2 cups corn kernels, plus corn milk if available

3 Tbsp diced red or green bell pepper (optional)

2 large eggs, lightly beaten

½ cup grated Cheddar

2 Tbsp unsalted butter, melted

Vegetable oil for pan-frying

Makes 6–8 servings

Stir together the flour, sugar, chili powder (if using), 1 tsp salt, and ¼ tsp pepper in a mixing bowl. Set aside.

Combine the corn and corn milk, if available, bell pepper (if using), eggs, ½ cup water, and the cheese in a bowl. Add to the flour mixture all at once. Stir just until the batter is evenly moistened. Stir in the melted butter.

Pour the oil into a large skillet to a depth of ¼ inch. Heat over medium heat until it registers 350°F on a deep-frying thermometer. Using a serving spoon and working in batches to avoid crowding, drop spoonfuls of batter into the hot oil to make 16 fritters in all. Pan-fry on the first side until golden brown and crisp, about 2 minutes. Turn once and fry until golden brown on the second side, 2 minutes more. Drain the fritters on absorbent towels and season with salt. Serve.

When fresh corn on the cob is available, cut the kernels from the ears of corn and then scrape the cobs with a table knife to release all the milk. Catch this milk in a bowl and add it to the batter. If needed, you can keep the first batches of fritters warm in a 200°F oven while you finish frying the rest.

pan-frying p. 34

preparing corn kernels p. 186

Vegetable Tempura

Dipping Sauce

2 green onions, minced

¼ cup soy sauce, plus as needed

2 Tbsp rice vinegar

2 Tbsp honey

1 Tbsp minced gingerroot

2 cloves garlic, minced

1 tsp dry mustard

1 tsp hot chili sauce, plus as needed

Batter

2 cups all-purpose flour

4 tsp baking powder

2 cups cold water

¼ cup dark sesame oil

1 cup red bell pepper strips

1 cup broccoli florets

1 cup quartered mushrooms

1 small zucchini, cut on the bias into ⅛-inch-thick pieces

Salt and freshly ground pepper

Vegetable oil for deep-frying

Makes 4–6 appetizer servings

For the dipping sauce, combine the green onions, soy sauce, ¼ cup water, the vinegar, honey, ginger, garlic, mustard, and hot sauce in a bowl. Cover and refrigerate to let the flavors blend for at least 1 hour or up to 12 hours. Taste and adjust the seasoning with soy sauce and hot sauce before serving.

For the batter, whisk together the flour and baking powder. Add the cold water and sesame oil all at once and whisk until about the thickness of pancake batter and very smooth. Refrigerate until ready to prepare the tempura.

Blot the vegetables dry, season with salt and pepper, and dip them in the batter to coat evenly.

Pour the oil into a tall pot to a depth of 5 inches. Heat over medium heat until the oil registers 350°F on a deep-frying thermometer. Working in batches to avoid crowding, slip the batter-coated vegetables into the hot oil. Deep-fry until the batter is golden brown and puffy, 3–4 minutes. Turn the vegetables if necessary to brown and cook evenly. Remove from the pot with tongs and drain briefly on absorbent towels.

Serve the vegetables at once, with the dipping sauce.

The popularity of these crisp, batter-dipped vegetables as an appetizer has spread beyond Japanese restaurants. Don't crowd the vegetables when frying, and be sure to let the oil come back up to the proper temperature before adding the next batch.

deep-frying p. 35

preparing ginger p. 181

Steamed Vegetable Medley

2 carrots, peeled and roll-cut into 1-inch pieces

1 cup small cauliflower florets

1 cup small broccoli florets

Salt and freshly ground pepper

1 Tbsp unsalted butter, softened

Makes 4 servings

Set a steamer basket in a pan with 1 inch of water (or over a pan if you are using a bamboo steamer). Bring the water to a boil over high heat and add the carrots to the steamer basket. Cover and steam for 3 minutes. Carefully remove the lid and add the cauliflower. Cover and steam for 2 minutes more. Remove the lid again and add the broccoli. Steam until all the vegetables are tender, about 4 minutes more. Taste and season with salt and pepper. Toss with the butter just before serving.

Wide, drum-shaped bamboo steamers, widely sold in kitchenware stores and Asian shops, are easy to use and steam a good quantity of vegetables at one time.

steaming p. 36

oblique or roll cut p. 17

Maple-Glazed Turnips

2 lb purple-top turnips

2 Tbsp unsalted butter
(divided use)

3 Tbsp maple syrup

¼ tsp ground cinnamon

1 pinch freshly grated nutmeg

Salt and freshly ground pepper

1 Tbsp chopped fresh flat-leaf
parsley

2 tsp fresh lemon juice

Makes 4 servings

Peel the turnips and cut into even 1-inch cubes.

Heat 1 Tbsp of the butter in a sauté pan over medium heat. Add the maple syrup, cinnamon, nutmeg, and salt and pepper to taste.

Add the turnips and then water to a depth of ¼ inch. Bring to a boil over high heat, reduce the heat to a simmer, cover, and pan-steam until the turnips are tender, 7–8 minutes.

Remove the cover from the pan and continue to cook the turnips until the water has cooked away and the syrup has glazed each piece evenly, about 3 minutes. Add the remaining 1 Tbsp butter to the pan with the parsley and lemon juice. Shake the pan until the butter is melted and the turnips are evenly coated. Taste and season with salt and pepper. Serve at once.

Pan-steaming, an excellent technique for cooking vegetables, uses a small amount of flavorful liquid in a covered pan. The quick cooking helps retain color, and the reduced liquid may be used to make a glaze or sauce.

zesting and juicing citrus p. 182

Zucchini with Tomatoes and Chorizo

1 large zucchini

1 Tbsp olive oil or vegetable oil

½ cup crumbled smoked
chorizo sausage

½ cup julienned red bell
pepper

2 Tbsp minced shallot

2 cloves garlic, finely minced

2 tomatoes, peeled, seeded,
and chopped, juices reserved

2 Tbsp minced fresh cilantro or
flat-leaf parsley

2 tsp fresh lemon juice

Grated zest of ½ lemon

Salt and freshly ground pepper

Makes 4 servings

Trim the ends of the zucchini and quarter lengthwise. Cut crosswise into ½-inch-thick slices and set aside.

Heat the oil in a skillet over medium heat. Add the chorizo and cook, stirring occasionally, until starting to brown and crisp, 2–3 minutes. Add the bell pepper, shallot, and garlic and cook, stirring occasionally, until softened, 2–3 minutes.

Add the zucchini with the tomatoes and their juices. (Add about 2 Tbsp water if the tomatoes are not juicy.) Cover and pan-steam over high heat until the zucchini are very tender, about 5 minutes.

Add the cilantro and lemon juice and zest and toss to blend evenly. Taste and season with salt and pepper. Serve at once.

Instead of zucchini, try other types of summer squash, such as yellow squash, flat oval sunburst or pattypan squash, or the delectable round, green *rond de Nice* squash. When choosing any summer squash, look for ones that are firm, slightly shiny, and smooth-skinned.

peeling and seeding tomatoes p. 184

julienne p. 17

Parsnip and Pear Purée

3 large parsnips

1 Bartlett pear

Salt and freshly ground pepper

¼ cup heavy cream, warmed

Makes 4 servings

Peel the parsnips and cut them into even 2-inch chunks. Peel the pear, halve it lengthwise, and scoop out the stem and core with a melon baller or spoon. Cut into even chunks.

Bring a large pot of salted water to a boil. Add the parsnips and cook for 12 minutes. Add the pear and cook until both the pear and the parsnips are soft enough to mash with a fork, about 10 minutes more. Drain well. Purée with an immersion blender or food mill or push through a sieve.

Add the warm cream to the parsnip and pear purée and stir until well combined. Taste and season with salt and pepper. Serve at once.

Parsnips and pears may seem an unlikely combination, but both are earthy and sweet. Try this dish with pork chops or roasted pork loin.

boiling and simmering p. 37

puréeing p. 47

French-Style Peas

8 pearl onions

4 Tbsp plus 1 tsp unsalted butter

2 cups fresh or thawed frozen peas

2 cups shredded Boston lettuce

½ cup chicken broth

Salt and freshly ground pepper

1 tsp all-purpose flour

Makes 4–6 servings

Bring a large pot of water to a boil. Add the pearl onions and blanch for 2 minutes. Scoop out the onions with a slotted spoon and rinse in cool water until cool enough to handle. Slip off the skins. Cut each onion in half (or quarters if they are more than 1 inch in diameter).

Heat the 4 Tbsp of butter in a saucepan over low heat and add the pearl onions. Cook, covered, until they are tender and translucent, about 4 minutes.

Add the peas, lettuce, broth, ½ tsp salt, and ¼ tsp pepper. Bring to a gentle simmer and re-cover the pan. Stew until the peas are fully cooked and tender, 3–4 minutes.

Mix together the remaining 1 tsp butter with the flour in a small dish to form a paste. Add to the pan and stir until the cooking liquid is lightly thickened. Taste and season with salt and pepper. Serve on warmed plates.

Stewing peas with pearl onions and fresh lettuce is a classic French preparation, making the most of the first offerings of the *potager*, or kitchen garden, in early spring. Here, the vegetable mixture is thickened with a *beurre manié*, a small knob of blended butter and flour.

boiling, parboiling, or blanching p. 37

thickening with roux and slurry p. 46

Ratatouille

2 Tbsp olive oil

3 cloves garlic, minced

2 yellow onions, diced

1 Tbsp tomato paste

¾ cup chicken broth

1 small globe eggplant, diced

1 zucchini, quartered lengthwise and sliced ½ inch thick

1 cup quartered mushrooms

1 green bell pepper, diced

2 tomatoes, peeled, seeded, and chopped

¼ cup chopped fresh flat-leaf parsley and basil

Salt and freshly ground pepper

Makes 4–6 servings

Heat the oil in a sauté pan over medium heat. Add the garlic and sauté until aromatic, about 1 minute. Add the onions and sauté until translucent, 4–5 minutes.

Add the tomato paste and cook over medium heat until it deepens in color and gives off a sweet aroma, about 1 minute. Add the broth and stir to deglaze the pan, scraping up any browned bits from the pan bottom.

Add the eggplant, zucchini, mushrooms, and bell pepper and simmer until the vegetables are tender but not falling apart, 10–12 minutes.

Stir in the tomatoes and continue to simmer until the tomatoes are heated through, 2–3 minutes. Add the herbs. Taste and season with salt and pepper, then serve.

This classic Provençal dish hails from the south of France, where it makes the most of the Mediterranean bounty of late summer. On a hot day, it can be served cool for a light supper or lunch dish.

peeling and seeding tomatoes p. 184

cleaning mushrooms p. 186

preparing bell peppers and chiles p. 183

Braised Red Cabbage

2 Tbsp vegetable oil

1 yellow onion, halved and thinly sliced

1 small head red cabbage, shredded

1 tart green apple, peeled, cored, and thinly sliced

1½ cups chicken broth

2 Tbsp red wine vinegar

1 cinnamon stick

1 pinch ground cloves

2 tsp sugar

Salt and freshly ground pepper

2 Tbsp currant jelly

1 tsp lemon juice, or to taste

Makes 6–8 servings

Heat the oil in a Dutch oven over medium-low heat. Add the onion and sauté until translucent, 6–8 minutes.

Stir in the cabbage and cook until limp, 3 minutes. Add the apple, broth, vinegar, cinnamon, cloves, sugar, 2 tsp salt, and pepper to taste. Raise the heat to high and bring to a boil.

Cover the pan, reduce the heat to low, and braise, stirring occasionally, until the cabbage is tender, about 30 minutes.

Remove from the heat and stir in the jelly and lemon juice. Taste and season with salt, pepper, and lemon juice. Remove the cinnamon stick before serving.

This German-inspired dish mixes sweet and tart to create a fine side dish for chops or game. While red cabbage is traditional (the acid of the vinegar helps set the bright magenta color), you can also use green cabbage or a crinkly-leaved savoy cabbage.

braising and stewing p. 40

shredding and chiffonade p. 17

Fennel and Orange Salad

2 fennel bulbs, trimmed and cored

2 oranges

1 Tbsp fresh lemon juice

2 Tbsp olive oil

1 Tbsp extra-virgin olive oil

Salt and freshly ground pepper

½ cup chopped fresh flat-leaf parsley

Makes 6 servings

Thinly slice the fennel bulbs with a sharp knife or a mandoline. Cut the skin from the oranges and cut the oranges into crosswise slices.

Whisk the lemon juice, olive oils, and salt and pepper to taste to make a vinaigrette. Reserve 2 Tbsp of the parsley for garnish. Put the fennel and remaining parsley in a bowl and toss with 3 Tbsp of the vinaigrette.

Season the orange slices with salt and pepper. Drizzle them with the remaining vinaigrette. Arrange the fennel and orange slices on chilled plates and garnish with the reserved parsley.

When you buy fennel, look for firm bulbs with no scarring or gouges. The tops should be firm with feathery green fronds. Trim away the tops at the top of the bulb. Cut through the bulb from the top through the root end to make halves or quarters. Slice the fennel thinly across the grain.

making vinaigrette p. 250

Corn and Jícama Salad

2 cups fresh or thawed frozen corn kernels, plus corn milk if available (p. 192)

2 cups finely diced jícama

1 Tbsp fresh lime juice

1 Tbsp minced fresh cilantro

¼ tsp ground cayenne pepper, or to taste

Salt and freshly ground black pepper

Makes 6–8 servings

Toss together the corn and corn milk, if available, jícama, lime juice, and cilantro in a serving bowl. Taste and season with cayenne, salt, and black pepper.

Refrigerate for at least 2 hours or up to 12 hours before serving.

Jícama, a tropical tuber, is roughly the size of a grapefruit, with a dusty brown skin. Inside, its flesh is crisp and white, with a mild flavor that marries well with the sweet corn and cilantro in this refreshing summer salad.

preparing corn kernels p. 186

dicing p. 17

Potatoes, Grains, and Legumes

The 1960s were a time of experimentation and rebellion. Not all of it happened during love-ins and marches on Washington, though; a major revolution began in the kitchen. We are indebted to that decade for ushering in flavorful, colorful dishes based on potatoes, grains, and legumes. Intrepid culinary adventurers of the era drew their inspiration from traditional ethnic cuisines, which often combine grains and beans to provide good-quality protein without the use of meat at every meal. At a time when parents worried that their children would succumb to malnutrition unless they ate plenty of meat, forward-looking chefs and home cooks of the 1960s realized that dishes based on potatoes, grains, and legumes are delicious and inexpensive, and can be a wholesome part of any diet.

Potatoes

Cuisines around the globe long ago embraced one of the New World's true culinary treasures, the potato. But its acceptance was not immediate, for two reasons. First, the earliest potatoes, dug in the high mountains of South America, were lumpy, bitter, watery tubers; and second, they belonged to the nightshade family, which also includes poisonous belladonna. But with improved breeding and selection—and the realization that not all members of that notorious plant family carry toxins—resistance melted away, and the unassuming potato joined other starches in kitchens across Europe and Asia. A full repertoire of potato dishes, from simply steamed or boiled new potatoes to more elaborate preparations like scalloped potatoes or French fries, soon developed.

The potato is one of nearly every kitchen's most versatile foods. It has complex carbohydrates, good proteins, and plenty of vitamins (including vitamin C), minerals, and fiber. Potatoes are also generally good keepers: with a little care, they can be held in storage for at least 2 weeks and usually longer. New potatoes are the exception; because of their tender, thin skins, they should be used within days of purchase.

Types of potato

The russet (or baking) potato and fingerling varieties are low-moisture, high-starch potatoes. They are good for baking and puréeing as well as good for frying because their low moisture content makes them less likely to cause oil to splatter. Their tendency to absorb moisture makes them a good choice for scalloped potatoes or other cream- or sauce-based dishes.

Moderate-moisture and -starch potatoes, commonly known as waxy potatoes, include all-purpose potatoes, red-skinned potatoes, and yellow-fleshed varieties such as Yellow Finn and Yukon gold. They hold their shape even after they are cooked through, making them a good choice for boiling, steaming, sautéing, roasting, braising, and making potato salads and soups.

High-moisture, low-starch potatoes include new potatoes (harvested when they measure less than 1½ inches in diameter) and some fingerling potatoes. New potatoes have tender skins that do not need to be peeled before cooking or eating. The naturally sweet, fresh flavor of potatoes in this category is best showcased by simple cooking techniques such as boiling, steaming, or oven-roasting with herbs.

Sweet potatoes have mellow gold or bright orange flesh. (What some Americans call yams are actually a variety of sweet potato and not a true yam.) The color advertises the tuber's significant quantities of beta carotene, a substance our bodies use to produce the vitamin A that we need. And, despite the name, sweet potatoes are not significantly higher in calories than white potatoes.

Selecting potatoes

Select potatoes that are firm and heavy for their size. The skin should be taut and dry. Green spots on the skin indicate the presence of an unpleasant (and mildly toxic) compound. Once you get them home, store them in a cool, dry area in a container that allows air to circulate. As potatoes age, they soften and wrinkle and the "eyes" may sprout. Discard potatoes that reach this state.

Preparing potatoes

The potato has a sweet, earthy flavor that requires very little adornment. But should you choose to gild the lily, the sky is the limit. Scalloped and whipped potatoes marry the potato with cream and butter for a suave texture. Fried potatoes develop a crunchy brown exterior and a moist interior when they come in contact with sizzling hot oil. A honey glaze brings out the natural flavor of sweet potatoes.

Grains and legumes

Grains and dried legumes—beans, lentils, and peas—are staple foods used throughout the world as the nutritious foundation of many meals. Most have relatively subtle flavors, making them eminently useful as palate cleansers and heat tamers. Since they carry other flavors well, they are often paired with small amounts of intensely flavored foods to bring them into balance. They absorb flavors as they cook, responding well to an array of aromatics and seasonings, and they reward you with soothing, soul-satisfying sustenance.

Selecting grains

Since we Americans opened up the global cupboard in our kitchens, boxes of converted rice have been joined by a rainbow of other rices—starchy round-grained Arborio for risottos; long-grain and fragrant rices such as basmati, jasmine, popcorn, and pecan rice for steaming or for pilafs; black rice, brown rice, red rice, and wild rice to add a robust flavor and color. But rice isn't the only grain that's available to us. Pearl barley, cracked wheat and bulgur, kasha, quinoa, millet, and teff are turning up on menus and supermarket shelves. One of the best ways to make an ethnic meal taste authentic is to include the appropriate grains. Even if you typically stick to one cooking style, substituting other grains for rice adds new flavors, textures, and colors to your meals.

When purchasing grains, look for stores with a good turnover of inventory, especially if you prefer to purchase in small quantities from bulk bins. Grains do have a long shelf life, but the older they are, the longer they take to cook and the more liquid they may require. And, as they age, their flavor can turn musty and stale. Keep whole grains in the refrigerator or freezer if you won't be using them within a few weeks of purchase, or their natural oils may become rancid.

Preparing grains

Grains have a substance and a subtle flavor that make them excellent accompaniments to a wide variety of foods. They can stand on their own, or they can readily adapt to a supporting role, carrying the flavors of other ingredients. Most grains cook quickly, few requiring more than 30 minutes. Some, notably bulgur, cook in 10 minutes or less. Consult the chart on page 204 for more information.

Selecting legumes

At one time, dried beans, lentils, and peas had all but disappeared from many kitchens across our nation—with the exception of the baked beans that almost invariably accompanied a baked ham supper or hamburgers and hot dogs at summer barbecues. When Tex-Mex and Southwestern cooking became popular, beans came back into their own. But these aren't the only cooking styles that employ a variety of

dried beans and peas. Any country or region with a rich peasant tradition has one or two bean dishes on its dinner table.

As with grains, choose dried legumes from a store with high turnover. Beans, lentils, and dried peas can be stored in plastic bags or other airtight storage containers for a few months and don't require refrigeration.

Preparing legumes

Although it is certainly fine to substitute one bean for another in many recipes, there is a noticeable difference in taste between favas and limas, black beans and kidney beans, and navy beans and black-eyed peas. Different types of beans require different cooking times. Lentils and split peas cook in about 30–45 minutes. Garbanzo beans (chickpeas) and lima beans can take up to 2 hours. Consult the chart on page 204 for more information. If time is short, use canned beans instead of cooking dried beans from scratch. Drain the beans and rinse them to remove the flavor of the canning liquid. This will also help reduce the sodium level, allowing you to season the dish to suit your own taste.

When you are planning a meal, use the recipes in this chapter as the main course, as an accompaniment to a meat or vegetable dish, or as a starter course for a more elegant meal. In addition to such favorite dishes as pilafs and risottos, grains and legumes are featured in salads, fritters, and pancakes. There is something honest and sustaining about these foods. Preparing them with care and attention is an excellent way to get back to basics in the kitchen.

Cooking grains and beans

TYPE OF GRAIN OR LEGUME	BASIC FORMULA FOR 4 SERVINGS	DESCRIPTION	COOKING TIME
Barley, pearl	1 cup grain + 2 cups liquid	Tender but still chewy, nutty taste	35–45 minutes
Kasha	1 cup grain + 2 cups liquid	Fluffy, chewy, and relatively dry	50–60 minutes
Quinoa	1 cup grain (rinsed thoroughly) + 2 cups liquid	Fluffy, round grain, delicate flavor	15 minutes
Rice, basmati	1¼ cups grain + 2 cups liquid	Long grains, not sticky, and slightly firm to the bite	25 minutes
Rice, long-grain, brown	1 cup grain + 3 cups liquid	Robust, chewy texture, pronounced flavor	40 minutes
Rice, long-grain, white	1¼ cups grain + 2 cups liquid	Long grains, not sticky, and firm to the bite	18–20 minutes
Rice, short-grain, brown	1 cup grain + 2½ cups liquid	Round, starchy grain, sticky consistency	35–40 minutes
Rice, short-grain, white	1¼ cups grain + 2 cups liquid	Round, starchy grain, sticky consistency	20–30 minutes
Rice, wild	1 cup grain + 3 cups liquid	Long grains, exterior just opening to expose grain	30–40 minutes
Black beans	1 cup beans soaked 4 hours and cooked in liquid to cover	Black throughout with creamy texture, skins soft enough to eat	1½–2 hours
Black-eyed peas	1 cup beans cooked in liquid to cover (no soaking required)	Tan with black spot, tender to the bite	1 hour
Garbanzo beans (chickpeas)	1 cup beans soaked 4 hours and cooked in liquid to cover	Light brown to yellow, tough skins rub away easily	2–2½ hours
Fava beans	1 cup beans soaked 12 hours and cooked in liquid to cover	Light brown to yellow, tough skins rub away easily	3–3½ hours
Great Northern (navy and cannellini)	1 cup beans soaked 4 hours and cooked in liquid to cover	Light beige, tender throughout, skins soft enough to eat	1½ hours
Kidney beans, red and white	1 cup beans soaked 4 hours and cooked in liquid to cover	Buff or deep maroon throughout with creamy texture, skins soft enough to eat	1 hour
Lentils	1 cup lentils cooked in liquid to cover (no soaking required)	Tender but still maintains shape	30–40 minutes
Lima beans	1 cup beans soaked 4 hours and cooked in liquid to cover	Light green, tough skins rub away easily	1–1½ hours

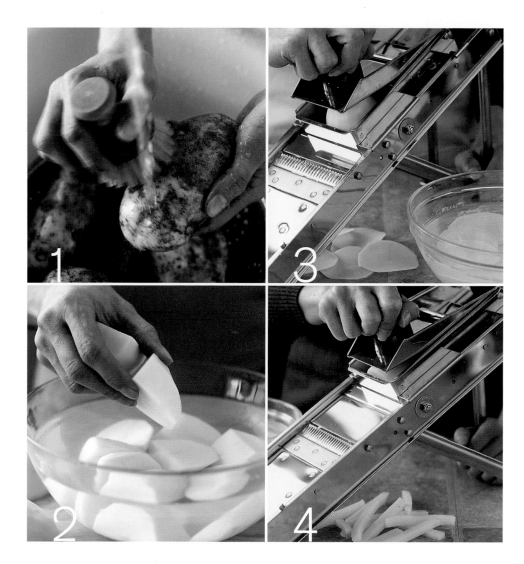

Preparing potatoes

Potatoes vary in size, color, and starch content, but their basic preparation is the same.

1 Scrubbing

With a stiff-bristled brush, scrub the potatoes well under running water. If needed, peel them, removing as thin a layer of the peel as possible. Tender-skinned ones, such as fingerlings or new potatoes, are best prepared unpeeled. A green tint on the skin of the potato indicates that it has been exposed to light long enough to produce a toxin called solanine, which is harmful when eaten in large quantities. Trim away completely any green areas, removing at least ¼ inch of the potato beneath the peel. If the eyes of a potato have sprouted, discard the potato.

2 Preventing discoloring

Raw potatoes will discolor after they are peeled, first turning light pink and, eventually, dark gray or black. To prevent this, submerge peeled or cut potatoes in cold water until time to cook. Avoid soaking the potatoes for extended periods of time, however, as they will become waterlogged and lose more nutrients. When possible, use the soaking water to cook the potatoes so any nutrients leached into it are retained. Extended soaking will also decrease the amount of starch in potatoes. Before roasting potatoes, dry them well with a clean cloth. If they go into the oven wet, they will stick to the pan and lose their crisp outer layers.

3 Making thin slices

To make potato chips or scalloped potatoes with ease, use a mandoline or slicer. For potato chips, adjust the slicing blade of the mandoline to about ¹⁄₁₆ inch. Have ready a bowl of cold water for holding the slices. Cut the potatoes in half crosswise, placing them cut side down on the work surface to prevent discoloration. Stand the mandoline firmly on its support legs, locking them fully open, or hold it securely at an angle to the work surface. Using the hand guard and positioning the potatoes cut side down, slice them with slow, smooth passes. For scalloped potatoes, widen the slice to ⅛–⅜ inch.

4 Making French fries

To make French fries using a mandoline, lock the ⅜-inch julienne blade into place. Cut a potato in half lengthwise and place it in the hand guard with its cut side facing down toward the blades. Press down evenly to cut long, thin pieces. Transfer the cut potatoes to a bowl of water to prevent discoloration.

Cooking rice and pilaf

Simple steamed rice and versatile pilaf can accompany a range of main dishes.

Steaming rice

In a heavy saucepan, combine the rice and water. Bring to a boil, then reduce the heat to medium and simmer the rice, uncovered, until most of the water has been absorbed. Cover the pan tightly, reduce the heat to low, and continue cooking the rice for 15–20 minutes. Do not lift the cover during this period of steaming. Remove the pan from the heat and let stand, still covered, for 10 minutes. Fluff the rice with a fork before serving.

Cooking pilaf

Pilaf may be made of rice or other grains such as barley or bulgur. Heat oil in a large, heavy, ovenproof pan. If the recipe calls for aromatics such as minced onion, cook until translucent before adding the grain. Stir in the grain and sauté, stirring frequently, until coated with oil and heated through. Carefully pour in hot broth and bring to a simmer, stirring the grains once or twice to prevent them from sticking to the bottom of the pan. Once the liquid is simmering and you've added any seasonings, cover the pot and finish cooking the pilaf either over very low heat or in a moderate oven. Cook until the grains are tender but still slightly firm. Remove pilafs from the heat and let rest, still covered, for about 5 minutes. Use a fork to gently separate and fluff the grains.

Preparing cereals and meals

Oatmeal, polenta, grits, and farina are all prepared by simmering and stirring cereal grains and meals.

Adding the cereal to the liquid

Cereals and meals can be cooked in water, broth, or milk. Bring the liquid up to a full boil, along with any desired seasonings or aromatics. Use one hand to add the measured cereal a little at a time or pour it slowly and gradually into the simmering liquid. Whisk or stir constantly with the other hand as you add the cereal to keep it from clumping together.

Simmering the cereal

Once you have added all the cereal, continue to cook over medium to low heat, stirring often. The more you stir, the creamier the finished dish will be. While it cooks, the cereal thickens and craterlike bubbles break the surface. When they are fully cooked, some cereals start to pull away from the sides of the pot as you stir. Serve soft and smooth directly from the pot.

Preparing legumes

Some chefs believe that soaking dried beans and other legumes before cooking gives a better texture.

Sorting and rinsing the legumes

Pour the legumes onto a baking sheet and, working methodically from one end to the other, carefully sort through them, removing discolored or misshapen pieces. Submerge in cold water, removing and discarding any that float to the surface. Drain the legumes and rinse them well with running water.

Soaking the legumes

Place the sorted and rinsed legumes in a container and add enough cool water to cover them by a few inches, about 4 times the volume of water to beans. Let the legumes soak in the refrigerator for at least 4 hours or up to overnight. For a quicker soak, place the sorted legumes in a pot and add enough water to cover by a few inches. Bring the water to a simmer. Remove the pot from the heat, cover, and let steep for 1 hour.

Cooking the legumes

Drain the soaked legumes, put in a large pot, and add enough water to cover the beans by about 2 inches. Bring the liquid to a full boil, then reduce the heat to maintain a simmer. Stir the beans occasionally as they cook and add more liquid if the level starts to drop. Most recipes tell you when to add various seasonings and flavorings, but the general rule is to add salt and any other acidic flavoring ingredients, such as tomatoes, vinegar, or citrus juices, only after the beans are nearly tender, to give them a smooth consistency.

Whipped Potatoes

2 lb russet potatoes, peeled and cut into large pieces

Salt and freshly ground pepper

2 Tbsp unsalted butter, softened

¼ cup whole milk, warmed

Makes 6 servings

Place the potatoes in a pot with cold water to cover by 2 inches. Salt the water. Gradually bring the water to a simmer over medium heat. Cover and simmer until the potatoes are easily pierced with a fork, 10–12 minutes. Drain and return them to the pan over low heat until no more steam rises from them. While still hot, purée the potatoes with a food mill or potato ricer into a heated bowl.

Add the butter and mix into the potatoes by hand or with the whip attachment of an electric mixer just until incorporated. Add the warm milk and stir to combine. Taste and season with salt and pepper. Whip the potatoes on medium speed until smooth and light. Serve at once.

You can make this classic comfort dish as rustic or as elegant as you like. For a home-style touch, use an old-fashioned potato masher to smash the potatoes, leaving some texture in the dish. Use a food mill or a potato ricer to purée the potatoes and give the dish a lighter-than-air texture.

preparing potatoes
p. 205

puréeing p. 47

VARIATIONS

Buttermilk Whipped Potatoes

Replace the milk with buttermilk. Add 1–2 Tbsp minced fresh chives along with the salt and pepper.

Roasted Garlic Whipped Potatoes

Roast 5 or 6 garlic cloves in a small baking dish in a 350°F oven until the flesh is soft and deep brown, about 20 minutes. Squeeze the garlic from the skin and mash with a fork to make a paste. Purée along with the potatoes and blend well to distribute the garlic evenly.

Whipped Sweet Potatoes

Replace the russet potatoes with sweet potatoes. Use the cooking liquid to replace half of the milk when whipping the purée. Season with ¼ tsp cinnamon, a few grains of nutmeg, and a few drops of fresh lemon juice.

Boiled New Potatoes with Fines Herbes

2 lb new or small potatoes, scrubbed and peeled if desired

3 Tbsp unsalted butter

3 Tbsp *fines herbes:* a mixture of chopped fresh flat-leaf parsley, tarragon, chives, and chervil

Salt and freshly ground pepper

Makes 6 servings

Cut the potatoes if necessary to make them even in size.

Place the potatoes in a pot with cold water to cover by 2 inches. Salt the water. Gradually bring the water to a simmer over medium heat. Cover and simmer until the potatoes are easily pierced with a fork, 10–12 minutes.

Drain the potatoes. Return them to the pot and let them dry briefly over very low heat until no more steam rises from the potatoes.

Melt the butter in a sauté pan over medium heat. Add the potatoes, rolling and tossing to coat them evenly with butter, and heat them through.

Add the *fines herbes* and season with salt and pepper. Toss the potatoes to distribute the seasonings. Serve immediately.

While the term "new potato" is often used to refer to any small red or white potato, a true new potato is a young potato, harvested while its skin is still thin and tender. You can find new potatoes in farmers' markets in early summer, or you can substitute any evenly sized, small boiling potatoes, such as Red Bliss.

preparing potatoes
p. 205

boiling and simmering
p. 37

French-Fried Potatoes

1½ lb russet potatoes

2½ cups vegetable oil

Salt

Makes 4 servings

Peel the potatoes and cut into ⅜-inch-thick matchsticks. Rinse, drain, and dry thoroughly. (Alternatively, the potatoes may be held in cold water until ready to cook. Remember to dry them thoroughly before cooking.)

Put the potatoes in a large cast-iron skillet or a 14-inch wok, preferably one with a handle. Add the oil and turn the heat to medium. Cook for 25 minutes, gently jiggling the pan from time to time. Do not stir, to avoid breaking the fries.

Turn the heat to high and cook the fries, stirring occasionally, until golden brown, 10–15 minutes. Transfer to paper towels to drain. Taste, season with salt, and serve immediately.

The technique used in this recipe differs from the classic restaurant approach to making French fries. The potatoes heat along with the oil. When the oil eventually reaches 350°F, the potatoes will start browning. Taking this virtually fool-proof approach means you don't need to use a deep-fat thermometer to maintain the perfect oil temperature.

making French fries
p. 205

deep-frying p. 35

Sweet Potato Chips

1 lb sweet potatoes, peeled

2½ cups vegetable oil

Salt

1 lime, cut into quarters

Makes 4 servings

Using a slicer or mandoline, slice the potatoes as thinly as possible.

Heat the oil in a deep pot or a 14-inch wok over high heat. The oil is ready when one of the potato slices slipped into it browns in 30 seconds.

Carefully add half of the potatoes to the oil. Fry, stirring frequently, until the potato chips are just starting to become crisp and turn a darker orange, 8–11 minutes. The timing will depend on the moisture level of the potatoes. Immediately remove the chips with a slotted spoon and transfer to paper towels to drain. Repeat to fry the rest of the potato slices.

Season with salt. Serve hot or at room temperature, accompanied with the lime wedges.

These deep-orange chips make a nice change from the usual potato chips. If you like spice, try adding a light dust of chili powder or cayenne pepper along with the salt.

preparing potatoes p. 205

deep-frying p. 35

Potatoes au Gratin

1 Tbsp unsalted butter

1½ lb red or Yukon gold potatoes

1 clove garlic, minced

Salt and freshly ground white pepper

1½ cups heavy cream, or as needed

Makes 6 servings

Preheat the oven to 325°F. Grease an 8 x 8–inch baking pan with the butter.

Peel the potatoes and use a slicer or mandoline to cut them into ¹⁄₁₆-inch-thick slices. Scatter the garlic in the prepared pan, then layer the potatoes, seasoning each layer with salt and pepper and drizzling with cream. Pour the last of the cream over the top and press into an even layer so that the cream just covers the top of the potatoes.

Cover with aluminum foil and bake for 45 minutes. Remove the foil. With the back of a large spoon, press on the potatoes to bring any juices and cream to the top. Bake, uncovered, until the potatoes are lightly browned on top and tender when pierced with a fork, 20–25 minutes more.

Dishes prepared "au gratin" are casseroles given a bubbly, golden-brown top in the oven or under the broiler. Slow baking helps the potatoes thoroughly absorb the cream.

preparing potatoes p. 205

roasting and baking p. 30

Potato Pancakes

3 all-purpose or yellow or white waxy potatoes (1½–2 lb)

½ yellow onion

2 tsp fresh lemon juice

1 large egg, lightly beaten

3 Tbsp all-purpose flour

1–2 Tbsp matzo meal

Salt and freshly ground pepper

Vegetable oil for pan-frying

Makes 14 pancakes; 4–6 servings

Scrub and peel the potatoes. Shred the potatoes and onion with a box grater into a bowl. Sprinkle with the lemon juice and toss to coat evenly.

Wring the grated potatoes and onion in cheesecloth or a flat-weave kitchen towel to remove excess moisture. You should have about 3 cups grated potato and onion. Transfer to a bowl and stir in the egg, flour, matzo meal, 1 tsp salt, and ½ tsp pepper.

Preheat the oven to 250°F. Pour the oil into a cast-iron skillet to a depth of ¼ inch and heat over medium heat until the oil shimmers.

Working in batches without crowding, drop the potato batter by mounded serving spoonfuls into the hot oil and flatten with the back of the spoon. Brown the pancakes on the first side, about 2 minutes. Turn them once and brown them on the second side, 2–3 minutes more. Remove with a slotted spoon and transfer to a baking sheet lines with paper towels to drain. Keep the pancakes warm in the oven while frying the remainder of the batter. Serve, very hot, as soon as possible.

Getting the liquid out of the grated potatoes is the secret to frying up a crisp, lacy potato pancake, so be sure to wring them thoroughly. Serve as an accompaniment to grilled or broiled meat, with sour cream and applesauce, or make smaller pancakes and serve as an elegant appetizer with caviar and crème fraîche.

pan-frying p. 34

preparing potatoes p. 205

Glazed Sweet Potatoes

3 sweet potatoes (about 2 lb)

3 cups finely diced fresh pineapple

1 cup sugar

4 Tbsp unsalted butter

1 Tbsp fresh lemon juice, or to taste

1 tsp ground cinnamon

Salt and freshly ground pepper

Makes 6–8 servings

Preheat the oven to 375°F. Blot the potatoes dry and pierce each in 2 or 3 places with the tip of a knife. Arrange in a single layer on a sheet pan. Bake the potatoes until very tender and cooked through, 30–40 minutes.

Meanwhile, combine the pineapple, sugar, butter, lemon juice, cinnamon, and salt and pepper to taste in a saucepan and bring to a simmer over medium heat. Continue to cook until slightly thickened, about 3 minutes. Set aside and cover to keep warm.

When the potatoes are ready, remove them from the oven. Reduce the oven temperature to 350°F. As soon as the potatoes are cool enough to handle, peel and cut them into slices or large chunks. Arrange the sweet potatoes in a 9 x 13–inch baking dish. Pour the glaze over them and bake until very hot, about 10 minutes.

You can use either pale gold or orange sweet potatoes in this dish. Orange-fleshed sweet potatoes tend to be more flavorful and a little moister than gold-fleshed ones, but when prepared this way, the differences are very slight.

preparing potatoes p. 205

roasting and baking p. 30

Herbed Pilaf

1 poblano chile, seeded and coarsely chopped

¼ cup chopped fresh basil

¼ cup chopped fresh mint

¼ cup chopped fresh oregano

2 tsp vegetable oil

1 Tbsp minced shallot or yellow onion

¾ cup long-grain white rice

Salt and freshly ground pepper

Makes 4 servings

Preheat the oven to 350°F.

In a small bowl, combine the chile, basil, mint, and oregano with 1½ cups water. Set aside.

Heat the oil in an ovenproof saucepan over medium heat and sauté the shallot until translucent, 5–6 minutes.

Add the rice and sauté until coated with oil and heated through, about 1 minute. Some of the rice may jump or pop. Add the herb mixture. Bring to a simmer, stirring the rice once or twice to prevent it from clumping together or sticking to the bottom of the pan.

Add ½ tsp salt and pepper to taste. Cover the pan and place it in the oven. Cook until the grains are tender to the bite, 12–14 minutes. Remove from the heat and let stand, covered, for 5 minutes to steam. Uncover and, using a fork, separate the grains and release the steam.

Taste and season with salt and pepper and serve the pilaf at once.

Originally from the Middle East, pilaf (also called *pilau*, *pullao*, *pilaw*, or *pilav*), is made from rice that's briefly sautéed in fat, then simmered with broth and seasonings, either over direct heat or in the oven. The initial sautéing gives the grains a nutty flavor and a firmer texture.

cooking rice and pilaf p. 206

making broth p. 45

VARIATIONS

Cilantro-Lime Pilaf

Omit the chile and herbs. Use 1½ cups chicken broth in place of the water. With a fork, gently fold 3 Tbsp minced fresh cilantro, 2 tsp fresh lime juice, and 1 tsp grated lime zest into the rice along with the salt and pepper. Proceed as directed above.

Middle Eastern Pilaf

Omit the chile and herbs. Use 1½ cups chicken broth in place of the water. Replace ¼ cup of the rice with orzo. Add it to the rice as it sautés, along with ½ tsp cinnamon and ½ tsp ground cumin. Increase the cooking time to 20–25 minutes. Gently fold 2 Tbsp toasted pine nuts into the rice with a fork as you adjust the seasoning with salt and pepper. Proceed as directed above.

toasting nuts p. 26

Curried Rice Salad

One 14-oz can coconut milk

1 cup long-grain white rice

¼ cup golden raisins

¾ cup olive oil (divided use)

2 Tbsp minced gingerroot

1 Tbsp curry powder, or to taste

1 small shallot, minced

1 Tbsp minced lemongrass

2 cloves garlic, minced

2 Tbsp cider vinegar

2 Tbsp fresh lemon juice

2 Tbsp honey

2 Tbsp chopped fresh mint, plus
1 Tbsp minced

Salt and freshly ground pepper

½ cup cooked peas

1 small Granny Smith apple,
peeled, cored, and diced

½ cup sliced green onion

½ cup toasted pumpkin seeds
or sliced almonds

Makes 6–8 servings

Bring the coconut milk and ¼ cup water to a boil in a medium saucepan. Add the rice, cover, reduce the heat to low, and simmer slowly until the liquid is absorbed, about 20 minutes. Remove from the heat and let cool.

Combine the raisins with ½ cup water and warm in a microwave oven for 40 seconds at full power. Or, combine in a small saucepan and warm over low heat. Allow the raisins to plump for about 10 minutes. Drain.

Meanwhile, to make a dressing, gently heat ¼ cup of the oil in a saucepan or sauté pan over low heat. Add the ginger, curry powder, shallot, lemongrass, and garlic. Sauté, stirring constantly, until very fragrant, about 30 seconds. Immediately remove from the heat and let cool. Combine the cooled oil and aromatics with the remaining ½ cup oil and the vinegar. Add the lemon juice, honey, minced mint, and salt and pepper to taste. Blend well.

Combine the cooled rice, peas, apple, green onion, pumpkin seeds, raisins, and chopped mint in a serving bowl. Toss lightly with the vinaigrette, adding just enough at first to moisten the rice (about ¾ cup), then more to taste. Taste and season with salt and pepper, plus additional curry powder, if desired. Serve at once.

Coconut milk adds a special creamy richness to the rice in this Asian-inspired salad. Look for cans of unsweetened coconut milk in the Asian foods section of the supermarket (check the ingredients list to make sure it's not the sweetened or flavored cream used for cocktails). When you open the can, don't worry if it has separated into a watery liquid and a white solid; it will melt back together as the rice cooks.

preparing ginger p. 181

toasting nuts p. 26

Bulgur with Dried Cherries and Apples

2 cups vegetable or chicken
broth or water

¾ cup bulgur

2 Tbsp coarsely chopped dried
cherries, plumped

2 Tbsp coarsely chopped dried
apples, plumped

½ tsp salt

Makes 4–6 servings

Bring the broth to a boil in a saucepan over high heat.

Add the bulgur in a stream, pouring it gradually into the broth, and stir well with a fork to remove any lumps. Reduce the heat to low and simmer until the grain has absorbed all the broth, about 15 minutes. Remove the pan from the heat.

Add the cherries, apples, and salt to the pan and fold in gently using a fork. Cover the pan and allow it to steam for about 10 minutes before serving, to allow the cereal to absorb the flavors of the fruit.

Combining grains with dried fruits gives a dish a sweet-tart flavor, making it a good candidate to pair with rich roasted meats or poultry such as pork or duck. This dish could also be served as a hot breakfast cereal, sprinkled with a little cinnamon sugar and drizzled with warmed milk.

**rehydrating and
plumping** p. 182

Quinoa Pilaf with Red and Yellow Bell Peppers

2 tsp vegetable oil

1 Tbsp minced shallot

1 clove garlic, minced

2 cups chicken broth

⅔ cup quinoa, rinsed in several changes of cool water

1 small bay leaf

1 sprig fresh thyme or ½ tsp dried

Salt and freshly ground pepper

½ cup diced roasted red bell pepper

½ cup diced roasted yellow bell pepper

Makes 6 servings

Heat the oil in a saucepan over medium heat. Add the shallot and garlic and sauté until aromatic and tender, 2–3 minutes.

Add the broth, quinoa, bay leaf, thyme, and ¼ tsp salt. Stir well with a fork, and bring the broth to a simmer over medium heat. Reduce the heat to low.

Cover the pot and simmer the quinoa over low heat (or in a 325°F oven) until tender and very fluffy, about 15 minutes.

Remove and discard the bay leaf and thyme sprig. Fluff the grains with a fork to break up any clumps, and fold in the bell peppers.

Taste and season with salt and pepper. Serve at once.

Quinoa (pronounced "KEEN wah") is one of the more ancient grains grown in the New World. When properly cooked, quinoa is a light, fluffy grain with a subtle flavor. Any leftovers could be combined with diced vegetables such as cucumbers, carrots, celery, avocado, and tomato and then dressed with a vinaigrette.

cooking pilaf p. 206

preparing bell peppers and chiles p. 183

Kasha with Spicy Maple Pecans

1 large egg white, lightly beaten

¾ cup kasha

1½ cups chicken broth or water

1 tsp unsalted butter

¼ tsp salt

¼ cup chopped toasted pecans

2 Tbsp maple syrup

1 pinch ground cayenne pepper

Makes 6 servings

Combine the egg white and kasha in a saucepan and cook over low heat, stirring constantly, until the kasha is evenly coated and the egg white is dry, about 2 minutes.

Add the broth, butter, and salt to the kasha and bring to a boil over high heat. Reduce the heat to low and simmer, covered, until the liquid is absorbed, about 15 minutes.

Remove from the heat, keep covered, and allow the kasha to steam for about 5 minutes.

While the kasha steams, put the pecans, maple syrup, and cayenne in a small skillet. Cook over low heat, stirring, until the pecans are well coated and the maple syrup has reduced to a very thick consistency, about 3 minutes.

Remove the lid from the kasha and fluff gently with 2 forks to remove any lumps. Scatter the spiced pecans over the kasha and serve.

Kasha, which is toasted buckwheat groats, has a delicious nutty aroma and flavor. The kasha is coated with egg white before cooking in order to prevent it from lumping once the liquid is added. You can use this recipe to prepare other grains, such as brown rice or pearl barley. Simply omit the first step of sautéing them in the egg white. Serve this dish with roasted chicken or turkey, or broiled bluefish or marlin.

toasting nuts p. 26

Soft Polenta

5 cups chicken broth or water

1½ tsp salt

1 cup coarse yellow cornmeal (polenta)

2 Tbsp unsalted butter

½ cup grated Parmesan (optional)

Makes 4 servings

Bring the broth to a boil in a heavy saucepan and add the salt.

To keep the polenta from becoming lumpy, add the cornmeal to the boiling broth very gradually, throwing in a few pinches to start and then adding it in a very thin stream, stirring constantly with a wooden spoon until all has been added. Simmer, stirring often, until the polenta pulls away from the sides of the pot but is still thin enough to fall from the spoon, about 45 minutes.

Remove the pot from the heat and blend in the butter and the cheese, if using. Serve at once as soft polenta.

Polenta is a thick porridge made from coarsely ground cornmeal. For a traditional presentation, prepare firm polenta, cut into squares, and top with a rich meat sauce.

preparing cereals and meals p. 206

making broth p. 45

VARIATIONS

Firm Polenta

For firm polenta, pour soft polenta into a buttered 8-inch baking pan and spread into an even layer about ¾ inch thick. Alternatively, pour into a buttered loaf pan. Cover and refrigerate until firm enough to cut into shapes, at least 2 hours and up to overnight. Once the polenta has cooled and firmed, use 3-inch cutters or a paring knife to cut into shapes as desired (triangles, squares, rectangles), or cut into ¾-inch-thick slices.

Sautéed Firm Polenta

To sauté firm polenta, heat 1 Tbsp *each* vegetable oil and butter in a sauté pan over medium-high heat until the butter stops foaming. Add the polenta pieces and sauté until golden brown on the first side, about 2 minutes. Turn once and continue sautéing over medium heat until the polenta is very hot and brown on the second side, about 2 minutes more.

sautéing and stir-frying p. 32

Grilled Firm Polenta

To grill, prepare a grill for a hot fire and grill the polenta until it is marked and very hot, about 2 minutes per side. Be sure to oil the polenta before grilling and use care when turning.

grilling and broiling p. 28

Southwest White Bean Stew

1½ cups dried navy beans, soaked for 4–12 hours

Salt and freshly ground pepper

2 tsp vegetable oil

1 yellow onion, diced

1 cup finely diced bell pepper

½ jalapeño, seeded and diced

8 cloves garlic, minced

2 cups chicken broth

1 tomato, peeled, seeded, and diced

¼ cup sherry wine vinegar

2 Tbsp minced fresh cilantro

Makes 8 servings

Drain the beans and put in a large pot. Add water to cover by 3 inches. Bring to a boil over high heat, then reduce the heat to medium and simmer until barely tender to the bite, about 45 minutes, stirring occasionally and adding water as necessary to keep the beans completely covered. Add 1 tsp salt and continue simmering until the beans are very tender and mash easily, 15–20 minutes more. Drain the beans, reserving about 1 cup of the liquid.

Purée 2 cups of the cooked beans in a food processor, adding cooking liquid if necessary, and combine with whole beans.

Heat the vegetable oil in a large saucepan over medium-high heat. Add the onion, bell pepper, jalapeño, and garlic and sauté until the onion is translucent, about 6 minutes. Add the bean mixture and broth and cook, stirring constantly, until the beans are heated through, about 10 minutes. Add the tomato and vinegar and continue to sauté until very hot. Taste and season with salt and pepper. Scatter with the cilantro just before serving.

Try using a mix of colored bell peppers for this stew. Green bell peppers, which are unripened, will be less sweet than the fully ripened orange, red, or yellow bell peppers.

preparing legumes p. 206

peeling and seeding tomatoes p. 184

Black Beans with Bell Peppers and Chorizo

1 cup dried black beans, soaked for 4–12 hours

Salt and freshly ground pepper

2 strips bacon, minced

¼ cup vegetable oil

1 yellow onion, diced

2 cloves garlic, minced

¼ lb chorizo sausage, sliced

1 red or green bell pepper, diced

½ cup thinly sliced green onion, white and green parts

1 Tbsp minced fresh basil

1 Tbsp minced fresh cilantro

2 tsp minced fresh oregano

Sour cream for serving (optional)

Makes 4 servings

Drain the beans and put in a large pot. Add water to cover by 3 inches. Bring to a boil over high heat, reduce the heat to medium, and simmer, stirring occasionally and adding water as necessary to keep the beans completely covered, until barely tender to the bite, 70 minutes. Add 1 tsp salt and continue simmering until the beans are very tender, 15–20 minutes more. Drain, reserving the cooking liquid.

Sauté the bacon in the oil in a large pot over medium heat until the bacon bits are crisped, 2–3 minutes. Add the yellow onion and garlic and sauté until lightly browned, 6–8 minutes. Add the chorizo and bell pepper; sauté until the pepper is tender, about 5 minutes.

Add the drained beans and enough of their cooking liquid to keep them moist (the consistency should be that of a thick stew). Simmer until all the flavors are developed and all the ingredients are heated through, 20–25 minutes. Add the green onion and fresh herbs. Taste and season with salt and pepper. Serve the beans with sour cream, if desired.

Slices of spicy Spanish chorizo sausage and a shower of fresh herbs blend well with the savory black beans in this Mexican-inspired bean stew. Serve with warmed tortillas and a dollop of sour cream.

preparing legumes p. 206

preparing bell peppers and chiles p. 183

Lentil Ragout

1 strip bacon, finely chopped

1 yellow onion, finely diced

1 stalk celery, finely diced

1 carrot, finely diced

1 clove garlic, minced

2 Tbsp tomato paste

2½ cups vegetable broth

1 cup green or brown lentils

1 bay leaf

1 sprig fresh thyme or
½ tsp dried

1 strip lemon zest

1–2 Tbsp sherry wine vinegar

Salt and freshly ground pepper

¼ cup fresh flat-leaf parsley,
chopped

Makes 6 servings

Put the chopped bacon in a saucepan and place over medium heat. Cook, stirring occasionally, until the fat is rendered and the bacon bits are crisped, 2–3 minutes. Remove the crisped bacon with a slotted spoon and transfer to paper towels to drain.

Add the onion, celery, carrot, and garlic to the fat left in the pan. Reduce the heat to low, cover, and cook without stirring for about 5 minutes. The onion should be very limp.

Raise the heat to high. Add the tomato paste and sauté, stirring constantly, until it darkens, about 3 minutes.

Add the broth, lentils, bay leaf, thyme, and lemon zest. Simmer over low heat, stirring occasionally, until the lentils are tender and have absorbed the liquid, about 30 minutes. (The lentils can also be cooked in a 350°F oven, tightly covered, for about 45 minutes.)

Remove and discard the bay leaf, thyme sprig, and lemon zest. Add the vinegar. Taste and season with salt and pepper. Fold in the parsley and serve at once.

Lentils can be found in a variety of colors and sizes. For this recipe, look for the commonly available brown lentils, or try substituting the smaller green lentils, also known as French lentils or *lentilles de Puy*.

sautéing and stir-frying p. 32

dicing p. 17

Apple-Sage Dressing

2 Tbsp unsalted butter, plus more for greasing pan

1 yellow onion, chopped

2 stalks celery, chopped

2½ cups chicken broth

2 Red Delicious apples, skin on, cored and diced

2 tsp chopped fresh sage

1 tsp chopped fresh thyme

Salt and freshly ground pepper

6 cups stale or lightly toasted bread cubes

¼ cup chopped fresh flat-leaf parsley

1 large egg white, lightly beaten

Makes 6 servings

Preheat the oven to 400°F.

Melt the butter in a large nonstick skillet over medium heat. Add the onion and celery and sauté until tender, about 5 minutes. Stir in the broth, apples, sage, thyme, ½ tsp salt, and pepper to taste. Bring just to a boil, then remove from the heat. Combine the apple mixture with the bread cubes, parsley, and egg white in a large bowl. Spoon into a buttered 9 x 13–inch baking dish.

Bake until golden brown on top, about 45 minutes.

A dressing is a stuffing that is baked outside the bird. To prepare a stuffed turkey or chicken safely, you must roast it until the stuffing temperature reaches 165°F. This means that there is a good chance that the bird's breast meat will be a little overcooked before the stuffing is done. Better to add some aromatics to the cavity instead of stuffing the bird and cook a dressing alongside.

dicing onions p. 180

Falafel

1 cup dried garbanzo beans (chickpeas), soaked for 12–24 hours

1 yellow onion, diced

3 cloves garlic

¼ cup fresh flat-leaf parsley leaves

1 tsp ground cumin

1 tsp ground coriander

1 tsp ground cayenne pepper

1½ tsp salt

1 tsp baking soda

2 Tbsp all-purpose flour

Vegetable oil for deep-frying

Makes 4 servings

Drain the garbanzos and rinse. Combine in a food processor with the onion, garlic, and parsley and grind to the consistency of coarse meal. Add the cumin, coriander, and cayenne and pulse to mix.

Dissolve the salt and baking soda in ¼ cup water in a large bowl. Add the garbanzo mixture and stir to mix.

Add the flour, 2 tsp at a time, until the mixture will hold together when molded. Mold into 8 flat, round disks, each 2 inches in diameter and ½–¾ inch thick.

Pour oil into a tall pot to a depth of 5 inches. Heat over medium heat until the oil registers 350°F on a deep-frying thermometer. Working in batches to avoid crowding the pot, deep-fry the disks until golden brown, 8–10 minutes. Transfer to paper towels to drain and serve at once.

Serve falafel in pita bread with lettuce, cucumbers, tomatoes, and a sauce of yogurt blended with tahini, salt, pepper, and a little lemon juice. Note that the beans are soaked for at least 12 hours, but not cooked, before grinding.

preparing legumes p. 206

deep-frying p. 35

Stewed Lima Beans with Tomato, Zucchini, and Parsley

1 cup dried lima beans, soaked for 4–12 hours

5–6 cups chicken broth or water, or as needed

1 Tbsp olive oil

2 cloves garlic, minced

1 zucchini, diced

1 plum (Roma) tomato, peeled, seeded, and chopped

3 Tbsp chopped fresh flat-leaf parsley

Salt and freshly ground pepper

½ tsp fresh lime juice, or as needed

Makes 6 servings

Drain the lima beans and rinse. Put in a large pot with broth to cover by 3 inches. Bring to a boil over high heat, then reduce the heat to medium and simmer until barely tender to the bite, about 40 minutes, stirring occasionally, and adding broth as necessary to keep the beans completely covered. Reserve about 1 cup of the cooking liquid. Drain in a colander, rubbing gently to remove the skins. Discard the skins.

Heat the olive oil in a saucepan. Add the garlic and cook until aromatic, about 1 minute. Add the zucchini and tomato and sauté until the zucchini is tender and heated through, about 10 minutes.

Add the lima beans to the pan, along with enough cooking liquid to keep them moist. Stew until heated through. Add the parsley, then taste and season with salt, pepper, and lime juice.

Best known for their starring role in succotash, oft-maligned lima beans have a mild, nutty-sweet flavor.

preparing legumes p. 206

peeling and seeding tomatoes p. 184

Vegetarian Chili

1½ cups dried pinto beans

1 Tbsp vegetable oil

1 yellow onion, chopped

3 cloves garlic, minced

2 tsp chili powder, or to taste

2 tsp dried oregano

1 tsp ground cumin

1 chipotle chile in adobo sauce, chopped

1 poblano chile, roasted, peeled, and seeded

4 cups vegetable broth, or as needed

2 cups peeled, seeded, and diced tomatoes, juices reserved

Salt and freshly ground pepper

½ tsp fresh lime juice, or to taste

½ cup sour cream

2 Tbsp minced fresh cilantro

Lime wedges, for serving

Makes 8 servings

Soak the beans for 4–12 hours, then drain.

Heat the oil in a large sauté pan over medium heat. Add the onion and sauté, stirring occasionally, until tender and translucent, 5–6 minutes.

Add the garlic and cook until aromatic, 1 minute more. Add the chili powder, oregano, and cumin and cook for 1 minute more. Be careful not to let the spices burn.

Add the drained beans, chipotle chile, poblano chile, and broth to cover by 2 inches and bring to a simmer. When the beans are starting to become tender, after about 1 hour, add the tomatoes and reserved juice. Cook until tender, 20 minutes more. Season with the salt, pepper, and lime juice.

Pass the sour cream, cilantro, and lime wedges at the table.

Three cups of canned beans may be substituted for the cooked dried beans in this recipe. Make sure to rinse the beans thoroughly before using. Since canned beans tend to be softer and blander, seasonings may need to be increased and cooking times decreased.

preparing legumes p. 206

roasting and peeling peppers p. 183

Beans and Greens Sauté

2 Tbsp olive oil

2 cloves garlic, chopped

1 lb beet greens, coarsely chopped into 1-inch pieces

1 cup cooked or canned navy beans, warmed

1 cup cooked or canned black beans, warmed

½ cup chicken broth

Salt and freshly ground pepper

Malt vinegar

Makes 4 servings

Heat the olive oil in a large skillet over medium heat. Add the garlic and sauté until aromatic, about 1 minute, taking care not to brown or scorch it. Add the beet greens and toss briskly with a wooden spoon. As the beet greens wilt and cook, add the warmed beans and broth and toss until the ingredients are well mixed and heated through. Taste and season to taste with salt, pepper, and vinegar.

Malt vinegar, a traditional British favorite to sprinkle on fish and chips, is made from the dried, powdered sprouts of barley or a similar grain. The flavor is sweeter and milder than that of other vinegars. If you prefer, you can use an herb-flavored, cider, or wine vinegar instead of the malt vinegar suggested in this recipe.

preparing legumes p. 206

Mixed Bean Salad

⅓ cup red lentils

Vinaigrette

¼ cup olive oil

1 small shallot, minced

1 clove garlic, minced

¼ tsp red pepper flakes

½ cup chicken or vegetable broth

2 Tbsp fresh lemon juice

2 Tbsp red wine vinegar

Cornstarch slurry: 1 tsp cornstarch blended with 1 tsp cold water

1 small tomato, peeled, seeded, and diced

1 Tbsp chopped fresh basil

1 Tbsp chopped fresh sage

Salt and freshly ground black pepper

1¼ cups cooked black beans (or one 15-oz can), rinsed and drained

1¼ cups cooked pinto or small red kidney beans (or one 15-oz can), rinsed and drained

1¼ cups cooked garbanzo beans (chickpeas) (or one 15-oz can), rinsed and drained

1 small red onion, finely diced

2 stalks celery, chopped

2 Tbsp chopped fresh flat-leaf parsley

Makes 10 servings

Bring 3 cups salted water to a rolling boil in a saucepan over high heat. Add the lentils, stir with a fork to separate, and adjust the heat to maintain a simmer. Cook until tender, 5–8 minutes. Drain immediately and rinse in cold water to stop the cooking. Set aside.

For the vinaigrette, heat the oil in a small saucepan over low heat. Add the shallot, garlic, and red pepper flakes and sauté until aromatic and tender, about 2 minutes. Add the broth, lemon juice, and vinegar and bring to a boil. While stirring, add enough of the cornstarch slurry to thicken the vinaigrette slightly. Remove from the heat and stir in the tomato, basil, and sage. Taste and season with salt and black pepper, and cover to keep warm.

Combine the lentils, black beans, pinto beans, garbanzo beans, onion, celery, parsley, ½ tsp salt, and ¼ tsp black pepper in a serving bowl. Toss lightly with the vinaigrette, adding just enough at first to moisten the beans, then more to taste. Cover and refrigerate for at least 8 hours or up to overnight to allow the flavors to blend.

Taste the salad and adjust the seasoning with salt and black pepper. Let the salad sit for 20 minutes at room temperature before serving to take the chill off and bring out the flavors.

Beans that will be served in salads or side dishes are best when cooked until they are tender all the way through but still retain their shape. For soups and purées, cook the beans longer, until they are very soft and beginning to break down on their own.

peeling and seeding tomatoes p. 184

making vinaigrette p. 250

Risotto with Asparagus Tips

1 lb fresh asparagus

Salt and freshly ground pepper

2½ cups chicken broth

½ cup dry white wine

3 Tbsp unsalted butter

½ cup finely minced yellow onion

1 cup Arborio rice

¼ cup grated Parmesan

Makes 4 first-course or side-dish servings

Cut the tips from the asparagus, about 2 inches long each, and parboil them for 3–4 minutes in boiling salted water until bright in color and just tender but not cooked through. Drain, refresh in cold water, drain well, and set aside. Reserve the rest of the asparagus for another use.

Combine the broth and wine in a saucepan and bring to a simmer over medium heat. Adjust the heat to maintain a gentle simmer.

Heat the butter in a large saucepan over medium heat. Add the onion and sauté, stirring frequently, until the onion is tender but not browned, about 5 minutes.

Add the rice and stir well to coat each grain with the butter.

Add about ½ cup of the warm broth mixture and cook the rice, stirring constantly, until the liquid has nearly cooked away. Repeat this process, adding ½ cup of the broth mixture at a time, until all of the broth has been added and the rice has the consistency of a smooth, creamy porridge and is just tender, with a little resistance to the bite. The total cooking time will be 18–20 minutes.

Remove the risotto from the heat and fold in the cheese and the reserved asparagus tips. Taste and season with salt and pepper.

The Arborio rice called for in this recipe is a special type of rice—a round, medium-grain variety—that develops a soft, creamy texture as starch is released during cooking. Other types of rice may be used in this dish, but they will not have the consistency associated with authentic risottos.

Risotto may be served in place of the pasta course in a traditional Italian-style meal, or try it as a side dish with a sautéed chicken breast.

boiling, parboiling, or blanching p. 37

VARIATIONS

Saffron Risotto

Omit the asparagus. Add ¼ tsp crushed saffron threads to the pan with the onion.

Shellfish Risotto

Add ½ lb shrimp, peeled and deveined, or 1–2 doz clams or mussels, scrubbed (and debearded if using mussels), during the last 10–12 minutes of cooking.

preparing shrimp p. 129

preparing mussels p. 129

Cheese-Filled Risotto Croquettes with Tomato Sauce

3 cups leftover cooked risotto

½ cup grated Parmesan

2 Tbsp heavy cream

2 Tbsp minced fresh flat-leaf parsley, chives, oregano, or basil

1 large egg yolk

Salt and freshly ground pepper

5 oz mozzarella or Fontina cheese

All-purpose flour for dredging

Egg wash: 1 large egg whisked with 2 Tbsp cold milk or water

1 cup fresh white bread crumbs

Vegetable oil for deep-frying

2 cups tomato sauce (p. 160)

Makes 8 appetizer servings

In a large bowl, combine the risotto with the Parmesan, cream, herbs, and egg yolk. Season with salt and pepper.

Cut the cheese into 16 cubes. Scoop up about 3 Tbsp of the risotto mixture and pack it around a cube of cheese to make a croquette, a ball the size of a Ping-Pong ball. Repeat to form 16 croquettes.

Put the flour, egg wash, and bread crumbs in 3 separate bowls. Dredge the croquettes in the flour, dip in the egg wash, and roll in the bread crumbs. Chill thoroughly, 2–24 hours.

Pour oil into a tall pot to a depth of 5 inches. Heat the oil over medium-high heat until it registers 375°F on a deep-frying thermometer. Deep-fry the croquettes in batches, without crowding, until they are evenly browned, 4–5 minutes. Using a slotted spoon or tongs, transfer to paper towels to drain briefly. Serve on a pool of warmed tomato sauce.

Known as *arancini*, or "little oranges," in Italian, these little balls, with their surprise melted cheese filling, are an excellent way to turn leftover risotto into a delectable hors d'oeuvre. They're so good, you might be inspired to make a batch of risotto (p. 224) just to enjoy in this form.

deep-frying p. 35

separating eggs p. 229

Grilled Tofu with Spicy Mango Glaze

Two 12-oz blocks extra-firm tofu

1 Tbsp minced shallot

2 Tbsp vegetable oil

2 cloves garlic, minced

1 ripe mango, chopped

2 cups ketchup

¼ cup chicken broth

3 Tbsp hoisin sauce

1 dried ancho chile, stemmed and seeded

2 Tbsp *each* bourbon and cider vinegar

2 tsp *each* Worcestershire sauce and lemon juice

1 Tbsp sugar

¼ tsp freshly ground pepper

Makes 4 appetizer servings

Slice the tofu blocks in half horizontally. Line a baking pan with several layers of paper towels, set the tofu on top, and cover with more paper towels. Top with a second pan, set a weight (such as 2 or 3 cans of beans) on top, to press the tofu. Refrigerate for 30–40 minutes or up to 12 hours.

Sauté the shallot in the oil in a large saucepan over medium-high heat until limp, about 1 minute. Add the garlic and cook, stirring often, 2 minutes more. Add the mango and the remaining ingredients and simmer until well flavored with a saucelike consistency, about 30 minutes. Let cool slightly, then carefully purée in batches in a blender to make a mango glaze.

Brush each piece of tofu generously with the mango glaze. Set aside to marinate for at least 20 minutes and up to 4 hours.

Prepare a grill for a medium-hot fire. Grill the tofu just long enough to mark on each side and heat through, about 2 minutes per side. Pass any remaining mango glaze on the side.

Fresh tofu comes in a variety of textures. For this recipe, look for extra-firm tofu, which slices well and keeps its shape during cooking. (Don't use soft, or silken, tofu, which will break up too easily on the grill.) Pressing excess water out of the tofu before using it will help the mango glaze form a better "skin" during grilling.

grilling and broiling p. 28

sautéing and stir-frying p. 32

8 Eggs

Eggs, with their unique packaging, sound nutrition, and countless uses, are arguably the perfect food. Yet they can challenge even the most accomplished cook, for their very simplicity demands nothing less than excellent timing and control over heat, and the cook's full attention. But their versatility and adaptability also make them great learning material for the novice, since their preparation requires nothing beyond very basic tools and techniques. Honest efforts are rewarded with an exquisite meal, whether a softly set poached egg or a tender rolled omelet, sunny-side up eggs or a silky-smooth quiche.

In this chapter we concentrate on eggs served as the main attraction, but they play an important supporting role in many other dishes, especially desserts. Eggs moisten batters and doughs, thicken dishes like custards, and enrich soups when added as a liaison. Mixed with milk or water, they make a glaze, known as egg wash, that gives baked goods a rich golden sheen. This versatile wash is also an effective adhesive for holding together stuffed pastas or pastries. Eggs can be used as a batter for pan-fried foods like zucchini or fish, or can help to hold a bread-crumb coating in place. Each use takes advantage of the particular qualities of the egg white and the egg yolk.

The egg white consists almost exclusively of water and a protein called albumen. When beaten, egg whites form a relatively stable foam that traps enough air to raise soufflés, cakes, pancakes, and mousses.

Egg yolks can also be beaten into a foam to make the base for certain types of sauce such as hollandaise and mayonnaise, sometimes referred to as emulsified sauces. In addition to protein, water, and fat, the yolk contains lecithin, a natural emulsifier that binds two ingredients that would otherwise separate after you mix them, like oil and vinegar.

Types of egg

Eggs are graded on the basis of external appearance and freshness. The top grade, AA, indicates that an egg is fresh, with a white that will not spread too much once the egg is broken, and a yolk that sits high on the white's surface.

Eggs are available in a number of sizes: jumbo, extra large, large, medium, and small. (Large eggs are used in the recipes throughout this book.) Younger hens produce smaller eggs, which are often regarded as better quality than larger eggs. Pasteurized eggs may be used in preparations such as salad dressings, desserts, and eggnog for which the traditional recipe calls for raw eggs. You can buy them in the dairy case, near the other eggs, sold in cartons or as pasteurized eggs in the shell.

For health reasons, many cooks use egg substitutes that are either entirely egg-free or produced from egg whites, with dairy or vegetable products substituted for the yolks. These substitutes are valuable for people who must follow a reduced-cholesterol diet.

Selecting eggs

Although eggs are not the only food that raises food safety concerns, their potential danger has received a great deal of public attention. A small percentage of eggs are contaminated with *Salmonella enteritidis,* which can cause illness if the bacteria are not destroyed through thorough cooking. The guidelines for selecting and storing eggs are essentially the same as for virtually any highly perishable food: select the food carefully from a reputable source, keep it cold and covered at home, use it within a reasonable period of time, and cook it to a safe doneness.

Buy eggs from a refrigerated case. Look at the packaging to be sure it is not dented or ripped. Inspect the eggs. The egg shells should be clean, without cracks, holes, or leaks. Once the egg shell is broken, it is easier for pathogens to pass through the membrane into the egg. To keep eggs wholesome at home, store them in the carton in the coldest part of the refrigerator. If the shells remain unbroken, your eggs will keep for 3 to 5 weeks held at 40°F or less. Once eggs are taken out of the shell, store them in clean containers, well covered, and use them within 2 days.

Whole eggs in the shell have membranes surrounding the white and yolk. When the egg is very fresh, the membranes keep the yolk anchored in the center of the white, protect the egg from contamination, and prevent loss of moisture through evaporation. As the egg ages, the membranes weaken.

When a very fresh egg is broken onto a plate, its yolk sits high and firm near the white's center. The white itself is compact and thick. The white of an older egg spreads thin and its yolk lies flat and breaks easily. A fresh egg in the shell sinks to the bottom of container of water, while an older egg floats, buoyed by the larger air space inside its shell created by moisture loss.

Preparing eggs

To be certain of destroying bacteria, cook boiled, poached, fried, or baked eggs until the yolk is solid. Cook scrambled eggs and omelets until they are no longer runny. Dishes like custards, stuffings, or meatballs must reach 160°F in order to destroy any existing bacteria. The recipes in this book have been adapted to heat eggs to a safe temperature, unless otherwise noted.

Eggs are a universally loved food. They are individually packaged and portion sized by nature. They keep well. And best of all, they are incredibly versatile and perfectly delicious.

Separating eggs

Separate eggs carefully to avoid breaking the yolk.

1 Setting up

Eggs separate most easily when they are cold, so keep them in the refrigerator until you are ready. Have 2 bowls ready to hold the whites and yolks separately, and crack each egg over an empty third bowl in case the yolk breaks. Egg whites that are to be whipped must be free from all traces of yolk, because the fat in the yolk inhibits the whites from foaming up. Be sure that the container you use to hold egg whites for whipping is perfectly clean, without a trace of grease, so that your foam will have the best possible volume. You can use lemon juice or white vinegar to wipe the bowl and the whisk to remove any fat.

2 Separating the eggs

Crack each egg's shell and carefully pull apart the halves. Gently pour the egg yolk back and forth from one half to the other, allowing the egg white to fall into the empty bowl. Drop the egg yolk into another bowl.

3 Keeping the white and yolk separate

Examine the white in the first bowl to be sure that it contains no bits of yolk. If it is clean, transfer it to the egg white bowl. If you see drops of yolk in the egg white, however, it cannot be used for whipping. Save it for adding to scrambled eggs, and wash out the bowl before separating the next egg.

Hard-boiling eggs

Eggs are cooked in the shell to make hard- and soft-boiled eggs and coddled eggs.

Cooking the eggs

Fill a deep pot with enough water to hold the eggs comfortably. Bring the water to a simmer for coddled and soft-boiled eggs. Hard-boiled eggs may be started in simmering or cold water. In either case, lower the eggs gently into the pot so they don't crack. If the eggs are added to simmering water, calculate the cooking time from the point when the water returns to a full simmer. If you started your hard-boiled eggs in cold water, pull the pot from the heat as soon as the water simmers. Cover the pot and let the eggs finish in the hot water for 20 minutes.

Peeling hard-boiled eggs

Eggs are easiest to peel while they are still warm. Place them under cold running water until they are cool enough to handle. Gently press down and roll the egg over a countertop to crack the shell before peeling. Peel the shell and membrane away with your fingers. The best way to prevent a green ring around the yolk is to avoid overcooking, and to cool and peel the eggs as soon as possible.

Whipping egg whites

Foamy whipped egg whites add a light texture and leavening power to a wide range of dishes.

1 Setting up

Egg whites foam best when there are no traces of fat in the whites themselves or on the equipment you use. Following the proper steps for separating eggs (see page 229) makes certain that no broken yolk mixes in with the whites. Choose a bowl large enough for the egg whites to triple in volume. Copper bowls react chemically with egg whites to create a foam with good volume and stability. If you don't have a copper bowl, you can add cream of tartar for stability. Wipe the bowl and whisk or beaters with lemon juice or white vinegar, and then again with hot water to remove any grease or oil. You will get the greatest volume if the egg whites are at room temperature when they are whipped. A 15-minute rest is usually enough time to warm up eggs taken from the refrigerator and separated while still cold.

2 Whipping the whites

Egg white foams start to deflate almost the moment you stop whipping them, so they are usually beaten and folded into a dish as the very last step in a recipe, to keep as much air as possible in the foam and the finished dish. Use a large, round balloon whisk or the wire whisk attachment of a stand mixer to incorporate as much air as possible. Begin whipping at a slow to moderate speed, until the whites loosen and become foamy. Then increase the speed to high and continue to whip. As more air is beaten into the whites, the texture becomes very smooth and the foam thickens enough to mound slightly, a stage called soft peak (shown at left). Ingredients like sugar or cream of tartar are gradually added starting at this point.

3 Egg white textures

Egg whites can be beaten to distinct stages, typically described as soft, medium, hard, and stiff peaks. "Soft peak" means that the foam is very glossy and moist. When you pull the whisk out of the bowl and turn it upright, look for soft peaks that fall over to one side. Egg whites whipped longer reach the "medium peak" stage. You will see distinct tracks left by the whisk or beaters as you whip. The peaks formed when the whisk is lifted retain their shape longer but are still glossy and smooth. This is the ideal stage for foams to be folded into batters or to make soufflés, since there is still enough flexibility for the whites to expand as they get hot without bursting. Once the "hard peak" stage is reached, the tips of the peaks are more pointed and hold their shape for a while before drooping. Beyond hard peak, egg foams approach their maximum volume and are at the "stiff peak" stage. Stiff foams tend to collapse easily and may start to lose their glossy sheen.

Frying eggs

From cheerful sunny-side up eggs with bacon to richly layered huevos rancheros, fried eggs are an essential part of breakfast.

1 Frying eggs

Use the freshest eggs possible for fewer broken yolks and find a smooth-surfaced skillet or griddle that is heavy enough to cook evenly. Break each egg separately into a small bowl. Heat the skillet or griddle over medium heat. Even if you are using a nonstick pan, add a small amount of flavorful fat, oil, or butter, to give good flavor and a crisp-edged texture to the eggs. Wait until the cooking fat is hot, then slide the eggs onto the skillet. Lower the heat to medium-low. Egg whites become opaque quickly, but an egg's doneness is determined by the yolk. Leave them soft and runny for "sunny-side up," or cook until firm or very firm ("medium" or "hard"). For "over-easy," "over-medium," or "over-hard" eggs, turn the eggs carefully with a spatula and cook for 30 seconds–2 minutes more.

Poaching eggs

Cooking eggs gently in water creates a tender, delicate texture that works for a variety of dishes.

1 Poaching eggs

Eggs should be poached in about 3 inches of water. Adding salt and a small amount of vinegar to the water prevents the whites from spreading too much and helps the egg proteins set faster. Bring the poaching water to a gentle simmer, about 180°F. The water should appear effervescent, with tiny bubbles collecting on the sides of the pan and breaking evenly over the surface. Adjust the heat to prevent a boil, as larger bubbles would break the egg. Use the freshest eggs possible for poaching, as they will have a more centered yolk and more compact white that will cook with a cleaner edge. Crack the egg first into a small cup or bowl, then gently slide the egg into the poaching liquid. As the egg drops to the bottom of the pot, the whites will set in a teardrop shape around the yolk. Work in small batches without crowding. Too many eggs will cause the temperature of the water to drop, extend the cooking time, and be more difficult to handle.

2 Trimming the eggs

After 3–4 minutes, lift the eggs out with a slotted spoon and drain on a clean towel to remove excess water. The whites should be set and opaque, while the yolks should be done to your liking. Trim away ragged edges on the egg whites with a paring knife or kitchen shears to form a compact oval shape.

Making scrambled eggs or rolled omelets

Depending on its filling, an omelet can be a simple breakfast for one or an impressive brunch for guests.

1 Mixing eggs

Although whole eggs are standard for making omelets, some recipes call for additional egg yolks for extra richness or more egg whites to reduce fat content. For best flavor, you should crack and blend the eggs just before cooking if possible, but if you need to streamline breakfast or brunch, you can make the mixture up to 12 hours in advance. Season the eggs well with salt and pepper. If you like, blend them with a small amount of water, broth, milk, or cream for a more tender texture. The omelet itself cooks in only a few minutes, so prepare any garnish or filling ahead of time.

2 Scrambling eggs

Heat a nonstick omelet pan or small skillet over high heat and add oil, butter, or a combination of both. Determining when the pan and fat are properly heated is key. Oil should shimmer but not smoke, while butter should melt and foam but not turn brown or black. Water droplets should skitter over the pan but not cook away instantly. Tilt the pan to coat its entire surface. Add the beaten eggs and use one hand to swirl the pan on the burner and the other to stir the eggs in the opposite direction, using a fork or heat-resistant rubber spatula. Once the eggs set into smooth, small curds and lose their glossy look, you can serve them as scrambled eggs.

3 Rolling an omelet

To make a rolled omelet, spread the curds in an even layer. If you are adding a filling, add it now in an even layer down the center of the omelet. Place one edge of the omelet pan on a work surface next to a serving plate and lift up the handle so that gravity can help roll your omelet. Using a rubber spatula or wooden spoon, lift the highest side of the omelet free of the pan and fold it over toward the center. Keep rolling the omelet over on itself until it is nearly out of the pan. Tilt the pan over the plate and push or roll the omelet out of the pan and onto a plate. Alternatively, simply fold the omelet in half to make a half-moon and slide it onto the plate. Rub the top of the warm omelet with a pat of butter to give it an attractive sheen.

Making a soufflé

Careful preparation of the soufflé dish, a hot oven, and close timing will ensure a light and puffy soufflé.

1 Preparing the dish

Soufflés are usually baked in a ceramic or glass dish or in individual ramekins. To encourage the best rise, soufflé dishes should have straight sides. To prepare one for filling, coat it generously and evenly with butter. For savory soufflés, dust the bottom and sides of the buttered dish with grated Parmesan cheese or bread crumbs. For sweet soufflés, dust the buttered dish with granulated sugar. These ingredients offer a rough texture to give the soufflé traction as it climbs. Put individual soufflé dishes on a baking sheet to make it easier to get them into and out of the oven.

2 Mixing the soufflé base

To make a soufflé, you need to combine a soufflé base and beaten egg whites. The base for soufflés is usually a thick sauce made of milk, egg yolks, butter, and flour. You can flavor the base with savory ingredients such as grated cheese, finely chopped vegetables, or small pieces of shellfish, or sweet ones like fruit or chocolate. Most recipes call for egg whites to be beaten to "soft or medium peaks (see page 230) just before they are to be blended with the base. The beaten egg whites will give both volume and structure to the soufflé as they expand in the hot oven. Fold the beaten egg whites into the base in two or three stages. The first addition will lighten the base so that subsequent additions will retain the maximum volume of air.

3 Baking the soufflé

Fill the prepared dish as soon as the egg whites are folded into the base. Spoon the batter into the dish gently to avoid deflating the batter. Be sure to wipe the rim and outside of the dish clean for a good, even rise and attractive appearance. As soon as the dish is filled, place the soufflé on the center rack of a thoroughly preheated oven. Soufflés bake in a hot oven so that the foamed egg whites expand while the base cooks quickly enough to stabilize the soufflé. Open the oven door as little as possible. Soufflés rise evenly and dramatically when the temperature stays steady. When a soufflé is fully baked, the sides appear fully set but tender, the top is browned, and a toothpick inserted near the center of the soufflé should come out clean. Serve the soufflé as soon as you take it from the oven.

Huevos Rancheros

Four 6-inch corn tortillas

1 cup canned refried beans

2 Tbsp unsalted butter or vegetable oil

8 large eggs

Salt and freshly ground pepper

½ cup grated Monterey Jack

1 avocado

2 tsp fresh lime juice

½ cup blackened tomato salsa (p. 259) or prepared salsa

½ cup sour cream

¼ cup fresh cilantro, coarsely chopped

1 green onion, white and green parts, thinly sliced on the bias

Makes 4 servings

Preheat the broiler.

Heat the tortillas by toasting them one at a time in a dry cast-iron skillet or directly over a gas flame until lightly toasted. Place on a baking sheet, spread each tortilla with ¼ cup of refried beans, and cover to keep warm.

Working in batches as needed, heat the butter in a large skillet over medium-high heat until it is very hot but not smoking and the foaming has subsided. Crack the eggs directly into the hot butter and reduce the heat to medium-low or low. Fry the eggs, shaking the pan occasionally to keep the eggs from sticking. Season the eggs with salt and pepper. Fry to the desired doneness (see page 228), about 2 minutes for "sunny-side up," 3 minutes for medium yolks, and 4 minutes for hard yolks. Or, once the whites are just opaque, turn the eggs and cook for 30 seconds more for "over easy," 1 minute more for "over medium," or 2 minutes more for "over hard."

Top each tortilla with 2 fried eggs and 2 Tbsp of the grated cheese. Slide the tortillas under the broiler to melt the cheese.

Meanwhile, dice the avocado and toss with the lime juice to prevent the avocado from discoloring.

Top each serving with 2 Tbsp salsa and 2 Tbsp sour cream. Divide the avocado among the tortillas. Garnish each tortilla with 1 Tbsp cilantro and 1 Tbsp green onion and serve.

Since avocados can still be rock-hard when they reach the market, it's a good idea to shop for these tropical fruits a few days before you need them. Ripen them at room temperature until they give slightly when pressed. To prepare, insert a knife into the bottom of the avocado. Cut in half lengthwise completely around the pit, then twist the two halves in opposite directions to loosen one half from the pit. Strike the pit carefully with a knife to lodge the blade in the pit, then draw it out. Scoop out the flesh in one piece with a large spoon.

frying eggs p. 231

zesting and juicing citrus p. 182

Eggs Benedict

2 tsp distilled white vinegar

1 tsp salt

8 large eggs

8 English muffin halves, toasted and buttered

8 thick slices Canadian bacon

Hollandaise sauce (p. 237) for serving

Makes 4 servings

Preheat the broiler. Combine 6 cups water with the vinegar and salt in a deep saucepan and bring to a bare simmer.

Break each egg into a cup and then slide the egg carefully into the water. Poach until the whites are set and opaque, about 3 minutes. Poach the eggs in batches to avoid overcrowding the pan.

Meanwhile, top each English muffin half with a slice of Canadian bacon and broil briefly to heat the bacon, 1–2 minutes.

Remove the eggs from the water with a slotted spoon. Blot on paper towels and trim the edges neatly, if desired.

Top each muffin half with a poached egg and coat with Hollandaise sauce. Serve at once.

Charles Ranhofer, chef of New York's renowned Delmonico's restaurant, created this dish for Mrs. LeGrande Benedict, a regular patron seeking something new. This richly layered concoction clearly reflects its Gilded Age origins.

poaching eggs p. 231

VARIATIONS

Farmer-Style Eggs

Make a creamed mushroom sauce to replace the Hollandaise sauce: Heat 1 Tbsp butter over low heat. Add 1 cup diced mushrooms (any type) and sauté until they start to release their juices, about 3 minutes. Fold in ½ cup sour cream and keep warm, but do not allow the mixture to boil. For each serving, replace the English muffin halves topped with Canadian bacon with buttered toast topped with a slice of tomato and a slice of ham. Broil as directed above, then top with poached eggs. Spoon ¼ cup of the mushroom mixture over each of the eggs.

cleaning mushrooms p. 186

Eggs Florentine

Make a bed of sautéed spinach to replace the Canadian bacon: Heat 2 Tbsp butter in a large sauté pan over medium heat and add 6 cups trimmed spinach leaves. Sauté until the spinach is dark green and wilted, about 2 minutes. Season with salt and freshly ground pepper. Divide the spinach among the English muffin halves, omit the broiling, and top with the poached eggs and Hollandaise as above.

preparing spinach and leafy greens p. 184

Hollandaise Sauce

2 Tbsp white wine vinegar or cider vinegar

¼ tsp cracked peppercorns

2 large egg yolks, lightly beaten

¾ cup unsalted butter, melted and kept warm

2 tsp fresh lemon juice, or as needed

Salt and freshly ground white pepper

1 pinch ground cayenne pepper (optional)

Makes 1¼ cups

Heat the vinegar and peppercorns in a small pan over medium heat. Simmer until nearly dry, 3–4 minutes. Add 2 Tbsp water and strain into a stainless-steel bowl, discarding the peppercorns.

Whisk the egg yolks into this mixture and set the bowl over a pot of barely simmering water. Cook, whisking constantly, until the yolks triple in volume and fall in ribbons from the whisk when it is lifted, about 4 minutes.

Remove the bowl of yolks from the heat and set on a damp towel to keep the bowl from slipping. Gradually ladle in the warm melted butter in a thin stream, whisking constantly. As the butter is blended into the egg yolks, the sauce will thicken. If it becomes too thick, you can add a little water or lemon juice to loosen the yolks enough to absorb the remaining butter.

Add the lemon juice, ½ tsp salt, ¼ tsp pepper, and the cayenne, if desired. Taste and adjust the seasoning. Keep the sauce warm in the top of a double boiler or in an insulated bottle, and serve within 2 hours.

This luxuriously rich egg-based sauce makes a wonderful accompaniment to poached salmon, steamed broccoli, or fresh asparagus. For best results, don't overheat or overcook the egg yolks, or the sauce may separate or "break" as the butter is added. If this happens, or if the eggs begin to scramble, try adding a small amount of cool water and whisking until smooth, straining out any bits of overcooked yolk as needed.

separating eggs p. 229

using a double boiler p. 269

Mayonnaise

2 large egg yolks

1 Tbsp white wine vinegar

1 tsp dry mustard

1½ cups vegetable oil

Salt and freshly ground white pepper

1 Tbsp fresh lemon juice, or as needed

Makes 2 cups

Combine the egg yolks, 1 Tbsp water, the vinegar, and mustard in a bowl set on a damp towel to keep the bowl from slipping. Whisk well with a balloon whisk until the mixture is slightly foamy, about 2 minutes.

Gradually add the oil in a thin stream, constantly beating with the whisk, until the oil is incorporated and the mayonnaise is thick.

Add ½ tsp salt, ¼ tsp pepper, and the lemon juice and whisk to combine. Taste and season with salt, pepper, and lemon juice. Use at once, or cover and refrigerate the mayonnaise for up to 3 days.

Use the freshest, highest-quality eggs you can find for this recipe. However, if you are concerned about using raw eggs, look for pasteurized eggs in the shell, which are usually found in the dairy case next to the liquid egg substitutes.

separating eggs p. 229

Souffléed Cheddar Omelet

8 large eggs, separated

Salt and freshly ground pepper

½ cup grated sharp Cheddar

2 Tbsp minced fresh chives

Unsalted butter for greasing pan

Makes 4 servings

Preheat the oven to 400°F.

Beat the egg yolks in a bowl until blended and season with salt and pepper. Stir in the cheese and chives.

Grease the entire interior surface of a 10-inch cast-iron skillet with butter. Place it in the oven to preheat while preparing the ingredients.

Meanwhile, beat the egg whites with a handheld mixer at low speed until they become foamy and start to thicken. Increase the speed and beat until they hold medium peaks when the whip is turned upright. Gently fold the beaten whites into the yolk mixture.

Pour the egg mixture into the preheated skillet. Set over low heat until the sides and bottom have set, about 1 minute. Return the pan to the oven and bake until the omelet is puffed but fully set and light golden on top, about 15 minutes. Serve at once.

A souffléed omelet takes a little more time and effort to make than a regular omelet, but the dramatic results are definitely worth it. In this cross between a soufflé and an omelet, the eggs are separated and the whites whipped to medium peaks. Folded back together and baked briefly in a hot oven, the omelet rises into a puffy golden mound.

whipping egg whites p. 230

folding p. 270

Shirred Eggs

2 Tbsp unsalted butter, melted

8 large eggs

Salt and freshly ground pepper

4 Tbsp heavy cream, warmed

Makes 4 servings

Preheat the oven to 350°F. Brush four 5-inch round shallow gratin dishes with the melted butter.

Break the eggs into a bowl one at a time (reserve the eggs for another use if the yolks break) and slide 2 into each dish. Place on a baking sheet.

Put the baking sheet in the oven and bake just until the undersides of the eggs have set, 1–2 minutes.

Season the eggs with the salt and pepper. Drizzle 1 Tbsp of the cream over the eggs in each dish. Bake the eggs until the whites are set and the yolks thickened, 6–8 minutes more. Serve at once.

Shirring, or baking with cream, is another versatile way of cooking eggs. You may place any desired accompaniments—Canadian bacon slices, sautéed mushrooms, or a little ratatouille—underneath the eggs as they cook.

roasting and baking p. 30

making custards p. 272

Corn and Pepper Pudding

2 Tbsp unsalted butter, plus more for greasing dish

½ cup minced yellow onion

½ cup chopped bell pepper

1 jalapeño, minced (optional)

2 cups whole milk

2 large eggs

¾ cup grated Monterey Jack

1 cup fresh or thawed frozen corn kernels

2 tsp chopped fresh cilantro

1 tsp sugar

¼ tsp ground cumin

Salt and freshly ground pepper

Makes 6 servings

Preheat the oven to 325°F. Grease an 8-inch baking dish with butter.

Heat the butter in a sauté pan over medium heat. Add the onion and sauté until translucent, 6–7 minutes. Add the bell pepper and the jalapeño (if using), reduce the heat to low, cover the pan, and cook until the bell pepper is tender, 3–4 minutes. Remove the cover and cook off any liquid over high heat, or remove from the pan and gently drain on absorbent towels. The draining is an important step, since excess liquid will affect the cooking time and final texture.

Whisk together the milk and eggs. Add the bell pepper mixture, cheese, corn, cilantro, sugar, and cumin. Mix together well and season the mixture with salt and pepper. Pour the mixture into the prepared dish. Place in a larger baking pan, set on the oven rack, and then add enough hot water to the pan to come two-thirds of the way up the side of the dish. Bake until a knife blade inserted in the center of the custard comes out clean, 30–45 minutes. Let stand for 15 minutes to allow the custard to set before serving warm.

Baking this savory custard in a hot-water bath, or *bain-marie,* helps the egg mixture to retain its silky texture as it cooks. When the custard is done, lift the baking dish out of the hot water and set on a counter to cool. Leave the water-filled pan to cool in the oven before removing.

preparing corn kernels p. 186

baking in a water bath p. 271

Carrot Timbales

1 Tbsp vegetable oil, plus more as needed for greasing molds

¼ cup minced onion

2 tsp minced shallot

4 carrots, peeled and coarsely chopped

¼ cup vegetable or chicken broth

1 small piece bay leaf

2 sprigs fresh flat-leaf parsley

2 large eggs

¾ cup heavy cream

Salt and freshly ground white pepper

Makes 6 servings

Preheat the oven to 325°F. Lightly oil six ½-cup soufflé molds.

Sauté the onion and shallot in the oil in a skillet over medium heat until limp, about 5 minutes. Add the carrots, broth, bay leaf, and parsley. Cover and simmer over low heat until the carrots are very tender and most of the broth has cooked away, 10 minutes. Remove and discard the herbs. Purée until very smooth, then let cool to room temperature.

In a separate bowl, blend the eggs, cream, ¼ tsp salt, and ⅛ tsp white pepper. Add to the cooled vegetables. Spoon the mixture into the molds, leaving ¼–½ inch of space at the top of each mold. Place in a baking dish, set on the oven rack, and then add enough hot water to come up to the level of the vegetable mixture in the molds. Bake until the timbales are set and a knife blade inserted in the center of a mold comes out clean, 18–20 minutes. Tip the timbales out of the molds onto warmed plates and serve at once.

The carrots in this savory custard recipe can easily be substituted with other vegetables, including broccoli, spinach, beets, or squash. A combination of vegetables, such as parsnips and carrots, or beets and acorn squash, is also interesting. Serve these rich, creamy timbales as an accompaniment to a grilled or roasted entrée, or feature them on their own as an appetizer. If desired, serve with a salsa or fresh tomato sauce (p. 160).

puréeing p. 47

baking in a water bath p. 271

Frittata

1 cup diced peeled waxy yellow
or white potatoes

Salt and freshly ground pepper

4 strips bacon, diced

Vegetable oil, if needed

1 yellow onion, diced

8 large eggs

Makes 4 servings

Place the potatoes in a pot with enough cold water to cover by 2 inches. Salt the water. Gradually bring the water to a simmer over medium heat. Cover and simmer until the potatoes are easily pierced with a fork, about 10 minutes.

Cook the bacon in an ovenproof nonstick or cast-iron skillet over low heat until crisp, 2–3 minutes. Using a slotted spoon, transfer the bacon bits to paper towels to drain, then reserve. Add vegetable oil to the bacon fat in the pan if needed to make 2 Tbsp.

Raise the heat to medium-low and add the onion. Cook slowly, stirring occasionally, until translucent, 8–10 minutes. Add the potatoes and sauté until lightly browned, 8–10 minutes more.

Meanwhile, beat the eggs until blended and season with ½ tsp salt and ¼ tsp pepper. Pour them over the ingredients in the skillet, and add the crisp bacon bits to the mixture, stirring gently.

Preheat the broiler. Reduce the heat to low, cover the skillet, and cook until the eggs are nearly set, 6–8 minutes. Remove the cover and place the skillet under the broiler to brown the eggs lightly, about 3 minutes, while watching carefully. Cut into wedges and serve at once.

This flat, Italian-style omelet makes a great brunch or supper dish without the one-at-a-time attention required for French-style rolled omelets. In Spain, where it's filled with sliced potatoes and onions, it's known as *tortilla*, while American menus sometimes call it a farmer's omelet. In Italy, thin wedges of frittata are a popular filling for *panini*, or hard-roll sandwiches.

sautéing and stir-frying p. 32

dicing onions p. 180

VARIATIONS

Vegetable Frittata

Replace the potatoes with ½ cup *each* peas, thinly sliced carrots, and asparagus sliced on the bias. Boil or steam the vegetables until they are tender, drain well, then add to the onion after it is translucent. Proceed as directed above.

boiling, parboiling, or blanching p. 37

steaming p. 36

Sausage Frittata

Substitute ½ lb sweet Italian sausage, removed from its casing and crumbled, for the bacon. Sauté until browned and cooked through, about 5 minutes, and drain on absorbent towels. Pour off all but about 2 Tbsp of the fat; it usually is not necessary to add more oil. Proceed as directed above.

Quiche Lorraine

roasting and baking
p. 30

Crust

1⅓ cups all-purpose flour

½ tsp salt

½ cup shortening

4 slices thick-cut bacon

1 Tbsp unsalted butter or vegetable oil

1½ cups heavy cream or crème fraîche

3 large eggs

Salt and freshly ground pepper

Makes one 9-inch quiche;
6–8 servings

Preheat the oven to 350°F.

For the crust, combine the flour and salt. Cut the shortening into the flour using a fork, a pastry cutter, or two knives until the mixture looks like extremely coarse meal. Add 4 Tbsp cold water and quickly stir together into a shaggy mass with a fork. Do not overwork the dough. Form into a disk, wrap well, and chill in the refrigerator for 15–20 minutes before rolling the dough into an 11-inch round on a floured work surface. Fold the round in half and gently place in a 9-inch quiche pan or tart pan with a removable bottom. Unfold the round and press gently into the pan without stretching the dough.

To prebake the crust, line the dough with waxed or parchment paper. Fill with pie weights or dried beans and bake until the crust is set and dry, but not browned, about 12 minutes. Remove from the oven and remove the weights and paper.

Sauté the bacon in the butter in a sauté pan over medium heat until browned, 2–3 minutes. Remove with a slotted spoon and drain on absorbent towels.

Whisk together the cream and eggs until blended. Season with salt and pepper.

Crumble the bacon evenly over the crust. Add the egg mixture gradually, stirring it with a fork to distribute the bacon evenly.

Set the quiche pan on a baking sheet and bake until a knife blade inserted in the center comes out clean, 40–45 minutes. Serve hot or at room temperature.

Originating in the Lorraine region in northeastern France, this savory quiche traditionally includes only bacon, cream, and eggs. With its buttery crust and gently puffed, golden custard, it makes an elegant luncheon dish with a simple green salad and a glass of wine. If desired, replace the cream, completely or in part, with half-and-half or whole milk.

VARIATION

Spinach Quiche

Substitute 1 lb fresh spinach, blanched for 30 seconds, drained, squeezed dry, and chopped coarsely, or thawed frozen spinach, for all or part of the bacon. Proceed as directed above.

boiling, parboiling, or blanching p. 37

Savory Cheese Soufflé

1 Tbsp unsalted butter, plus more as needed for greasing

2 Tbsp all-purpose flour

1½ cups whole milk

Salt and freshly ground pepper

4 large eggs, separated

½ cup grated Parmesan (divided use), plus more for dusting

⅓ cup grated Gruyère or Emmenthaler cheese

Makes 4 appetizer servings

Preheat the oven to 425°F.

To make the soufflé base, melt the butter in a pan over medium heat and stir in the flour. Cook over low to medium heat, stirring frequently with a wooden spoon, to make a blond roux, about 5 minutes. Add the milk, whisking well until the mixture is very smooth. Season with salt and pepper. Simmer over low heat, stirring constantly, until very thick and smooth, about 5 minutes.

Put the egg yolks in a bowl and whisk them lightly. While whisking constantly, slowly ladle a small amount of the hot soufflé base into the egg yolks. Return the tempered yolks to the rest of the base and continue to simmer, stirring constantly, until thickened, 3–4 minutes. Do not allow the mixture to boil. Taste and season with salt and pepper.

Grease four ½-cup soufflé molds liberally with butter. Lightly dust the interior of the molds with grated Parmesan, tapping out the excess.

Fold together the soufflé base, ¼ cup of the Parmesan, and the Gruyère until the cheeses are evenly distributed. Adjust the seasoning with salt and pepper.

Just before baking, beat the egg whites until they hold soft peaks when the whisk is turned upright. Add about one-third of the beaten whites to the soufflé base and gently fold until incorporated. Fold in the remaining beaten whites in one or two more additions.

Spoon the soufflé batter into the prepared molds to within ½ inch of the rims. Wipe each rim clean. Tap the soufflés gently on the counter to settle the batter. Sprinkle the soufflé tops with the remaining Parmesan, about 1 tsp per soufflé.

Place the soufflés on a baking sheet and bake undisturbed until they are puffy and a knife blade inserted in the center of a mold comes out relatively clean, 16–18 minutes. Serve immediately.

The eggs for soufflés must be whipped just before baking, but that doesn't mean you can't plan ahead. The soufflé base may be cooled, refrigerated, and held for up to 2 days. Let the base warm up for 30 minutes at room temperature. Stir vigorously to loosen the base before folding in the beaten egg whites.

making a soufflé p. 233

tempering eggs p. 272

folding p. 270

Rolled Omelet

2 large eggs

1 Tbsp whole or low-fat milk, heavy cream, or water (optional)

Salt and freshly ground pepper

1 tsp unsalted butter, plus more as needed for coating omelet (optional)

3 Tbsp grated or crumbled cheese such as Cheddar, Gruyère, Asiago, manchego, Havarti, Monterey Jack, goat cheese, cream cheese, or feta

2 tsp minced fresh chives, tarragon, or flat-leaf parsley (or a combination)

Makes 1 serving

Break the eggs into a bowl. Add the milk, if using. Season with salt and pepper and whisk until evenly blended.

Have a serving plate ready by the stove. Heat the butter in a small nonstick omelet pan over high heat, tilting the pan to coat the entire surface.

Pour the egg mixture into the pan and scramble it with the back of a fork or wooden spoon as you gently shake the pan. Keep moving the pan and utensil at the same time until the egg mixture has coagulated and is nearly set, 2–3 minutes. Gently press the eggs down into an even layer and top with the cheese.

Lower the heat and let the egg mixture finish cooking without stirring, 15–20 seconds. Sprinkle with the herbs.

Tilt the pan and slide a fork or spoon under the omelet, to be sure it is not sticking. Slide the omelet to the front of the pan and use a fork or a wooden spoon to roll the edge nearest the handle toward the center of the omelet.

Tip the pan, rolling the omelet onto the serving plate. To give the omelet additional sheen, rub the surface lightly with butter.

Speedy cooking is the secret to a truly moist, tender omelet. If you are going to make several omelets in a row, have everything ready before you begin. Finished omelets can keep warm in a 200°F oven, but it's best to serve each as it's made.

making scrambled eggs or rolled omelets p. 232

VARIATIONS

Spinach Omelet

Heat 1 Tbsp butter in a large sauté pan over medium heat and add 2 cups trimmed spinach leaves. Sauté until the spinach is tender and fully cooked and any liquid has cooked away, about 2 minutes. Remove from the pan, chop finely and blend with about 1 Tbsp heavy cream. Fold this mixture into the eggs before cooking, then proceed as directed.

preparing spinach and leafy greens p. 184

Mushroom Omelet

Heat 2 tsp butter over low heat. Add ½ cup diced mushrooms (any type) and sauté until they start to release their juices, 2–3 minutes. Fold in 2 Tbsp sour cream and keep warm, but do not allow the mixture to boil. Season with salt and pepper. Proceed as directed above, spooning the mushroom mixture onto the omelet just before rolling.

cleaning mushrooms p. 186

Starters
9 # and Salads

A multicourse meal is a clear signal that the occasion is special. We don't always have the time or energy to cook several dishes for an ordinary meal. Still, even a weekday dinner can benefit from the civilizing influence of a separate first course. Salads made from crisp, colorful greens that have been carefully rinsed, spun dry, and dressed with a perfectly balanced vinaigrette make superb first courses. Or serve a fresh grapefruit half, a plate of sliced vine-ripened tomatoes drizzled with olive oil, or artichokes, steamed until tender and served with a vinaigrette for dipping. These simple foods are not difficult to prepare—and don't require a recipe.

Starters

French for "outside of the work," *hors d'oeuvre* refers to the bite-sized nibbles served to guests while they mingle and wait to be seated at the dinner table. Most hors d'oeuvres are finger foods, small enough to eat in one or two bites, and require no plates or utensils.

Appetizers are served as the first course; in other words, they are part of the meal itself, instead of a prelude like hors d'oeuvres. The success of a first course depends upon a number of factors. The appetizer or salad you select should have some relationship with the dishes that are going to follow. It is also important to remember that this is the first course, not the entrée. Keep the portions small enough just to take the edge off an appetite.

For a memorable dining experience, you can create a "tasting menu," a selection of starters and salads served in lieu of a single entrée or multicourse meal. The dishes may be suited to the weather or the season, taking advantage of seasonal ingredients, and the array of small plates creates the effect of a celebratory banquet.

Salads

In the United States, salads often begin a meal, although in Europe they generally appear after the main course as a palate refresher. In a meal of several courses, a salad might precede a warm first course, such as pasta or a soup, or it may be served alongside another dish, like a terrine or a savory tart. Often light and refreshing, salads are an excellent foil to rich foods. Whether a plate of carefully composed vegetables or an informal toss of spring greens, a salad provides a pleasant counterpoint to the richer elements of the meal.

The lettuces you choose determine a green salad's character. They may be mild or spicy. You can add bitter greens, fresh herbs, or even edible flowers to your salad for more flavor, colors, and texture. Or look for prepared salad blends, derived from such traditional combinations as French mesclun, which includes different greens according to the season.

The greens are the foundation of a salad, but garnishes add crucial color, texture, and flavor. Most important, the dressing ties all of a salad's components together. The dressing should contribute a distinct flavor without overpowering the greens, especially in salads of delicate spring greens. Sturdier greens can stand up to thicker, creamier dressings with more assertive flavors.

Side salads include potato and pasta salads, marinated vegetable salads, bean salads, and even fruit salads. These are perfect to accompany a lunch or dinner entrée. You can also make an array of these salads and serve a small portion of each one as a sampler plate.

When you carefully select a variety of ingredients and combine them in a single dish, you are making a composed salad. Chef's salads, Cobb salads, and Greek salads all fall into this category. Composed salads feature foods with contrasting colors, flavors, textures, heights, and temperatures.

Preparing starters and salads

Since the first course will set the stage for the entire meal, select the most delicious raw materials you can find. This does not mean the most expensive. It is simple enough to purchase a big tin of beluga caviar and trim the crusts off little toast points. The real goal, however, is to bring out the very best from simple foods.

Just as you should select the ingredients for appetizers and salads with great care, you should select the recipes with equal care. Consider the entire menu and choose an appetizer that is not too similar to the main course. If your main course includes mushrooms, for example, a mushroom-filled strudel to start is probably not the best choice. Similarly, note the tastes and preferences of the people you intend to feed. Salads and starters are a great way to introduce new ingredients or flavors, but you also want to please your friends and family.

Choose simple fare to introduce a complex or hearty main course. This is good advice on two counts. First, you want everyone to appreciate all the flavors, aromas, and textures of the meal's centerpiece rather than feeling overwhelmed by the starter. Second, you want to be able to sit down with everyone and enjoy the meal. However, if your main course is a simple grilled or sautéed dish that doesn't demand a lot of last-minute fussing, you might prefer a more elaborate first course.

This chapter includes some favorite starters and salads, but you can find more options throughout the other chapters of this book. For instance, try the tamarind grilled seafood (page 132), but thread the seafood onto smaller skewers to pass as hors d'oeuvres. Serve 2 or 3 ravioli or tortellini (pages 166–168) as a first course, instead of the main event. Start a wonderful springtime meal with delicious peas that have just arrived at market (page 196). Or enjoy risotto croquettes (page 225), made smaller than usual to eat as finger food.

Making crêpes

The thinner the crêpe, the better—with each new batch, practice until you find the right amount of batter and level of heat for your pan.

1 Making the batter

Crêpe batters have a more liquid consistency than other pancake batters. Whisk well to remove any lumps, then let the batter rest for 30–60 minutes to ensure tender crêpes.

2 Preparing the pan

Crêpes are typically prepared in a small, flat, round pan with short, sloped sides. Small nonstick skillets also work well. Heat the pan over medium heat and grease with butter or oil to prevent sticking (or, in the case of nonstick pans, to add flavor).

3 Cooking the crêpes

With a ladle or small measuring cup, quickly pour a small amount of batter into the pan. Immediately tilt and swirl the pan to spread the batter in a thin, even layer that just covers the bottom of the pan. Cook for a few minutes, then check the doneness of a crêpe by carefully lifting one edge and looking underneath it for a golden color with specks of light brown. With a metal spatula, loosen the edge of the crêpe from the pan, turn, and cook on the other side until golden. Crêpes are easily made in advance. Cool them completely on baking sheets lined with parchment or waxed paper, then stack the crêpes with parchment or waxed paper between each one. They can be wrapped well and refrigerated or frozen for later use.

Using phyllo dough

Cover the thin, delicate layers with a towel while working, to keep them moist and pliable.

Using frozen dough

Allow at least 12 hours for frozen phyllo to thaw in the refrigerator, or 5 hours at room temperature. Have at hand the prepared filling, a pastry brush, a sharp knife, and baking sheets to hold finished pastries before you unwrap the pastry sheets. Unwrap the sheets and unfold on a work surface. To keep the dough flexible as you work, cover the sheets with plastic wrap and then a lightly dampened towel. Lift 1 sheet at a time from the stack and re-cover the unused sheets. Brush melted butter over the surface of the pastry sheet. For the best texture, sprinkle bread crumbs over the butter to absorb excess moisture and keep the layers separate. Continue stacking sheets and brushing them with butter; some recipes call for 3 or 4 sheets, others may require 5 or 6. When finished, brush the top of the formed pastry or pastries with butter for a golden brown finish. Refrigerating the pastries before baking helps the layers to remain distinct and allows them to rise higher.

Preparing salad greens

Select a well-balanced mixture of textures and flavors for a refreshing interlude in any meal.

Washing greens

All salad greens, including prepackaged salad mixes and "triple-washed" bags of spinach, must be washed before serving. Separate lettuce or other heads of greens into leaves. If necessary, trim the coarse ribs or stem ends. To remove the core from heads of lettuce, gently rap the core on a hard surface. This will break the core away from the leaves and allow it to be pulled away easily. Tighter heads may require trimming the core with a paring knife. Fill a sink or large bowl with cool water. Plunge the greens into the water, lifting them gently in and out of the water to loosen sand and grit. Drain the water and repeat the washing as many times as needed until the water is clear.

Drying and storing greens

It is important to dry greens completely, as any residual water will dilute the flavor of the salad and prevent the dressing from coating the leaves properly. A spinner is the most effective tool for drying greens. Do not overcrowd the spinning basket, preventing the water from spinning off completely. Once greens are cleaned and dried, they can be refrigerated for up to 2 days before you dress and serve them. Store washed and dried greens in shallow containers, covered with a clean, damp cloth to keep them crisp. Do not stack the greens too deep, as the weight of the top leaves can bruise the bottom leaves.

Making vinaigrette

A vinaigrette is a popular and simple sauce that works as a salad dressing, marinade, or dip.

Selecting the ingredients

The typical ratio for vinaigrettes of 1 part vinegar to 3 parts oil works well as a starting point, but different types of oil, acidic ingredients, and other flavorings may affect the portions. Vinegars range widely in flavor and acidity, from a complex red wine vinegar to a delicate, fruity pear vinegar. An assertive oil is often blended with a less intense one to produce a more balanced flavor. Other acidic ingredients include fresh citrus juices or fruit purées. Additionally, both oils and vinegars can be infused with herbs or spices. For a typical tossed salad, plan on 1–2 tablespoons vinaigrette per 1-cup serving of greens.

Making the vinaigrette

Prepare the vinaigrette in a blender or whisk it together in the salad bowl itself. A vinaigrette is an emulsion, or blend of 2 liquids that do not mix easily, achieved through the suspension of tiny droplets of one liquid throughout another to create a smooth consistency. Vinaigrettes prepared by machine hold their emulsions longer than those whisked together by hand. The mixture can gain stability as well as flavor from natural emulsifying agents such as mustard and garlic. First, combine the vinegar with the seasonings, including any emulsifier. (Reserve fresh herbs for adding at the end.) Next, begin drizzling in the oil while blending or whisking constantly, until all of the oil is incorporated and the dressing begins to thicken. Vinaigrettes left to sit generally revert to their original, unemulsified state, so take the time to re-whip any vinaigrette that was made ahead of time before you serve it. Vinaigrettes can be refrigerated, but are best used within 3 days.

Tasting the vinaigrette

Always taste and adjust the ingredients as you make a vinaigrette. Before using the dressing, be sure to toss it with a few salad greens as described below. Simply tasting the vinaigrette "straight" or dunking a leaf into it does not give a true read of how it will taste when served as part of a salad.

Dressing salad greens

To dress a tossed salad, place the greens in a large bowl and drizzle a small amount of the dressing over them. Use tongs, salad spoons, or your hands to toss the salad gently in a lifting and rolling motion. Cover the greens evenly and lightly with the dressing. Since greens begin to wilt as soon as they are dressed, toss the salad just before serving for the best flavor and texture.

Hummus

1¼ cups cooked garbanzo beans (chickpeas), or one 15-oz can, rinsed and drained

2 Tbsp tahini paste

2 Tbsp fresh lemon juice, or to taste

1 Tbsp extra-virgin olive oil, plus more for drizzling (optional)

1 clove garlic, minced

Salt and freshly ground pepper

Makes 4 servings

Combine the garbanzo beans, tahini, lemon juice, olive oil, garlic, and 1 tsp salt in a food processor or blender and purée until a paste forms. Add water 1 Tbsp at a time and continue to purée until the mixture has a light, spreadable consistency, similar to mayonnaise.

Transfer the hummus to a bowl, taste, and season with lemon juice, salt, and pepper. Drizzle a little additional oil over the surface, if desired.

This popular Middle Eastern dip makes a wonderful sandwich filling for pita bread, with sliced cucumbers, onions, tomatoes, and lettuce. You can also try adding a pinch of cumin or some freshly chopped parsley for a different flavor. Look for tahini in natural foods stores or in the ethnic-foods section of your supermarket.

puréeing p. 47

zesting and juicing citrus p. 182

Romesco Sauce

2 dried ancho chiles

Boiling water as needed

4 Tbsp extra-virgin olive oil (divided use)

4 cloves garlic, halved

1 slice French or Italian bread, cubed

3 plum (Roma) tomatoes, peeled, seeded, and chopped, or 3 canned tomatoes

½ cup slivered toasted almonds

¼ cup red wine vinegar

½ tsp ground cumin

1 pinch ground cayenne pepper, or to taste

Salt and freshly ground black pepper

Makes 4 servings

Place the ancho chiles in a small bowl and add enough boiling water to cover them completely. Allow the chiles to steep until they are very tender, about 10 minutes. Drain, remove and discard the stems and seeds, and reserve the flesh.

Heat 1 Tbsp of the olive oil in a small skillet over low heat. Add the garlic and sauté until deep golden brown and aromatic, about 5 minutes. Remove the garlic and set aside. Add the bread cubes to the same oil and sauté until evenly toasted, about 1–2 minutes.

Combine the reserved anchos, the sautéed garlic, the toasted bread cubes, the tomatoes, almonds, vinegar, cumin, and cayenne in a blender or food processor. Purée until smooth. Then, with the machine running, add the remaining 3 Tbsp olive oil. Taste and season with salt and black pepper. Serve at room temperature.

This full-flavored Catalan sauce is often paired with seafood in Spain. It's also excellent with steamed green or white asparagus, cauliflower, or broccoli.

toasting nuts p. 26

puréeing p. 47

Roasted Pepper and Goat Cheese Canapés

2 Tbsp golden raisins

2 Tbsp dry sherry wine

4 Tbsp olive oil

2 Tbsp balsamic vinegar

1 tsp Dijon mustard

Salt and freshly ground pepper

½ cup diced, seeded tomato

½ red onion, thinly sliced

5 kalamata olives, pitted and cut into strips

2 Tbsp minced fresh cilantro, plus leaves for garnish

½ jalapeño, seeded and minced

1 clove garlic, minced

1 red bell pepper, roasted

1 yellow bell pepper, roasted

1 green bell pepper, roasted

8 slices whole-wheat bread

½ cup crumbled fresh goat cheese

¼ cup sour cream

Makes 16 hors d'oeuvres;
6–8 servings

Combine the raisins with the sherry and warm in a microwave oven for 40 seconds at full power. Or, combine in a small saucepan and warm over low heat. Allow the raisins to plump for about 10 minutes. Drain, reserving the liquid.

Whisk together the olive oil, vinegar, mustard, ¼ tsp salt, and ¼ tsp pepper in a large bowl. Add the tomato, onion, olives, minced cilantro, jalapeño, and garlic and stir to combine. Let the dressing rest while preparing the bell peppers.

Remove and discard the skin, seeds, and stems from the roasted bell peppers. Cut the peppers lengthwise into ⅛-inch-wide strips and add to the dressing. Add the plumped raisins and toss well. Set aside to marinate for at least 30 minutes or up to 2 hours.

Preheat the oven to 425°F. Punch out 2 circles from each bread slice with a 2-inch round cutter. Transfer to a baking sheet and toast in the oven until evenly browned and crisp, 3–4 minutes.

Whisk together the goat cheese and sour cream and transfer to a piping bag fitted with a round tip (about ¼-inch-diameter hole).

To assemble the canapés, pipe the goat cheese mixture in a ring around the edges of the toasted rounds. Or, spread or spoon the goat cheese on the toast circles. Mound about 1 Tbsp of the pepper salad in the center of each canapé and top with a cilantro leaf.

Easy to pick up, neat to eat, canapés are probably the best-known type of hors d'oeuvre. The base is a small piece of bread or toast, often cut into a decorative shape; the topping is up to you. Here, a chunky, smoky-sweet roasted pepper salad is matched with a creamy blend of goat cheese and sour cream.

preparing bell peppers and chiles p. 183

piping p. 271

Gravlax

1 salmon fillet, skin on
(about 3 lb)

¼ cup fresh lemon juice

2 Tbsp aquavit or gin (optional)

Cure

½ cup salt

¼ cup sugar

2 Tbsp freshly ground pepper

½ cup coarsely chopped
fresh dill

Makes 12–14 servings

Remove the pinbones from the salmon and center it skin side down on a large piece of cheesecloth. Brush the lemon juice and the aquavit, if using, over the salmon.

For the cure, combine the salt, sugar, and pepper. Pack evenly over one side of the salmon. (The layer should be slightly thinner where the fillet tapers to the tail.) Cover with chopped dill.

Wrap the salmon loosely in the cheesecloth and place it in a large baking pan. Top with a second large baking pan, and press with a 2-lb weight (a few cans of beans or a brick work well).

Refrigerate and let the salmon cure for 3 days. After the third day, gently scrape off the cure. Slice the gravlax as thinly as possible against the grain, on the diagonal. Hold your knife to slice at a 30-degree angle. Arrange on a platter or plates and serve.

Fishermen in Scandinavia once prepared this unsmoked, salt-cured salmon by packing salt and sugar over freshly filleted salmon. They buried the fish near a stream or river, and continued on their way upstream. When they returned, they would "harvest" the buried fish.

preparing salmon fillets p. 127

Seviche of Snapper

½ lb snapper fillet

2 Tbsp fresh lime juice

1 Tbsp extra-virgin olive oil

1 tsp minced jalapeño, seeded

1 clove garlic, minced

¼ tsp salt

⅛ tsp freshly ground pepper

2 plum (Roma) tomatoes

½ small red onion

1 green onion

4 tsp chopped fresh cilantro
or flat-leaf parsley

Makes 4 appetizer servings

Cut the snapper into small dice or strips.

Combine the lime juice, olive oil, jalapeño, garlic, salt, and pepper in a bowl and whisk to blend well. Add the snapper and toss to coat evenly. Cover and refrigerate for at least 8 hours or up to overnight.

As close as possible to the time you wish to serve the seviche, prepare the other vegetables. Peel and seed the tomatoes and cut into neat dice or julienne. Cut the red onion into very thin slices and separate the slices into rings. Cut the green onion, white and green parts, very thinly on the bias.

Fold the cilantro into the seviche and mound it on a chilled platter or individual plates. Scatter the tomato, red onion, and green onion on top of the seviche.

Other seafood may be used in this dish, including scallops, tuna, swordfish, squid, or monkfish. Fish with a relatively firm texture, like that of snapper, is the best choice. Select fish that is perfectly fresh, since the fish is "cooked" only by the acidity of the lime juice. Serve avocado slices as an accompaniment, and garnish the plates or platter with additional sliced tomatoes and sprigs of cilantro.

julienne p. 17

peeling and seeding tomatoes p. 184

Forest Mushroom Strudel

14 Tbsp unsalted butter
(divided use)

2 Tbsp minced shallot

1 clove garlic, minced

½ lb assorted mushrooms, such
as stemmed shiitake, cremini,
and white, coarsely chopped

3 Tbsp dry white wine

¼ cup crumbled fresh goat
cheese

1 tsp chopped fresh flat-leaf
parsley

1 tsp chopped fresh chervil

1 tsp chopped fresh chives

Salt and freshly ground pepper

3 sheets phyllo dough

3 Tbsp dried bread crumbs

Makes 4 appetizer servings or
8–10 hors d'oeuvre servings

Melt 2 Tbsp of the butter in a sauce pan over medium heat. Add the shallot and garlic and sauté until soft and translucent, about 3 minutes. Add the mushrooms and wine and continue to cook until the mushrooms release their moisture and it cooks away, 8–10 minutes. Remove from the heat and allow to cool thoroughly.

Preheat the oven to 400°F. Have ready a baking sheet. When the mushroom mixture is cool, add the goat cheese and herbs and mix in well to form a paste. Taste and season with salt and pepper.

Melt the remaining 12 Tbsp butter in a small saucepan over medium-low heat. Lay out a phyllo sheet on the baking sheet and brush with warm melted butter. Scatter lightly with 1 Tbsp bread crumbs. Top with the second and third sheets, brushing each time with butter and scattering with bread crumbs. Form the mushroom mixture into a cylinder at one long end of the phyllo sheets. Roll up the mixture in the phyllo, and brush the entire outside of the pastry with butter.

Use a small, sharp knife to make parallel diagonal cuts in the cylinder, about 1 inch apart, to mark portions. Do not cut more than one-third of the way through the pastry before baking. Bake until golden brown, 15–20 minutes. Allow to cool slightly before slicing all the way through the cuts. Serve warm.

Although goat cheese is called for in this recipe, cream cheese, ricotta, or mascarpone may be used in its place. Using an assortment of wild mushrooms boosts flavor and texture, although the strudel is still delicious made with only white mushrooms. This dish makes a nice appetizer but may also be served as a main course when paired with a salad or fresh vegetables.

using phyllo dough
p. 249

cleaning mushrooms
p. 186

making bread crumbs
p. 26

Quick Chicken Liver Terrine

10 oz chicken livers

8 Tbsp unsalted butter

1 shallot, minced

Salt and freshly ground white
pepper

½ tsp ground cinnamon

1 pinch ground nutmeg

¼ cup dry Marsala wine

¼ cup heavy cream

Makes 6 servings

Trim the chicken livers of any connective tissue. In a large sauté pan, melt the butter over medium heat and cook the shallot until translucent, about 3 minutes. Add the livers and sauté until cooked through, about 7 minutes. Add ½ tsp salt, ¼ tsp white pepper, cinnamon, and nutmeg to taste, then add the Marsala. Purée the mixture in a blender or food processor.

In a mixing bowl, whip the cream until it holds soft peaks when the whisk is turned upright. Fold the whipped cream into the puréed mixture and pour into a 6-cup terrine mold. Cover with plastic wrap and refrigerate overnight.

Serve the terrine directly from the terrine mold.

If you like, substitute dry sherry or port for the Marsala in this recipe. Serve with crackers or toast points.

puréeing p. 47

whipping cream p. 269

Pizza Margherita

¾ cup warm (105–115°F) water

2½ tsp (1 package) dry yeast

1 tsp honey

1⅓ cups bread flour

1 cup semolina flour

¼ tsp salt

Vegetable oil for coating

Cornmeal for sprinkling (optional)

Topping

1 Tbsp extra-virgin olive oil

1 Tbsp chopped fresh basil

1 tsp chopped fresh oregano

1 clove garlic, minced

Freshly ground pepper

1 cup tomato purée

4 plum (Roma) tomatoes, sliced

4¼ oz part-skim mozzarella, thinly sliced

¼ cup grated Parmesan

Makes 4 individual pizzas or 1 large pizza

Combine the water, yeast, and honey in a large bowl. Stir in just enough of the bread flour to make a batter about the consistency of buttermilk. Cover and let proof in a warm place until the surface is puffy, about 1 hour.

Add the remaining bread flour, the semolina flour, and the salt. Knead in a stand mixer fitted with a dough hook on medium speed, or by hand, until the dough is smooth, springy, and elastic, 4 minutes with the mixer or 10 minutes by hand. Rub the dough lightly with oil, place in a clean bowl, and cover with a cloth. Let the dough rise at warm room temperature until doubled in volume, about 1½ hours.

Punch down the dough, sinking your fist into it to deflate it, and divide into 4 equal pieces for individual pizzas or leave whole for a large pizza. Form the dough into smooth ball(s), cover, and let rise again until doubled in volume, 45–60 minutes.

Preheat the oven to 450°F. Lightly oil a 16-inch pizza pan or a large baking sheet with vegetable oil or scatter with cornmeal.

On a lightly floured surface, roll and stretch out the ball(s) of dough to an even ¼-inch thickness. If the dough has not relaxed properly, it may spring back as you stretch it; simultaneously spinning and stretching the dough will help. (This may be accomplished flat on a work surface or by spinning and tossing it into the air, then catching the disk on the back of your hands. Avoid tearing the dough or creating very thin patches.) Transfer the dough round to the prepared pan.

For the topping, mix together the olive oil, basil, oregano, garlic, and pepper to taste. Spread this mixture evenly over the pizza dough. Spread evenly with the tomato purée and top with the sliced tomatoes and mozzarella. Scatter the Parmesan over the top.

Bake until the dough is golden brown and the toppings are very hot, 20–30 minutes for 1 large pizza or 10–12 minutes for individual rounds. Cut into wedges and serve at once, or let cool for 5–10 minutes and serve warm.

Avoid the temptation to add too many toppings; a pizza should be more bread than topping. In fact, the basic dough in this recipe may be used to prepare a delicious grilled bread as well as the base for pizza. Shape the dough as you would for individual pizzas, and then grill it over hot coals for about 2 minutes on each side, until it is blistered and browned. After the dough is turned, drizzle with olive oil and scatter it with fresh herbs such as oregano, basil, thyme, or rosemary.

roasting and baking
p. 30

Spinach and Arugula Salad with Strawberries

Vinaigrette

1 Tbsp red wine vinegar

1 Tbsp balsamic vinegar

¼ tsp salt

3 Tbsp olive oil

2 cups baby spinach leaves

2 cups arugula leaves

1 cup sliced strawberries

Freshly ground pepper

Makes 4 servings

For the vinaigrette, measure the vinegars and salt into a salad bowl, then gradually add the oil while whisking until emulsified.

Add the greens to the vinaigrette and toss gently, using a lifting motion. When the greens are lightly coated, transfer to chilled plates, top with the strawberries, and finish with a generous grinding of pepper.

Tossed salad lends itself to innumerable variations. When creating a new one, remember to use light dressings with delicate greens and more robust dressings with more strongly flavored greens. Choose garnishes, if desired, according to the season, your intended presentation, and the other flavors in your meal.

preparing spinach and leafy greens p. 184

making vinaigrette p. 250

VARIATIONS

Boston Lettuce with a Lemon, Dill, and Parsley Vinaigrette

Replace the olive oil with vegetable oil and use 1 Tbsp white wine and 2 tsp lemon juice in place of the vinegar. Whisk the vinaigrette together with 2 tsp *each* minced fresh dill and parsley. Replace the greens with 2 small heads Boston lettuce, leaves torn into bite-sized pieces. Replace the strawberries with ½ cup haricots verts, blanched, and ¼ cup thinly sliced radish. Toss as directed above.

boiling, parboiling, or blanching p. 37

Frisée with Goat Cheese and Almonds

Replace the greens with 2 cups frisée (or chicory, tender yellow inner leaves only) and 2 cups mixed mild greens. Dress the greens as directed above, then finish each salad with a broiled goat cheese button (use four 1-oz "buttons," or cut a log into 1-inch pieces; press fresh white bread crumbs over the surface and broil until the cheese is hot and the bread crumbs on the top turn golden brown) and 1 Tbsp toasted sliced almonds.

grilling and broiling p. 28

toasting nuts p. 26

making bread crumbs p. 26

Celeriac and Tart Apple Salad

½ cup all-purpose flour

2 Tbsp fresh lemon juice, plus more as needed

½ lb celeriac (celery root)

Dressing

3 Tbsp crème fraîche

3 Tbsp mayonnaise (p. 237)

1 Tbsp Dijon mustard

1 Tbsp fresh lemon juice

1 tsp sugar

Salt and freshly ground pepper

1 Granny Smith apple

Makes 4 servings

Put 4 cups water in a bowl with the flour and 2 Tbsp lemon juice. Whisk to combine and make a *blanc*.

Cut away the outer rind of the celeriac and cut into matchsticks about 1½ inches long. As they are cut, place them in the *blanc* to prevent discoloring.

Bring a large pot of water to a boil, to which 2 Tbsp lemon juice has been added for each 4 cups water.

For the dressing, whisk together the crème fraîche, mayonnaise, mustard, lemon juice, sugar, and salt and pepper to taste in a serving bowl.

Rinse the celeriac, then add to the boiling water and cook until tender. Drain, plunge into a bowl of cold water, and drain again on absorbent towels.

Peel, core, and dice the apple. Fold the apple and celeriac into the dressing. Taste and season with salt and pepper before serving.

Celeriac, also known as celery root, discolors quickly once it is cut. To prevent browning, the cut celeriac in this recipe is held in a *blanc* (a mixture of water, flour, and an acid such as lemon juice), which slows the discoloring.

boiling and simmering p. 37

julienne p. 17

Blackened Tomato Salsa

5 plum (Roma) tomatoes

1 Tbsp olive oil or vegetable oil

1 Spanish onion, cut into ¼-inch-thick slices

½ dried chipotle chile or canned chipotle in adobo sauce, plus as needed

Salt

Warmed flour tortillas or corn chips for serving

Makes about 3 cups; 6 servings

Place the tomatoes on a wire rack directly over a gas burner or under a preheated broiler. Turn frequently until they are evenly blackened on all sides, about 45 seconds. When cool enough to handle, slip off the blackened skins, core and seed the tomatoes, and chop them coarsely. Place in a bowl and set aside.

Heat the oil in a large sauté pan over medium heat. Add the onion slices and cook on both sides until they are a very deep brown, 15–20 minutes.

Coarsely chop the onion. Combine the tomatoes, onion, chile, and ¼ tsp salt in a blender or food processor. Purée the mixture in short pulses to make a relatively even purée. Taste and season with salt and chipotle (and ¼ tsp adobo sauce, or to taste, if using).

Serve warm or at room temperature with tortillas or chips.

Spanish onions are large yellow cooking onions, usually sold loose in bins. Chipotle chiles, which are jalapeño peppers that have been dried and smoked, contribute a distinctive smoky flavor to this salsa. To store the salsa, cover and refrigerate for 3–4 days.

grilling and broiling p. 28

puréeing p. 47

Niçoise Salad

4 new red potatoes

Salt

½ lb green beans

½ cup julienned red onion

2 Tbsp chopped fresh flat-leaf parsley

2 tsp capers, rinsed and chopped

½ cup vinaigrette (p. 258)

2 cups mixed greens

One 12-oz can tuna, drained and flaked

2 plum (Roma) tomatoes, peeled and quartered

2 large eggs, hard boiled, peeled, and quartered

8 anchovy fillets

16 pitted Niçoise or kalamata olives

Makes 4 servings

Place the potatoes in a saucepan with enough cold water to cover by 2 inches. Salt the water. Gradually bring the water to a simmer over medium heat. Cover and simmer until the potatoes are easily pierced with a fork, 10–12 minutes. Drain, cool under running water, and quarter the potatoes.

Trim the ends of the green beans. Simmer in ½ inch of water over medium heat until barely tender, 4–5 minutes. Drain and cool under running water.

Toss together the green beans, potatoes, onion, parsley, and capers. Add the vinaigrette and toss.

Arrange the greens on a platter. Place the tuna in the center. Arrange the bean and potato mixture around the tuna. Garnish the plate with the tomatoes, eggs, anchovies, and olives.

For the most authentic flavor in this dish, seek out imported Italian tuna packed in olive oil. Cut from the belly of the fish, this tuna is a little fattier and more flavorful than other canned tunas.

preparing salad greens p. 250

hard-boiling eggs p. 229

VARIATIONS

Greek Salad

Substitute 2 cups romaine lettuce for the mixed greens. Toss together ½ cup *each* diced or sliced cucumber, red onion, and tomato. Scatter evenly over the romaine, drizzling with any vinaigrette that remains in the bowl. Top with ½ cup crumbled feta cheese, 4 pickled peppers, and 16 kalamata olives. Serve with stuffed grape leaves (p. 263).

Cobb Salad

Make a lettuce base as for the Greek salad above. Then top as follows, arranging the ingredients in rows or strips: 1 cup diced turkey breast meat, 1 cup diced avocado, 1 cup diced tomato, ½ cup crumbled blue cheese, and ½ cup crumbled cooked bacon. Top with ¼ cup minced or bias-cut green onions.

Crêpes with Zucchini and Mushroom Filling

Crêpes

¾ cup all-purpose flour

Salt

1 cup whole milk

1 large egg

1 Tbsp unsalted butter, melted and cooled to room temperature, or vegetable oil

Zucchini and Mushroom Filling

1 Tbsp olive oil

2 green onions, white and green parts, sliced thinly on the bias

1 clove garlic, minced

½ cup sliced white or wild mushrooms

½ cup shredded zucchini

1 plum (Roma) tomato, peeled, seeded, and chopped

1 tsp chopped fresh tarragon leaves or ½ tsp dried

½ cup crumbled feta cheese

1 tsp fresh lemon juice, or as needed

Freshly ground pepper

Vegetable oil for pan

Makes 4 servings

For the crêpes, sift the flour and ⅛ tsp salt together into a bowl. In another bowl, whisk together the milk, egg, and butter until evenly blended. Add all at once to the dry ingredients. Stir just enough to make a smooth batter. Let the batter rest, refrigerated, for at least 2 hours or up to overnight. If the batter has lumps, strain through a sieve before preparing the crêpes.

For the filling, heat the olive oil in a skillet over high heat. Add the green onions and garlic and sauté for 2–3 minutes. Add the mushrooms and continue to cook, stirring occasionally, until the mushrooms release their moisture and it cooks away, about 5 minutes more. Add the zucchini, tomato, and tarragon and sauté until the moisture has cooked away, 10 minutes more. Remove from the heat and fold in the feta cheese. Taste and season with lemon juice, salt, and pepper.

Heat a crêpe pan or small nonstick skillet over medium-high heat and brush liberally with oil. Ladle about ⅓ cup of the batter into the crêpe pan. Lift the pan from the heat and tilt and swirl to completely coat the pan with a thin layer of batter. Cook on the first side until set and lightly browned, about 1½ minutes. Turn or flip the crêpe and finish cooking on the second side, 30–45 seconds more. Flip the crêpe out of the pan onto a plate lined with parchment or waxed paper. Repeat with remaining batter to make 8 crêpes in all.

If needed, reheat the filling over low heat, stirring occasionally, about 5 minutes. Place 2 Tbsp of the warm filling in the center of each of the warm crêpes. Fold the right side to the middle and roll up the crêpe. Serve at once.

The filling for these delicate crêpes may be prepared, cooled, and refrigerated for up to a day. Reheat before serving by warming gently in a 200°F oven. The crêpes may also be made in advance, separated with squares of parchment or waxed paper, and wrapped tightly and refrigerated for up to 3 days, or frozen for up to 6 weeks.

making crêpes p. 249

peeling and seeding tomatoes p. 184

Stuffed Grape Leaves

¼ cup olive oil

½ cup finely diced yellow onion

2 cloves garlic, chopped

½ cup long-grain white rice

2 cups peeled, seeded, and diced tomato or canned diced tomato

Salt and freshly ground pepper

2 Tbsp chopped fresh flat-leaf parsley

2 Tbsp toasted pine nuts (optional)

16 brined or fresh grape leaves

2 cups vegetable broth, or as needed

2 Tbsp fresh lemon juice

Lemon wedges for serving

Makes 16 hors d'oeuvres;
6–8 servings

Heat the oil in a sauté pan over medium-low heat. Add the onion and garlic and sauté until aromatic but not colored, 6–8 minutes. Add the rice and stir to coat with the oil. Add the tomato, ½ tsp salt, and ¼ tsp pepper. Stir and cook to heat through, about 2 minutes. Transfer to a bowl and mix in the parsley and pine nuts (if using). Set aside and let cool.

If using brined grapes leaves, trim the stems, rinse the leaves thoroughly, and pat dry. If using fresh grape leaves, choose unblemished flexible leaves and rinse them thoroughly; drop the leaves into rapidly boiling salted water and blanch until softened, about 1 minute. Scoop out, plunge into a bowl of ice water, and drain.

Place the grape leaves, smooth side down, on a work surface. Place 2 Tbsp of the rice mixture in the center of each leaf. Roll one long side of each grape leaf around the filling once, then fold in the sides to enclose the ends of the roll. Repeat with the remaining leaves. If the leaves are small, you can overlap several to give enough surface area to roll up the filling.

Place a rack on the bottom of a Dutch oven. (This will prevent the stuffed grape leaves from sticking.) Place the rolls, seam side down and side by side but with a little space between them, on top of the rack.

Pour in the broth, adding more as needed to cover the rolls, and add the lemon juice. Use a weighted plate to keep the rolls submerged and under pressure. Bring the broth to a simmer over medium heat and adjust the heat to maintain a gentle simmer. Braise until the rice is fully cooked, about 1 hour. The grape leaves may be served now, or allowed to cool in their cooking liquid to room temperature, then covered and refrigerated for at least 3 hours or up to overnight; they may be served cold. Serve with lemon wedges.

These tangy little rolls, also known as *dolmata* or *dolma*, are Greek in origin. Some versions include ground lamb; others, like these, are stuffed with a savory vegetarian mixture of aromatic rice studded with pine nuts and spritzed with fresh lemon juice. Look for brined grape leaves in shops specializing in Mediterranean products, or in well-stocked supermarkets. If you live near a vineyard or in an area where grapevines flourish wild, you may be able to find fresh grape leaves. (Avoid vines that are treated with sprays or that grow near highways.)

boiling, parboiling, or blanching p. 37

toasting nuts p. 26

Vietnamese Fried Spring Rolls

Filling

2 dried tree ear mushrooms

4 water chestnuts, finely minced

⅓ cup picked crabmeat

5 or 6 medium shrimp, peeled, deveined, and minced

¼ lb ground pork butt

⅓ cup minced green onion

1 tsp minced gingerroot

1 clove garlic, minced

2 tsp Vietnamese fish sauce (nuoc mam)

2 tsp dry sherry wine

¼ tsp freshly ground white pepper

1 egg, lightly beaten

Wrappers

4 Tbsp sugar

16 rice paper rounds (9 inches in diameter)

Dipping Sauce

¼ cup Vietnamese fish sauce (nuoc mam)

⅓ cup sugar

3 Tbsp fresh lemon juice

3 Tbsp rice vinegar

1 garlic clove, finely minced

2 tsp chili sauce

4 cups peanut oil for frying

Fresh chives for garnish

Makes 16 rolls; 4 appetizer servings

For the filling, place the mushrooms in a small bowl with warm water to cover and heat in a microwave oven for 40 seconds at full power. Or, combine in a small saucepan and warm over low heat. Allow the mushrooms to plump for 10 minutes. Drain and blot dry. Mince finely and combine with the remaining ingredients for the filling.

For the wrappers, stir the sugar into 4 cups warm water in a large, shallow bowl. Moisten 1 wrapper in the sugar water until it is pliable, about 10 seconds, and place it on a clean kitchen towel. Put ⅓ cup of the filling 1 inch from the bottom of the wrapper. Fold the end over the filling and fold in each side of the wrapper and roll to enclose completely. Moisten the end of the wrapper with additional water if needed to seal. Place seam side down on a baking sheet lined with parchment or waxed paper. Repeat with the remaining wrappers and filling.

For the dipping sauce, whisk together the fish sauce, sugar, lemon juice, vinegar, 2 Tbsp water, the garlic, and the chili sauce in a small bowl. Cover and refrigerate while heating the oil.

Pour the peanut oil into a deep pot with tall sides to a depth of 3 inches and heat over medium-high heat until it registers 350°F on a deep-frying thermometer. Deep-fry the rolls in batches until golden brown, about 4 minutes.

Garnish with chives and serve with the dipping sauce.

Known as *cha gio,* these crunchy rolls are traditionally served during Vietnam's Tet Festival, the Lunar New Year celebration in early February that also marks the beginning of spring.

deep-frying p. 35

rehydrating and plumping p. 182

10 Kitchen Desserts

In the professional kitchen, the more time-consuming and elaborate desserts, such as pastries, cakes, and tortes, are the domain of the pastry chef. Smaller restaurants without a pastry chef rely on the regular kitchen staff to produce what are known as "kitchen desserts." Simple fruit desserts, custards, puddings, crêpes, and soufflés all fall into this category. These sweets have all the hallmarks of a good homemade dessert: easily made, with simple ingredients like farm-fresh eggs, sweet butter, sugar, heavy cream, perfectly ripe fruit, or good-quality chocolate. They are soul-sustaining and satisfying.

Fruit

A generous bowl of perfect berries or a tree-ripe pear is pure luxury all on its own. Adding a dollop of sweetened cream, shredded herbs, or a splash of a liqueur are all ways of elevating the dish to another level. You can blanket sliced peaches or plums with a foamy sabayon sauce and broil them to create a fruit gratin. Fruit fritters pair contrasting textures and flavors in a dessert that you can eat with your fingers. You can sauté some fruits, especially apples, plums, and pears, and then wrap them in a crêpe.

Custards

Many of the desserts in this chapter, including the ice creams, soufflés, puddings, and many sauces, are based on a combination of eggs, cream (or milk), and sugar—a basic custard. Bake a basic custard mixture and you get crème caramel and its close relations, crème brûlée and bread pudding. Stir that same mixture over the gentle heat of a water bath and the result is a dessert sauce known variously as custard sauce, crème anglaise, or *zuppa inglese*. In addition to using it as an accompaniment to something else, you can cool it and then fold in flavorings and whipped cream or a meringue to make a Bavarian cream. Freeze Bavarian cream in a collared mold for a frozen soufflé or parfait.

Puddings and pastry cream

When you heat a basic custard, whether you bake it or stir it over direct heat, the eggs in the mixture are what thickens it. (To read more about how eggs behave when you cook them, turn to Chapter 8.) When you make a pudding or pastry cream, you may replace the thickening effect of the eggs—all of the eggs or just some of them—with flour or cornstarch. Pudding is a delightful dessert served on its own, perhaps topped with a spoonful of whipped cream. Pastry cream, however, is a building block to use as a filling or to create one of the most spectacular offerings in the kitchen dessert repertoire, the hot dessert soufflé.

Soufflés

A soufflé is made by folding beaten egg whites into pastry cream. Then, as the mixture cooks in a hot oven, the egg white foam expands, while the pastry cream bakes into a network that just barely supports the soufflé as it rises high above the rim of the dish. Add flavor and color to soufflés by blending into the pastry cream base ingredients like fruit purées, liqueurs, melted chocolate, or extracts. A dessert soufflé does call for some advance planning. When it comes out of the oven, someone should be ready and waiting to enjoy it.

Frozen desserts

When you make a custard sauce and then stir or agitate it as it freezes, the result is ice cream. French ice cream generally relies upon egg yolks and cream, while American-style ice cream may be slightly less rich, made with a combination of cream, milk, and whole eggs. The Italian version of ice cream, gelato, is typically made with milk and plenty of eggs. All of these desserts are churned as they are frozen.

You can use this same freezing method to produce sorbet. Instead of using custard as the base, however, mix fruit juice or fruit purée with a sugar syrup. Since sorbet doesn't have the butterfat of ice creams, it has a lighter, icier texture. Flavor a sorbet base with infusions of tea, spices, or herbs. The base mixture of a granita is essentially the same as for a sorbet. However, instead of being constantly churned like sorbets, granitas are left to freeze undisturbed in shallow containers. Once they freeze solid, they are scraped by hand into flakes. The result is that granitas have a grainier, icier texture than sorbets.

Dessert sauces

In addition to versatile custard sauce, make chocolate sauce, caramel sauce, and a selection of fruit sauces part of your repertoire. Custard sauce should be enjoyed within a few days, but chocolate and caramel sauces can be made in large quantities and held for weeks. You can enjoy a farm-stand splurge all through the year if you make a garnet red raspberry sauce and freeze it.

A stash of dessert sauces in your freezer or refrigerator makes it easy to add great taste and color to simple slices of pound cake, angel food cake, or sponge cake. Fold a sauce into whipped cream for a quick filling or icing. Bring fruit sauces out at breakfast to drizzle on pancakes or waffles.

In the best of all possible worlds, each meal would be a ritual, a chance to step outside the daily crush of meetings and appointments, deadlines and demands. We don't always have the luxury of the time required to plan an entire menu, shop, and then prepare the meal. But when life is at its most hectic, it becomes even more meaningful to sit down with friends and family to share a cup of coffee or tea and a simple homemade dessert when the day has at last wound down.

Whipping cream

Heavy cream may be whipped to soft or medium peaks for use in sweet and savory applications.

1 Whipping in air

Use a balloon whisk or electric mixer to whip cream. Chilling the cream as well as the bowl and whisk or beaters helps produce a more stable foam that holds volume when folded into other ingredients. Begin whipping the cream at a moderate speed. Once the cream begins to thicken, increase the speed and continue to whip until the cream reaches the desired thickness. Cream may be whipped to soft peaks or medium peaks (see page 230); avoid beating cream to stiff peaks, as it will lose much of its flexibility as well as its sheen and velvety texture. Cream will eventually turn to butter if the whipping continues. For best results, sugar and other flavorings should be added after the cream is whipped to soft peaks. When cream is sweetened with confectioners' sugar and flavored with vanilla, it is called chantilly cream.

Using a double boiler

Egg-based sauces are best prepared with controlled heat.

1 Setting up a double boiler

A double boiler is a saucepan with a second pan or bowl that nests on top. Steam from water simmered in the bottom pan rises and heats the top pan or bowl, so food placed in the top receives even, gentle heat that never rises above the temperature of the steam. If you do not own a specially made set of double boiler pans, place a heatproof bowl over a saucepan, making sure it fits the pan snugly. There should be at least 3 inches between the bottom of the bowl and the bottom of the pan. Fill the bottom pan with 1 inch of water and heat just to the point of simmering. Place the food to be heated in the top, then set it over (but not touching) the simmering water. Do not let the water boil; adjust the heat to maintain a slow simmer.

Using prepared puff pastry dough

Work quickly to prevent warming the dough.

Thawing slightly and rolling out

Thaw frozen puff pastry as directed on the package, letting the dough soften just until it becomes pliable but is still cool to the touch. Keep the dough chilled, taking out only the amount you will work with during a short period of time. If the dough becomes too warm, the butter in between the thin layers will begin to melt into the flour, making the finished pastry gummy and less flaky. Use a sharp knife when cutting and shaping the dough. Clean cuts ensure even rising. If you need to roll the dough to make it thinner, use gentle, even pressure and avoid running your roller over the edge of the dough. Refrigerate the puff pastry after forming and before baking. Chilling helps keep the layers distinct, ensuring the best rise in the oven and flakiness in the finished dish.

Folding

This gentle technique combines a light mixture such as beaten eggs with a heavier base to produce mousses and soufflés.

1 Lightening the base

Put the heavier base mixture (for example, a soufflé base) into a bowl large enough to hold the base and the foam easily, and to permit you to work freely. Stir or whip the base to make it as light and smooth as possible. As you mix a foam and a base together, even if you use a very gentle touch, the foam starts to deflate. Blending a small portion of the foam first with the base lightens the base and makes it easier for you to fold in the remaining foam while keeping as much volume as possible. Use a rubber spatula with a long handle or a whisk to blend one-fourth to one-third of the foam with the base.

2 Folding in the remaining foam

After the base is lightened, add the remaining foam in two or three more additions. Use a sweeping and lifting motion to fold the mixtures together. Sweep the spatula or whisk down under the base, pressing its edge against the bowl, and then bring it up through the center of the base and foam in a circular motion toward your body. Twist your wrist so that the spatula edge cuts cleanly through the base as you sweep up. Give the mixing bowl a quarter turn and repeat the folding motion until the mixtures are blended, with no streaks or clumps of foam.

Melting chocolate

Use gentle or brief heat to melt chocolate.

1 Heating gently

Cut the chocolate into small pieces with a sharp knife. Place in the top of a double boiler (see page 269). As it melts, stir frequently with a wooden spoon or rubber spatula. Alternatively, to use a microwave to melt chocolate, put the chocolate in a nonmetal bowl and use a low to medium power setting and keep the cooking time very brief, just a few seconds at a time. The chocolate should look glossy and become lighter in color but still retain the shape it had before melting. Stir to liquefy. Once the chocolate is melted, it is a good idea to let it cool to room temperature, and to stir in a bit of the batter or base it will be blended into so that it mixes in easily without hardening.

Baking in a water bath

Water helps control temperatures when baking delicate dishes such as those containing eggs.

1 Setting up the water bath

A water bath consists of a container or containers, such as a baking dish or ramekins, placed inside a larger, shallow pan filled with warm water. Foods with a large amount of eggs, such as custards or bread puddings, are baked in the dish while benefitting from the insulation that the water provides; otherwise, the harsh heat of the oven could cause the eggs to curdle. To prepare a water bath, select a shallow pan large enough to hold the dish or ramekins that will be filled with food. There should be space all around each dish. To avoid spilling water, place the pan with the dish or ramekins of food onto the oven rack and then fill the pan with hot water to reach halfway up the sides of the dish or ramekins. Bake as directed. Remove the dish or ramekins from the pan and let the water cool before removing the pan from the oven.

Piping

Even pressure and steady movements produce decorative shapes.

1 Filling the bag

Pastry bags can be used with tips for decorative piping or without them for making plain round shapes with meringues, doughs, or cheeses. To fill a pastry bag, position the tip securely in the bag's opening or in a coupler or tipholder. Fold down the bag's top to create a wide cuff, then transfer the piping ingredient to the bag with a large spoon. Support the bag with your free hand while filling it. Use a tall container to support the bag if you need to use both hands, folding down the cuff around the edge of the container. Fill the pastry bag only two-thirds full, as you will need excess cloth to twist it securely closed.

2 Closing the bag

Twist the bag to close, compressing the mixture and releasing any air pockets before starting to pipe.

3 Piping

Holding the bag at a 45-degree angle, use your dominant hand to slowly and steadily squeeze the bag and your other hand to guide and steady the tip. Release pressure on the bag as you lift it away to make clean lines without thin tails. For decorative work, you may want to test the piping on parchment or waxed paper first to adjust your pressure to the consistency of the filling. After each use, wash tips and reusable pastry bags thoroughly in warm, soapy water and dry them completely inside out.

Making custards

Egg-based custard requires some attention but adds rich flavor and silky texture.

1 Types of custard

Smooth and liquid stirred custard is used as the base for ice creams and mousses or as a sauce on its own, known as *crème anglaise;* when starch is added, it becomes pastry cream, used as a filling or base for dessert soufflés. Stirred custards have a soft "set" because keeping the mixture in motion prevents proteins from setting in a uniform network. Baked custards are not disturbed as they cook, so they set firmly, often firm enough to unmold or even slice.

2 Tempering eggs

When eggs are added to a large amount of hot liquid, such as a pot of milk or cream, they must be tempered first so that they do not curdle. Whisk the eggs or egg yolks in a small bowl until smooth. While whisking constantly, slowly pour a small amount of the hot liquid into the eggs. Then, stir this mixture back into the pot. This technique heats the eggs more gradually than simply stirring them into a hot liquid all at once. After the eggs are added, the liquid may be heated, but do not bring it to a boil or the eggs will curdle.

3 Making stirred custards

Once eggs, milk or cream, and the other ingredients in a custard are combined over heat, stir the mixture constantly with a wooden spoon or heatproof rubber spatula. Take care to reach into the corners of the pan, where scorching or curdling is most likely to occur. When the mixture thickens enough to coat the back of the spoon, remove the pan from the heat. Transfer to a bowl or continue to stir for a minute, since heat retained in the pan can curdle or scorch the mixture. If the custard is not perfectly smooth, strain it through a fine-mesh sieve. To prevent a skin from forming on the custard sauce as it cools, place a piece of waxed or parchment paper directly on the surface.

4 Making baked custards

For baked custard, pour the combined eggs, milk, and other ingredients into a buttered pudding mold or custard cups and bake in a water bath (see page 271). Test a baked custard for doneness by gently shaking it. While the custard should look "set," the center should still jiggle slightly. The custard will continue to cook slightly and set further after removal from the oven. If desired, chill baked custards thoroughly and unmold by placing a plate over the custard mold and inverting the plate and mold together.

Making ice cream and frozen desserts

Once you master the basic principles and a few simple recipes, you can experiment with flavoring ingredients to create endless variations.

1 Filling the canister

All ice cream machines include a canister to hold the ice cream base while it is simultaneously frozen and stirred. This agitation of the base prevents it from freezing into a solid mass. Fill the canister no more than two-thirds full to allow room for the ice cream base to expand as it freezes.

2 Freezing the base

Old-fashioned ice cream machines have canisters that must be surrounded with ice to freeze the base (and rock salt to prevent the ice from melting too quickly), and the base is agitated by a hand-cranked dasher, or paddle. Modern models replace the ice with canisters that may be placed in the freezer for several hours before being filled with the base. They may be agitated by hand cranking or electric motor. Consult the manufacturer's instructions for your particular machine.

3 Making the ice cream

The stirring motion of the dasher lightens the texture of ice cream by incorporating air into the base as well as discouraging the formation of large ice crystals. Nearly constant stirring ensures a smooth, creamy dessert rather than a coarse and icy consistency. Let freshly made ice cream rest, or ripen, in the freezer for at least 30 minutes and up to 2 hours before serving. This firms the ice cream and allows its flavors to blend.

Testing sugar in sorbet

A precise balance of sugar and liquid is required for a sorbet to freeze properly.

The egg test

While the proportions of the sorbet recipes in this book were carefully tested for the home cook, if you decide to create your own sorbet, you will need to test the proportions of sugar and water. Although an inexpensive hydrometer can measure the exact density of the fruit and sugar syrup mixture, the classic test involves floating an egg in the sorbet base. Wash a raw, whole egg in the shell and place it in the sorbet mixture. When the base contains the proper amount of sugar, the egg will float to the top and expose an area of its shell that is the size of a nickel. If a greater area of the shell is exposed, the mixture is too sweet and requires more water to freeze properly. If the egg sinks or exposes too little of its shell, then you will need to add more sugar or sugar syrup.

Making sugar syrup

Combine sugar and water and heat until the sugar is completely dissolved to make sugar syrup.

1 Dissolving the sugar

Also known as simple syrup, sugar syrup adds flavor, moisture, and sweetness to many desserts. Use caution when heating sugar, for it can cause bad burns. Choose a heavy saucepan to help prevent the sugar from burning. Combine the sugar and water in the saucepan and bring to a boil just to dissolve the sugar. The syrup should be very clear with no undissolved sugar crystals. To check, drag a spoon across the bottom of the pan. It should feel smooth, not gritty. Note that flavoring ingredients, such as spices or liqueurs, may be added to the syrup as it comes to a boil.

Making caramel

As it cooks, sugar changes from solid to liquid and from white to clear to a deep golden brown.

1 Caramelizing sugar

To caramelize sugar, boil sugar syrup (left) until it darkens to the desired color. You may gently swirl the pan over the heat to cook the sugar evenly. The darker the color, the harder the caramel will set when it cools and the deeper its flavor will be. Once the sugar has dissolved into a syrup, stop stirring and start using a wet pastry brush to wipe down the sides of the pan with water to dissolve any sugar crystals that form. Crystals of sugar clinging to the spoon or the pan sides can cause the sugar syrup to crystallize and become grainy. Although it may take a while for the sugar to begin coloring, once it starts caramelizing, it will darken quickly.

2 Combining caramel and other ingredients

Caramelized sugar is used at different stages for different desserts and candies, and each stage may be determined by the sugar's temperature. For the recipes in this book, sugar is caramelized only to the first stage and then used in simple recipes such as crème caramel. To minimize spattering as you blend the caramel with other ingredients, heat any liquid ingredients that you plan to stir into the caramelized sugar. Add all liquids carefully, away from the heat, and be prepared for the hot caramel to foam and splatter.

Crème Caramel

Unsalted butter, softened, for greasing

Caramel

6 Tbsp sugar

4 drops fresh lemon juice

Custard

⅔ cup whole milk

⅔ cup heavy cream

6 Tbsp sugar (divided use)

½ vanilla bean

2 large eggs

1 large egg yolk

Makes 4 servings

Preheat the oven to 325°F.

Lightly grease the bottom and sides of four ½-cup ramekins with the butter.

For the caramel, combine the sugar and lemon juice in a small, heavy skillet. Cook over medium heat, stirring gently with a wooden spoon until the sugar melts, about 1 minute. Continue to cook without stirring until the sugar turns a deep golden brown, about 2 minutes. Immediately remove from the heat and divide the caramel evenly among the ramekins.

For the custard, combine the milk, cream, 3 Tbsp of the sugar, and the vanilla bean in a small saucepan and bring to a boil over high heat, stirring constantly. Remove from the heat, then remove the vanilla bean and reserve it for another use.

In a bowl, whisk to combine the remaining 3 Tbsp sugar with the eggs and egg yolk. While whisking constantly, slowly pour a small amount of the hot milk mixture into the egg yolk mixture to temper the eggs. Stir the tempered egg mixture into the pan with the remaining hot milk mixture. Divide the custard evenly among the ramekins and place in a baking pan. Place the baking pan with the ramekins in the oven and pour hot water into the pan to come two-thirds of the way up the side of the ramekins.

Bake until the custards are set but still jiggle in the middle when gently shaken, about 35 minutes.

Refrigerate for at least 12 hours or up to 2 days before serving. To serve, run a thin knife under hot water and run the knife around the edge of the custard. Unmold the custard onto a small plate. The caramel in the bottom of the cup will form a sauce.

When caramelizing sugar, adding a small amount of lemon juice or corn syrup helps prevent sugar crystals from forming and making the caramel turn grainy.

making caramel p. 274

tempering eggs p. 272

baking in a water bath p. 271

Chocolate Mousse

2 large egg yolks

1½ Tbsp brandy

2 Tbsp sugar (divided use)

¾ cup coarsely chopped bittersweet chocolate, melted, plus more for garnish

1 large egg white

½ cup heavy cream

Makes 4 servings

Combine the egg yolks with the brandy and 1 Tbsp of the sugar in the top of a double boiler or a stainless-steel bowl set over simmering water. Whisk until the mixture is thick, light, and very warm, about 110°F, 6–8 minutes.

Add the melted chocolate. Remove from the heat and whip with a handheld mixer on high speed until cool.

In another bowl, combine the egg white with the remaining 1 Tbsp sugar and whisk until it holds a medium peak when the whisk is turned upright.

In a third bowl, whip the cream until it holds soft peaks when the whisk is turned upright.

Add one-third of the egg white to the chocolate mixture and gently fold until incorporated. Fold in the remaining egg white, then fold in the whipped cream until just blended.

Pipe or spoon into serving dishes, cover, and chill for at least 3 hours or up to 24 hours before serving.

To garnish, use a vegetable peeler or paring knife to scrape curls from the bar of chocolate. Scatter over the mousse before serving.

Choose a good bittersweet (but not unsweetened) chocolate for this luscious dessert. Many chocolate manufacturers list the percentage of cocoa solids in their product; the higher the percentage, the more intense and less sweet the flavor. Taste-test a few brands to find your favorite. This dish includes raw egg whites; substitute pasteurized eggs if you are concerned about possible health risks.

melting chocolate p. 270

whipping egg whites p. 230

piping p. 271

Cappuccino Smoothies

2 cups brewed espresso or double-strength coffee, chilled

1 pint coffee ice cream

6 cups ice

1½ cups milk

Whipped cream for topping

Ground cinnamon for sprinkling

Makes 6–8 servings

In a blender, in batches as needed, blend the espresso, ice cream, ice, and milk until smooth. Divide among 6–8 stemmed glasses. Top each with a dollop of whipped cream and a sprinkle of cinnamon. Serve with a straw.

For a mocha cappuccino, substitute chocolate sorbet for the ice cream and chocolate milk for the regular milk. Sprinkle cocoa or chocolate shavings instead of cinnamon.

whipping cream p. 269

Lemon Mousse

2 tsp powdered unflavored
gelatin

3 Tbsp sugar (divided use)

Cornstarch slurry: 1 Tbsp
cornstarch blended with
1 Tbsp cold water

1 large egg yolk

3 Tbsp fresh lemon juice

2 large egg whites

Makes 4 servings

Scatter the gelatin over the surface of 2 Tbsp warm water. Let sit until the gelatin swells and "blooms," about 5 minutes.

Combine 1½ Tbsp of the sugar and ½ cup water in a saucepan. Bring to a boil over high heat to make a sugar syrup.

Meanwhile, whisk the cornstarch slurry with the egg yolk in a stainless-steel bowl.

While whisking constantly, slowly pour a small amount of the hot sugar syrup into the yolk mixture to temper. Stir the tempered yolk mixture back into the hot syrup and stir gently over the heat just until it boils.

Add the gelatin, stirring well to mix evenly. Add the lemon juice, stir to blend, and strain through a fine-mesh sieve into a clean bowl.

Combine the egg whites and the remaining 1½ Tbsp sugar in the bowl of a stand mixer or a metal mixing bowl and set over simmering water. Heat, stirring frequently, until the egg whites are hot (140°F) and the sugar has dissolved; continue to heat for 3 minutes.

Transfer the bowl to the mixer fitted with the whisk attachment or use a handheld mixer to whip the egg whites on medium-low speed until foamy and just starting to thicken. Increase the speed slightly and continue to whip until the whites are glossy and thickened and hold a stiff peak when the whisk is turned upright, making a meringue.

Fold the meringue into the lemon mixture in 2 or 3 additions, mixing just until evenly blended. Spoon immediately into parfait glasses or other molds. Chill for at least 3 hours or up to 24 hours before serving.

Use unflavored gelatin for this recipe, not flavored and sweetened gelatin-dessert powder. Always let gelatin soften ("bloom") in a cool liquid first. If dry gelatin is put directly into a hot liquid, it will seize up and form rubbery lumps.

whipping egg whites
p. 230

folding p. 270

using a double boiler
p. 269

Gratin of Fresh Berries

2 cups fresh berries such as strawberries, blueberries. blackberries, boysenberries, or raspberries

Sabayon

½ cup sugar

¼ cup sweet white wine

3 large egg yolks

½ cup heavy cream

Makes 4 servings

Preheat the broiler. Arrange the berries on a flameproof plate or in individual ramekins, in concentric circles or as desired.

For the sabayon, combine the sugar, wine, and egg yolks in the top of a double boiler or in a stainless-steel bowl set over simmering water. Whisk until light and foamy and approximately 165°F, 3–4 minutes. The sabayon should fall in ribbons from the whisk when it is lifted. Remove from the heat and allow to cool slightly.

Meanwhile, in a mixing bowl, whip the cream until it holds soft peaks when the whisk is turned upright. Add one-third of the whipped cream to the cooled sabayon and gently fold until incorporated. Fold in the remaining whipped cream. Spoon over the berries.

Slide the dish(es) under the broiler just to brown the sabayon, 30–45 seconds. Serve at once.

Sabayon, a frothy custard sauce, is made from egg yolks flavored with sugar and dessert wine. Whisked over simmering water until lightly thickened and foamy, it can be served on its own or, as here, folded into whipped cream and lightly gratinéed. In this recipe, try a light dessert wine like muscat, vin santo, or a late-harvest Gewürztraminer or Riesling.

grilling and broiling p. 28

whipping cream p. 269

using a double boiler p. 269

Fruit Fritters

1 large egg

1 Tbsp sugar

6 Tbsp dry white wine

6 Tbsp apple juice

1 pinch salt

½ tsp grated lemon **zest**

½ tsp grated orange zest

1½ cups all-purpose flour, sifted

2 cups strawberries

4 bananas

Vegetable oil for deep-frying

Fruit sauce, such as brandied cherry coulis (p. 291), for serving

Whipped cream for serving

Makes 4 servings

Whisk the egg and sugar in a bowl until foamy and slightly thickened, about 5 minutes. Add the wine, juice, salt, and zests and mix thoroughly. Add the flour and blend until smooth. Let rest, covered, for 1 hour.

Hull the strawberries and cut them in half. Peel the bananas and cut them into ½-inch-thick slices. Add the strawberries and bananas to the batter and toss gently to coat the fruit with batter.

Pour oil to a depth of 5 inches in a deep pot and heat over medium heat to 350°F on a deep-frying thermometer. Use a large spoon to scoop up 2 strawberry pieces and 2 banana slices for each fritter and use another spoon to push gently into the hot oil. Continue adding fritters to the hot oil, but do not crowd the pot. Deep-fry until light golden brown, about 5 minutes. Using a slotted spoon, transfer the fritters to absorbent towels to drain. Repeat with the remaining fruit and batter. It is best to serve fritters immediately, but if necessary, they can be kept warm in a 200°F oven while finishing the remaining fritters; leave uncovered to maintain crispness.

Serve with fruit sauce and whipped cream.

To choose the best strawberries, use both your eyes and your nose. Avoid berries with white or greenish tips or tops, which indicates an underripe berry. The berries should have a full, sweet aroma. Finally, always check the bottom of the basket for damp spots caused by squashed or rotting berries.

deep-frying p. 35

zesting and juicing citrus p. 182

Bread and Butter Pudding

¼ cup raisins

⅓ cup rum

8 slices enriched bread, such as challah or brioche, cut into 1-inch cubes

3 Tbsp unsalted butter, melted and kept warm, plus more as needed for greasing

2 cups whole milk

3 large eggs, lightly beaten

1 large egg yolk, lightly beaten

⅓ cup sugar

½ tsp vanilla extract

¼ tsp ground cinnamon

Makes 4–6 servings

Preheat the oven to 350°F. Combine the raisins with the rum and warm in a small saucepan over low heat. Remove from the heat and allow the raisins to plump for about 10 minutes. Drain and reserve.

Meanwhile, drizzle the bread cubes with the melted butter, spread on a baking sheet, and toast in the oven, stirring once or twice, until golden brown, 10–12 minutes.

Combine the milk, eggs, egg yolk, sugar, vanilla extract, and cinnamon and stir until the sugar has fully dissolved.

Grease a 2-qt shallow casserole, 8-inch square baking dish, or individual ¾-cup ceramic ramekins with butter and place in a larger rectangular baking dish. Add the bread cubes and raisins to the ramekins or dish and ladle the milk mixture over the bread, reserving about ¾ cup. Refrigerate the bread pudding(s) and the reserved milk mixture for about 30 minutes while the bread absorbs the liquid.

Preheat the oven again to 350°F. Spoon the remaining custard mixture on top of the soaked bread. Place the baking pan containing the ramekins in the oven, and pour hot water into the pan to come two-thirds of the way up the side of the ramekins or dish.

Bake until the custard is set but still jiggles in the middle when gently shaken, about 30 minutes for small ramekins and 50 minutes for a larger baking dish. Let stand for 15 minutes after removing it from the oven. The pudding may be served warm or chilled.

Soft, egg-enriched challah bread makes a wonderful addition to this homey baked dessert. Similar in ingredients to French toast, this pudding also makes a great brunch dish.

baking in a water bath p. 271

separating eggs p. 229

Rice Pudding

⅓ cup long-grain white rice

2½ cups whole milk

¼ cup sugar

1 cinnamon stick

1 orange slice, about ½ inch thick, peel on, seeds removed

1 pinch salt

1 tsp vanilla extract

Makes 4 servings

Rinse the rice in several changes of cool water and let drain. Combine the milk, sugar, cinnamon, orange slice, and salt in a saucepan and bring just to a boil over high heat. Add the rice to the milk mixture, reduce the heat to low, and simmer, partially covered, until the rice is tender, 25–35 minutes. Remove the saucepan from the heat, cover, and let the pudding stand, covered, for 10 minutes.

Remove the orange slice and cinnamon stick and stir in the vanilla extract. Cool slightly and spoon into a serving dish or 4 custard cups. Chill before serving, at least 3 hours or up to 24 hours.

Rinsing the rice helps wash off excess starch from the outside of the grains, which in turn will keep the rice from sticking together and forming clumps in the finished pudding.

making custards p. 272

Apple Crêpes

Dessert Crêpes

2 large eggs

¼ cup confectioners' sugar

½ cup whole milk

1 cup all-purpose flour

1 cup heavy cream

¼ tsp vanilla extract

Vegetable oil for pan

Apple Filling

2 Granny Smith apples

¼ cup firmly packed light brown sugar

4 Tbsp unsalted butter (divided use)

⅓ cup cider or apple juice

2 Tbsp Calvados

½ cup heavy cream, whipped to medium peaks

Makes 4 servings

For the crêpes, combine the eggs and confectioners' sugar and whip until foamy and slightly thickened, about 5–7 minutes. Stir in the milk. Add the flour and mix until smooth. Add the cream and the vanilla extract and mix until smooth.

Heat a crêpe pan or small nonstick skillet over medium-high heat and brush liberally with oil. Ladle about ⅓ cup of batter into the pan. Lift the pan from the heat and tilt and swirl to completely coat the pan with a thin layer of batter. Cook on the first side until set and lightly browned, about 1½ minutes. Turn or flip the crêpe and finish cooking on the second side, 30–45 seconds more.

Repeat with remaining batter to make 8 crêpes in all. (Crêpes may be prepared up to 2 days in advance. To hold them, place squares of parchment or waxed paper between the crêpes, wrap well, and refrigerate. Or, freeze them for up to 1 month. Thaw at room temperature. If crêpes are made in advance, warm them gently in a 200°F oven while preparing the filling.)

For the apple filling, peel, core, and slice the apples thinly. Heat a sauté pan over medium high heat. Add the brown sugar in an even layer and heat until the sugar begins to melt, about 1 minute. Add 2 Tbsp of the butter and stir to combine. Add the sliced apples to pan and coat with the brown sugar and butter mixture. Sauté the apples until they are softened and very hot, 3–4 minutes.

Divide the apple mixture evenly among the crêpes and roll the crêpes around the filling. Place in a baking dish and keep warm in a 200°F oven.

In the same pan used for the apples, combine the cider and Calvados, stir to dissolve any remaining sugar and reduced juices, and bring to a simmer. Continue to simmer until slightly reduced, 2–3 minutes. Swirl in the remaining 2 Tbsp of butter. Keep hot.

Serve the crêpes on warmed plates and spoon some of the pan sauce over them. Top with a dollop of whipped cream.

Calvados is an apple brandy made in Normandy, the northwestern province of France known for its abundant apple orchards. Besides apples, Normandy is also known for its excellent dairy products, especially butter and cream, making this dessert a real speciality of the area.

making crêpes p. 249

whipping cream p. 269

Orange Soufflé

1 Tbsp butter, softened, for greasing molds

5 Tbsp granulated sugar (divided use) plus more for dusting

2 egg yolks

2 Tbsp all-purpose flour

⅛ tsp salt

¾ cup milk

½ tsp vanilla extract

2 Tbsp orange juice concentrate, thawed

1½ tsp grated orange zest

5 large egg whites

Confectioners' sugar for dusting

Makes 4 servings

Preheat the oven to 400°F. Lightly grease four 6-oz soufflé molds with the butter. Dust with granulated sugar to coat the butter evenly, emptying out any excess. Wipe the rims clean.

In a bowl, blend 2 Tbsp of the granulated sugar, the egg yolks, flour, and salt. Set aside.

Heat the milk and remaining 3 Tbsp sugar in a small saucepan over medium-high heat. Bring to a boil and remove from heat. Whisk in the vanilla extract and let cool slightly.

Gradually add the warm milk to the egg yolk mixture, whisking constantly. Return the mixture to the saucepan over medium heat. Whisk constantly until the mixture thickens and comes to a boil, about 1½ minutes, to make a pastry cream. Remove from the heat.

Transfer the pastry cream to a bowl and place over a pan of cold water. Whisk until the pastry cream is cool, about 5 minutes. Add the orange juice concentrate and zest to the pastry cream. Set aside.

Whip the egg whites to medium peaks with a handheld mixer. Add one-third of the whipped whites to the pastry cream and gently fold in just until incorporated. Add the remaining egg whites and fold in just until incorporated. Divide evenly among the prepared soufflé molds on a baking sheet and bake undisturbed until the tops are golden brown and the soufflés appear set but soft, 18–20 minutes. Sift a little confectioners' sugar over the top of each soufflé and serve at once.

To produce the lightest, puffiest soufflé, whip your egg whites to medium, not stiff, peaks before folding them into the pastry cream base. While folding, keep in mind that it's better to leave a few patches of whipped egg white than to deflate the mixture by overfolding.

making a soufflé p. 233

whipping egg whites p. 230

tempering eggs p. 272

VARIATIONS

Almond Soufflé

Use finely chopped toasted almonds in place of the granulated sugar coating. Replace the orange juice concentrate and zest with ½ tsp almond extract and 1 Tbsp Amaretto.

Coffee Soufflé

Add 2 tsp instant coffee or espresso powder to the milk mixture. Replace the orange juice concentrate and zest with 1 Tbsp Kahlúa.

Pithiviers

8 Tbsp unsalted butter, softened

⅓ cup sugar

⅓ cup almond paste

¾ tsp vanilla extract

3 large eggs

1 lb frozen puff pastry, thawed

1 Tbsp light corn syrup, heated

Makes 6–8 servings

Preheat the oven to 375°F.

Beat the butter in a bowl with a wooden spoon until creamy, about 2 minutes. Add the sugar and continue to beat until the mixture is light and fluffy in both appearance and texture. Stir in the almond paste, breaking it into pieces to make it easier to blend, and the vanilla extract. Add 2 of the eggs, 1 at a time, beating well after each addition to prevent separation.

Lightly beat the remaining egg with 1 tsp water to make an egg wash.

Unfold the puff pastry and cut out two 8-inch rounds. Place 1 round on a baking sheet. Spread the almond mixture in the center of the round, leaving a 1½-inch border on all sides. Lightly brush the border with some of the egg wash. Place the second pastry round on top of the filling and line up the edges of the 2 circles. Gently press the edges together to force out any air bubbles along the edge. Chill the pastry for 20 minutes.

Crimp the edges with the tines of a fork. Brush the pastry all over with egg wash and, using a sharp knife, score a spiral pattern in the top of the puff pastry. Be careful not to slice through the pastry.

Bake until golden brown, 35–40 minutes.

Brush the top of the pastry with the corn syrup. Raise the oven temperature to 425°F. Return the *pithiviers* to the oven and bake until the corn syrup becomes golden, 2–3 minutes more. Be careful not to overcook, as corn syrup burns easily.

Let the *pithiviers* cool slightly before slicing and serving.

Named after a town in the Loire region, this French cake is a tradition for the Feast of Epiphany. On January 6, the twelfth day after Christmas (also known as the Feast of the Three Kings), a ring, bean, or small ceramic figurine is tucked into this pastry. The one who gets the surprise in his or her piece becomes the "king" for the day. Look for almond paste in the baking section of most supermarkets.

roasting and baking p. 30

using prepared puff pastry dough p. 269

French-Style Ice Cream

6 large egg yolks

2 cups sugar (divided use)

3 cups heavy cream

1 vanilla bean, split lengthwise

Makes about 1¼ quarts; 8 servings

Whisk together the egg yolks with ½ cup of the sugar until thickened.

Combine the cream, the remaining 1½ cups sugar, and the vanilla bean in a heavy saucepan over medium heat. Bring to a simmer, stirring constantly.

While stirring constantly, slowly pour about 1½ cups of the hot cream mixture into the beaten yolks to temper them. Stir the tempered egg mixture into the remaining cream mixture and continue to cook over low heat, stirring constantly, until the custard is thick enough to coat the back of a spoon, 5 minutes.

Immediately pour the custard through a fine-mesh sieve into a bowl. Put about 2 inches of ice in a larger bowl, add water to cover the cubes, and set the bowl with the custard in the ice bath. Stir the custard every few minutes until it is quite cool, about 1 hour.

With the tip of a paring knife, scrape the seeds from the vanilla pod into the custard, then discard the pod.

Cover and refrigerate the custard for at least 4 hours or up to overnight. Freeze in an ice cream maker according to the manufacturer's instructions. Pack the ice cream in storage containers and place in the freezer for at least 2 hours before serving.

This is a classic custard-based ice cream, flavored generously with vanilla. In some parts of the country it is still known as "frozen custard." Because of the delicate nature of the custard, it is important to cool it as quickly as possible. Cooling it over an ice bath is the safest way to ensure a wholesome and delicious ice cream. Refrigerating the ice cream base for at least 4 hours before churning is an important step in getting the right texture.

making ice cream and frozen desserts p. 273

tempering eggs p. 272

VARIATIONS

Cinnamon Ice Cream

Add 2 cinnamon sticks to the cream and, if desired, replace the vanilla bean with ½ tsp vanilla extract. Proceed as directed above, removing the cinnamon sticks along with the vanilla bean.

Peach or Apricot Ice Cream

Peel and pit 1 lb peaches and cut into slices or chunks. You should have about 3 cups. Toss with a few Tbsp sugar. Purée 2 cups of the fruit and lightly crush the remainder. Proceed as above, stirring the purée into the ice cream base. Churn in the ice cream machine for 15 minutes, then stop the machine and add the crushed peaches. Finish freezing according to the manufacturer's instructions.

Lemon Sorbet

1¼ cups sugar

½ cup fresh lemon juice

1 large egg white

Makes 8 servings

Combine the sugar with 3½ cups water and stir until the sugar is fully dissolved. Add the lemon juice.

Whip the egg white until foamy. Add to the sugar syrup, mixing well. Chill in the refrigerator for 1 hour.

Freeze in an ice cream maker according to the manufacturer's instructions. Serve the sorbet directly from the ice cream maker as an ice, or place it in the freezer for at least 2 hours before serving.

If too much sugar is added to the sorbet, it will be too dense to freeze properly, so follow the recipe carefully.

making ice cream and frozen desserts p. 273

making sugar syrup p. 274

Fresh Ginger Granita

3 Tbsp thickly sliced gingerroot

1½ cups sugar

2 tsp fresh lime juice

Makes 8 servings

In a blender or food processor, purée the ginger with 1 cup water. Combine the ginger purée and sugar with 2½ cups additional water in a saucepan. Bring to a bare simmer over high heat. Do not allow to boil.

Strain the mixture through a fine-mesh sieve, add the lime juice, and pour into a baking pan. Place in the freezer. You may stir the granita every 15–20 minutes until it is evenly frozen with large crystals, about 2 hours, or let it freeze without stirring until solid, about 4 hours, then use a metal serving spoon to scrape it into a light, granular texture.

Present this and other frozen desserts in well-chilled bowls or plates to prevent them from melting too quickly.

preparing ginger p. 181

puréeing p. 47

Grand Marnier Parfaits

2 cups heavy cream

8 large egg yolks

¾ cup granulated sugar

5 Tbsp plus 8 tsp Grand Marnier

Grated zest of 1 orange

Unsweetened cocoa powder
for dusting (optional)

Confectioners' sugar for
dusting (optional)

Makes 8 servings

Whip the cream in a chilled bowl until it holds a soft peak when the whisk is turned upright. Refrigerate until ready to use.

Prepare eight ½-cup ramekins by wrapping the outside of each with a parchment paper collar extending 1 inch above the rim. Secure with tape or string. Set on a baking sheet.

Whip the egg yolks in the bowl of a stand mixer fitted with the whisk attachment or with a handheld mixer on medium speed until light and thickened.

Meanwhile, combine the granulated sugar and 6 Tbsp water in a small, heavy saucepan and bring to a full boil over high heat, stirring to dissolve the sugar. With the mixer on low speed, slowly add the sugar syrup to the egg yolks. Continue whipping until the mixture cools to room temperature.

Fold the 5 Tbsp Grand Marnier and the orange zest into the egg-yolk mixture. Add one-third of the reserved whipped cream to the egg-yolk mixture and gently fold until incorporated. Fold in the remaining whipped cream.

Pour the egg mixture into the ramekins to a depth of ½ inch above the rim of each ramekin. Freeze for 3–4 hours.

To serve, unwrap the collars from the ramekins. Pierce 2 holes through each parfait and pour ½ tsp Grand Marnier into each. If desired, use a sieve to dust with cocoa powder and confectioners' sugar and serve at once.

These are parfaits in the French sense—a frozen soufflé that combines whipped cream with a custard base. Here, the base is flavored with the classic French orange-flavored liqueur Grand Marnier. Since the soufflé is frozen, not baked, there's no oven heat to puff up the soufflé. Wrapping a parchment-paper collar around the soufflé dishes allows the dishes to be filled above the rim. When the parchment is removed just before serving, the soufflé stands tall.

Note that this dish includes eggs that may be only partially cooked.

making sugar syrup
p. 274

Chocolate Sauce

1¼ cups half-and-half

3 Tbsp sugar

3 Tbsp unsalted butter

10 oz semisweet or bittersweet chocolate, finely chopped

¼ cup liquor (optional)

Makes 2½ cups

Combine the half-and-half, sugar, and butter in a heavy saucepan over medium heat. Carefully bring just to a boil, then remove from the heat.

Add the chocolate and stir until it melts. When the mixture has cooled completely, add the liquor, if using. Serve at once.

The chocolate sauce may be stored in the refrigerator. To rewarm, heat gently in a heavy saucepan over low heat, or briefly in the microwave on medium power.

Vary the flavor of this sauce by using different chocolate and liquor combinations as desired. Try dark rum, brandy, bourbon, Grand Marnier, Amaretto, Kahlúa, or Tia Maria.

melting chocolate p. 270

Caramel Sauce

1 cup sugar

Few drops fresh lemon juice

1 pinch salt

½ cup heavy cream, warmed

2 Tbsp unsalted butter

Makes 1¼ cups

Combine the sugar, 3 Tbsp water, the lemon juice, and salt in a heavy saucepan over medium heat. Cook, stirring gently with a wooden spoon, until the sugar melts, about 1 minute. Continue to cook without stirring until the sugar turns a deep golden brown, about 2 minutes more.

Remove from the heat and carefully add the cream. Stir until smooth and evenly blended. Add the butter and stir gently to blend. Serve at once.

The caramel sauce may be stored in the refrigerator. To rewarm, heat gently in a heavy saucepan over low heat, or briefly in the microwave on medium power.

Since sugar burns easily, be sure to use a heavy pot to prevent scorching when making this caramel. A few drops of lemon juice help prevent the caramel from forming sugar crystals and becoming grainy. Carefully add the warmed cream off the heat, as the hot caramel will foam up and may spatter when the liquid is added. Serve over ice cream or use as a topping for purchased profiteroles, filled with pastry cream or ice cream.

making caramel p. 274

zesting and juicing citrus p. 182

Brandied Cherry Coulis

¾ cup pitted fresh or frozen
cherries

½ cup dry red wine

6 Tbsp sugar

2 Tbsp brandy

1 small pinch ground cinnamon

Makes about 1½ cups

Combine the cherries, ¾ cup water, the wine, sugar, brandy, and cinnamon in a small saucepan over low heat. Simmer until the cherries are tender, 8–10 minutes. Purée in a blender or food processor until smooth. Strain through a fine-mesh sieve and let cool.

Transfer to a squeeze bottle or a cup with a spout and use to decorate plates.

Dress up a simple slice of angel food cake with a drizzle of this dazzling ruby-red cherry sauce. Mixed with additional warmed, whole pitted cherries, it can also be used as a filling for dessert crêpes.

puréeing p. 47

Lemon Curd

8 Tbsp unsalted butter
(divided use)

12 Tbsp sugar (divided use)

½ cup fresh lemon juice

2 tsp finely grated lemon zest

5 large egg yolks

Makes 1½ cups

Combine 4 Tbsp of the butter, 6 Tbsp of the sugar, and the lemon juice and zest in a nonreactive saucepan. Bring the mixture to a boil over medium heat.

Meanwhile, whisk together the egg yolks and the remaining 6 Tbsp sugar in a bowl.

Remove the pan from the heat. While whisking constantly, slowly pour one-third of the hot lemon mixture into the egg yolk mixture to temper the eggs. Stir the tempered egg mixture into the remaining hot lemon mixture and continue to cook over medium heat, stirring constantly, just until the mixture comes to a boil.

Remove from the heat and stir in the remaining 4 Tbsp butter.

Strain the curd through a fine-mesh sieve into a nonreactive bowl. Put about 2 inches of ice in a larger bowl, add water to cover the cubes, and set the bowl with the curd in the ice bath. Stir the custard every few minutes until it is quite cool, about 1 hour. Cover with parchment or waxed paper, pressing it directly onto the surface of the curd to prevent a skin from forming, and chill for at least 3 hours or up to 2 days before serving.

To make a delicious filling or topping for pound cake or sponge cake, fold the lemon curd in up to 1 cup of heavy cream, whipped to medium peaks. Lemon curd also makes a wonderful spread for toasted English muffins or crumpets.

tempering eggs p. 272

zesting and juicing citrus p. 182

CONVERSIONS AND EQUIVALENTS

Useful measures

3 tsp = 1 Tbsp

4 Tbsp = ¼ cup

16 Tbsp = 1 cup

1 cup = ½ pt = 8 fl oz

2 cups = 1 pt

2 pt = 1 qt

4 qt = 1 gal

1 stick butter = 8 Tbsp = 4 oz = ½ cup

To convert Fahrenheit to Celsius

Subtract 32. Divide result by 9. Multiply result by 5 to get Celsius.

To convert Celsius to Fahrenheit

Divide by 9. Multiply result by 5. Add 32 to get Fahrenheit.

Useful temperatures

Water freezes at 32°F, 0°C.

Water boils at 212°F, 100°C.

Experienced home cooks have traditionally relied on pinches, dashes, and a little of this or that. They know when a food is done cooking by touch or feel. They can accomplish this feat because they have become accustomed over time to the way foods look when they are done, what their hands and fingertips can hold, how fast salt pours from their shaker, how full their pans and bowls typically look when making a particular dish.

However, you may want to follow the measurements given in a recipe exactly the first time you make it, then make adjustments to suit your taste. If you are reading and using these recipes in a kitchen outside the United States, you will most likely need to convert to metric measurements for weight, volume, and temperature. The unit of measure for oven temperatures in some areas also differs from those in the U.S.; "gas marks" are used instead of a Fahrenheit or Celsius temperature. The information in the following charts allows you to make a variety of conversions—pounds to kilograms, ounces to grams, cups to milliliters and liters, Fahrenheit to Celsius, and volume to weight.

Recipes and grocery stores don't always speak the same measurement language. You might buy something as a bunch or a can, but need to use it as a cup or a tablespoon. The ingredient equivalents charts (see pages 294–97) offer estimates of how many whole onions will give you a cup of diced or how many slices of bread you'll need for a cup of crumbs. These charts should help you to buy and use what you need with as little waste as possible.

Temperature conversions

GAS MARK	FAHRENHEIT	CELSIUS	DESCRIPTION
1	275	120	very slow oven
2	300	150	slow oven
3	325	160	slow oven
4	350	180	moderate oven
5	375	190	moderate oven
6	400	200	hot oven
7	450	230	very hot oven
8	475	250	very hot oven

Weight conversions

U.S. UNIT	METRIC (ROUNDED)
½ oz	15 g
1 oz	30 g
2 oz	55 g
3 oz	85 g
4 oz (¼ lb)	115 g
8 oz (½ lb)	225 g
1 lb (16 oz)	455 g
5 lb	2.25 kg
10 lb	4.5 kg

To convert ounces and pounds to grams

Multiply ounces by 28.35 to determine grams; divide pounds by 2.2 to determine kilograms.

To convert grams to ounces or pounds

Divide grams by 28.35 to determine ounces; divide grams by 453.59 to determine pounds.

To convert fluid ounces to milliliters

Multiply fluid ounces by 29.58 to determine milliliters.

To convert milliliters to fluid ounces

Divide milliliters by 29.58 to determine fluid ounces.

Volume conversions

VOLUME MEASURE	U.S. VOLUME	METRIC (ROUNDED)
1 tsp	⅕ fl oz	5 ml
1 Tbsp	½ fl oz (3 tsp)	15 ml
⅛ cup	1 fl oz (2 tbsp)	30 ml
¼ cup	2 fl oz	60 ml
⅓ cup	2⅔ fl oz	80 ml
½ cup	4 fl oz	120 ml
⅔ cup	5⅓ fl oz	158 ml
¾ cup	6 fl oz	180 ml
1 cup	8 fl oz	240 ml
¾ pt (1½ cups)	12 fl oz	360 ml
1 pt (2 cups)	16 fl oz	480 ml
1 qt (2 pt)	32 fl oz	950 ml (1 L)
1 gal (4 qt; 16 cups)	128 fl oz	3.75 L

Ingredient equivalents

INGREDIENT	VOLUME	WEIGHT (U.S.)	WEIGHT (METRIC)
Apple			
1 medium	1 cup sliced	4.2 oz	119 g
Asparagus			
1 bunch	2 cups	9.5 oz	269 g
Bacon			
1 cooked strip, crumbled	2 Tbsp	.75 oz	21 g
Baking powder	1 tsp	.15 oz	4 g
Baking soda	1 tsp	.18 oz	5 g
Beans			
black, garbanzo (chickpeas), lima, pinto	1 cup dried	6.5 oz	184 g
cannellini	1 cup dried	7.25 oz	206 g
Bell pepper	1 cup diced	5.2 oz	147 g
1 medium	1⅓ cups diced (approx.)	7 oz	198 g
Bread crumbs			
5 slices bread	1 cup crumbs	3.5 oz	100 g
Broccoli	1 cup florets	2.5 oz	71 g
1 head	3½ cup florets (approx.)	8.75 oz	248 g
Butter			
1 stick	8 Tbsp	4 oz	113 g
1 lb whole	1¼ cups clarified	12 oz	340 g
Cabbage	1 cup shredded	3.3 oz	94 g
1 small head	8 cups shredded (approx.)	26 oz	737 g
Capers	1 Tbsp	.25 oz	6 g
Carrot	1 cup diced	5 oz	142 g
1 medium	⅔ cup diced (approx.)	3.3 oz	94 g

Ingredient equivalents (continued)

INGREDIENT	VOLUME	WEIGHT (U.S.)	WEIGHT (METRIC)
Cauliflower	1 cup florets	4.7 oz	133 g
1 head	3¾ cups florets (approx.)	18 oz	510 g
Celeriac (celery root)	1 cup diced	3 oz	85 g
1 medium	3½ cups diced (approx.)	12 oz	340 g
Celery	1 cup diced	4 oz	113 g
1 stalk	½ cup diced (approx.)	2 oz	57 g
Cheese			
hard (e.g., Parmesan)	1 cup grated	3.75 oz	106 g
medium (e.g., Cheddar)	1 cup shredded	3 oz	85 g
soft (e.g., fresh goat or blue)	1 cup crumbled	4.75 oz	135 g
Chocolate chips	1 cup	5.5 oz	156 g
Coconut (fresh)	1 cup	2.75 oz	78 g
Coconut (dried)	1 cup	2.4 oz	68 g
Corn	1 cup kernels	5.75 oz	163 g
1 ear	½ cup kernels (approx.)	2.75 oz	78 g
Cornstarch	1 Tbsp	.3 oz	8.5 g
Eggplant	1 cup diced	3 oz	85 g
1 medium globe	3 cups diced (approx.)	9 oz	255 g
Garlic	1 Tbsp minced	.25 oz	8 g
1 clove	1 tsp minced (approx.)	.125 oz	3 g
Gingerroot	1 tsp grated	.15 oz	4 g
Green onion	1 cup sliced	2 oz	57 g
1 medium	¼ cup sliced (approx.)	.5 oz	14 g
Ham	1 cup minced	4 oz	113 g
Herbs (dried)	1 Tbsp	.08 oz	225 mg
Herbs (fresh)	1 Tbsp minced	.115 oz	3 g

Ingredient equivalents (continued)

INGREDIENT	VOLUME	WEIGHT (U.S.)	WEIGHT (METRIC)
Honey	1 Tbsp	.75 oz	21 g
Jalapeño	1 tsp minced	.10 oz	3 g
1 medium	2 Tbsp minced (approx.)	.5 oz	14 g
Jícama	1 cup diced	4.5 oz	128 g
Juniper berries	1 Tbsp	.176 oz	5 g
Kale	1 cup chopped	2.5 oz	71 g
Leek	1 cup sliced	4 oz	113 g
1 leek, white and green parts	1¼ cups sliced (approx.)	6 oz	170 g
Lemon			
1 medium, juiced	3 Tbsp	1.5 oz	43 g
1 medium, zested	2 tsp	.10 oz	3 g
Lentils	1 cup dry	6 oz	170 g
Lime			
1 medium, juiced	3 Tbsp	1.5 oz	43 g
1 medium, zested	2 tsp	.10 oz	3 g
Mushroom	1 cup sliced (approx.)	2 oz	57 g
1 large white mushroom	¼ cup sliced (approx.)	.5 oz	14 g
Mustard (prepared)	1 Tbsp	.5 oz	15 g
Nuts	1 cup chopped	4 oz	113 g
Onion	1 cup diced	4 oz	113 g
1 medium	1¾ cups diced (approx.)	7 oz	198 g
Orange			
1 medium, juiced	½ cup	4 oz	113 g
1 medium, zested	1 Tbsp	.25 oz	6 g
Peas	1 cup	3.5 oz	99 g
Pepper (ground)	1 tsp	.07 oz	2 g

Ingredient equivalents (continued)

INGREDIENT	VOLUME	WEIGHT (U.S.)	WEIGHT (METRIC)
Potato	1 cup diced	5 oz	142 g
1 medium russet	1 cup diced (approx.)	5 oz	142 g
1 medium Yukon gold	¾ cup diced	4 oz	113 g
1 medium red potato	½ cup diced	2 oz	57 g
1 medium sweet potato	1 cup diced	4.5 oz	128 g
Radish	1 cup sliced	4 oz	113 g
Raisins	1 cup	6 oz	170 g
Rice			
converted, long grain	1 cup uncooked	6.5 oz	184 g
Saffron threads	1 tsp crushed	.025 oz	710 mg
Salad Greens			
green leaf lettuce, Boston lettuce	1 cup	2 oz	57 g
arugula	1 cup	2.5 oz	70 g
escarole	1 cup chopped	2.5 oz	71 g
Salt (table)	1 tsp	.25 oz	7 g
Seeds (sesame, cumin, fennel, etc.)	1 tsp	.20 oz	6 g
Shallot	1 tsp minced	.125 oz	3.5 g
1 medium	2 Tbsp minced (approx.)	.75 oz	20 g
Spices (ground)	1 tsp	.07 oz	2 g
Spinach	1 cup chopped	2.75 oz	78 g
1 bunch	4 cups chopped (approx.)	10.5 oz	298 g
Tomato			
1 medium	1 cup chopped	5.75 oz	163 g
Turnip	1 cup diced	4.5 oz	128 g
Zucchini	1 cup diced	4 oz	113 g
1 medium	2 cups diced	8 oz	227 g

INDEX